MW01120212

Carol Ann Duffy

Jane Dowson

Carol Ann Duffy

Poet for Our Times

palgrave
macmillan

Jane Dowson
De Montfort University
Leicester, UK

ISBN 978-1-137-41562-2   ISBN 978-1-137-41563-9   (eBook)
DOI 10.1057/978-1-137-41563-9

Library of Congress Control Number: 2016938778

Printed on acid-free paper

This Palgrave Macmillan imprint is published by Springer Nature
The registered company is Macmillan Publishers Ltd. London

For Tim

I.M. Diana Widdows 1922–2015

Acknowledgements

I am grateful to the staff at The Saison Poetry Library, London and The Scottish Poetry Library, Edinburgh for their invaluable resources and assistance. Profound thanks go to Bernadette Hyland who sourced the article in Manchester's *City Life* magazine. Robert DiNapoli kindly agrees to my extensive extracts from his valuable article on word-play and poetry. With characteristic generosity, Carol Ann Duffy has granted permission to quote extracts from her poems, for which I am hugely grateful. The book could not have been completed without the term's Research Leave granted by De Montfort University, Leicester or the support of my colleagues during that time. I thank Andy, Damir, and students on the Contemporary Poetry module for sharing my enthusiasm for this project. For their forbearance and encouragement, my love goes to friends, family and especially Tim, to whom the book is dedicated. It also commemorates the life of my mother who passed on to me her love for poetry.

ABBREVIATIONS

Poetry Volumes by Carol Ann Duffy

Bees	*The Bees* (London: Picador, 2011)
FG	*Feminine Gospels* (London: Picador, 2002)
MT	*Mean Time* (London: Anvil, 1993)
NCPC	*New and Collected Poems for Children* (London: Faber & Faber, 2009)
Near	*Near* (London: Faber & Faber, 2012)
NSP	*New Selected Poems 1984–2004* (London: Picador, 2004)
PMP	*Penguin Modern Poets 2: Carol Ann Duffy, Vicki Feaver, Eavan Boland* (Harmondsworth: Penguin, 1995)
Pamphlet	*The Pamphlet* (London: Anvil, 1998)
Rapture	*Rapture* (London: Picador) 2005
RL	*Ritual Lighting: Laureate Poems* (London: Picador, 2014)
SFN	*Standing Female Nude* (London: Anvil, 1985)
SM	*Selling Manhattan* (London: Anvil, 1987)
TOC	*The Other Country* (London: Anvil, 1990)
William	*William and the Ex-Prime Minister* (London: Anvil, 1992)
WW	*The World's Wife* (London: Macmillan, 1999)

| PBS | *Poetry Book Society Bulletin* |

CONTENTS

CHAPTER 1

Poet for Our Times

Carol Ann Duffy is one of the freshest and bravest talents to emerge in British poetry—any poetry—for years. (Boland 1993)

The effortless virtuosity, drama and humanity of Carol Ann Duffy's verse have made her our most admired contemporary poet. (Winterson 2009)

It's particularly apt to honour a laureate who so energetically challenges Auden's oft-quoted line 'poetry makes nothing happen'. (Wilkinson 2014)

Introduction: 'How Poetry / Pursues the Human'

Due to her originality, unusual range, prolific output, and swelling influence, Carol Ann Duffy is a major poet of the late twentieth and early twenty-first centuries. For over thirty years, she has been lauded as one of the most gifted, relevant, and versatile poets of her time. She has published ten main poetry collections—along with pamphlets, poetry selections, poems for children, and edited collections—starting with *Standing Female Nude* (1985) that received the Scottish Arts Council book award. The many subsequent prizes included: the Somerset Maughan for *Selling Manhattan* (1987); the Cholmondley (1992); the Forward and Whitbread for *Mean Time* (1993); the T.S. Eliot for *Rapture* (2005), and the 2012 PEN/Pinter Prize, aptly given for work of 'outstanding literary merit' that casts an 'unflinching, unswerving' gaze upon the world and shows a 'fierce intellectual determination ... to define the real

© The Editor(s) (if applicable) and The Author(s) 2016
J. Dowson, *Carol Ann Duffy*,
DOI 10.1057/978-1-137-41563-9_1

1

truth of our lives and our societies'.[1] Duffy was awarded an OBE in 1995, a National Endowment for Science Technology and Art (NESTA) in 2000, and a CBE in 2002. In 2009, she became the first female Poet Laureate of the United Kingdom, a post that crowned the ways in which Duffy raises poetry's profile and that entrenched 'woman' and 'poet' as respected adjuncts. The laureateship further released her passionate labour towards enhancing the place of poetry in contemporary culture. In 2015, she was made a Dame, the female equivalent of a knighthood, and hailed 'a great public poet who deserves her public honour' (Wilkinson 2014).

When Duffy was appointed Laureate, reviewers concurred on how her appeal is both deep and broad: 'As one of the bestselling poets in the UK, Duffy has managed to combine critical acclaim with popularity: a rare feat in the poetry world' (Flood 2009); 'Carol Ann Duffy is that rare thing—a poet whose work is loved by children and adults alike, critics as much as the public' (Cooke 2009). Not only is her poetry printed in the broadsheets and analysed in academic works, but it also appears in popular magazines, tabloid newspapers, and Internet forums. She has worked in primary and secondary schools where her poems have long been on exam syllabuses at GCSE, Advanced, and Scottish National and Higher levels. She has published several poetry books for children, winning the coveted Signal Prize for Children's Verse (1999), and edited *A Laureate's Choice: 101 Poems for Children* (London: Macmillan Children's Books 2012) and two anthologies aimed at teenagers, *Stopping for Death* (1996) and *I Wouldn't Thank You for a Valentine* (1992). She has also edited: *Anvil New Poets 2 No. 2* (1995); *Times Tidings: Greeting the Twenty-First Century* (1999); *Hand in Hand: An Anthology of Love Poetry* (2001); *Out of Fashion: An Anthology of Poems* (2004); *Answering Back: Living Poets Reply to the Poetry of the Past* (2007); *To the Moon: An Anthology of Lunar Poetry* (2009); *Jubilee Lines: 60 Poets for 60 Years* (2012); and *1914: Poetry Remembers* (2013). Her individual poems have been claimed for several territories, appearing in exhibitions and anthologies organized by timescale, nationality, gender, sexuality, or theme—from childhood, generations, and love, to films, short stories, memory, and the millennium.[2] These anthologies

---

[1] The words are taken from Harold Pinter's Nobel Speech, cited on The PEN Pinter Prize website. http://www.englishpen.org/prizes/pen-pinter-prize/

[2] '-/-/99' (*NCPC* 139) was displayed during the Salisbury Festival, *Last Words* (25–31 October 1999) and printed in the anthology, *Last Words*, ed. Don Paterson and Jo Shapcott (London: Picador 2001).

target many audiences, including new parents, lovers, cancer sufferers, and poetry buffs. She is counted as British, English, and Scottish, and her poems are translated into Chinese, French, German, Hungarian, Italian, Polish, and Spanish. From the United States, she received the Lannan Literary Award for Poetry in 1995 and the E.M. Forster award in 2000. Duffy writes opera librettos, is sometimes accompanied by musician John Sampson, and performs with the poetry band LiTTLe MaCHiNe. Her poetry has been set to music and read on the radio.

The breadth of her readership, subject matter, and literary complexity, makes Duffy magisterial but also vulnerable to disparagement. A furore over 'Education for Leisure' (*SFN* 15) exemplifies the battle involved in being a fresh brave voice against the conservative watchdogs in Education and the Arts. As the title indicates, the poem captures the restlessness of a youth for whom 'leisure' is a euphemism for unemployment. The dramatic monologue invites sympathy for the youth's disempowerment and subsequent impulse for violence: 'I get our bread-knife and go out. / The pavements glitter suddenly. I touch your arm'. In 2008, when an external examiner, Pat Schofield, complained that the poem glorified knife-crime, the AQA exam board ordered schools to remove from its GCSE syllabus an anthology containing the poem. Duffy's riposte, 'Mrs Schofield's GCSE' (*Bees* 15), displays her wit, compassionate politics, and how her imagination is first and foremost literary. She parodies exam-speak and cites fragments of violent threats or acts in Shakespeare's plays, always compulsory on the National Curriculum—'You must prepare your bosom for his knife, / said Portia to Antonio in which / of Shakespeare's Comedies? Who killed his wife / insane with jealousy?'—then commends the purpose and power of poetry. Mrs Schofield allegedly called the poem '"a bit weird"' and continued, '"But having read her other poems I found they were all a little bit weird. But that's me"' (Addley 2008). This 'weirdness' is, of course, what makes Duffy's work original and affecting. A typical line, 'a bowl of apples rotten to the core' ('Disgrace', *MT* 48), blends the pleasant image of a fruit dish, evocative of a still life painting or homely domestic space, with a disturbing voiceover that all is not well. This tendency to make something familiar seem alien signals what Freud famously called 'unheimlich' ('uncanny'), and pushes the reader to a new awareness, which in Freudian terms would be about something repressed. Thus, the speaker in 'Education for Leisure' is a recognizable stereotype whose social disaffection represents a segment of society that we might wish to ignore but are uncomfortably pushed to face, contemplate, and even find sympathetic. We also see how Duffy is 'for our times'—historically specific and enduringly relevant—for although written during the 1980s, the poem is also pertinent to the economic recession that began in the mid-2000s.

While the spat over 'Education for Leisure' is amusing and Duffy the clear winner, the notorious comments from the Oxford Chair of Poetry in 2012 give more pause. In a lecture, 'Poetry, Policing and Public Order', Sir Geoffrey Hill made a denigratory remark about one of Duffy's poems: '"My simultaneous incompatible response is this is not democratic English but cast-off bits of oligarchical commodity English such as is employed by writers for Mills & Boon and by celebrity critics appearing on A Good Read or the Andrew Marr show"' (Flood 2012). Although Duffy graciously ignored the hubristic slight, it was reported in *The Daily Telegraph*, *The Daily Mail*, and *The Guardian*—right wing and left wing, broadsheet and tabloid papers, all of which proved loyal to her.[3] *The Daily Mail* clearly welcomed her appeal to readers who might not naturally read poetry: 'She claims to have grown up in a "bookless house" and has become a passionate advocate for the teaching of poetry in schools and the popularization of the art among the young' (Gayle 2012). It printed 'Remembering a Teacher', the poem that Hill dismissed as juvenile, and referred to an interview for *The Guardian* in which Duffy had allegedly said that mobile phone texts and Facebook could foster poetry writing due to their methods of condensing language. Importantly, Hill and the paper misrepresented her remarks and less reported was his approval of 'The Christmas Truce' as something '"radically different"' (Flood 2012). Thus, the media can both shape and topple a poet's status by stirring controversy and preferring gossip to plaudits. However, as Lemn Sissay comments on Hill's attack, the dispute over what makes good poetry and who should read it prove that 'Poets are at the heart of revolution because revolution is the heart of the poet. Poets see things because they won't look anywhere else. They are single-minded in their pursuit of the poem' (2012).

Given the accolades, it might seem unthinkable that Duffy's rightful status is not secure but the atavistic chauvinism in classing Duffy as a 'Mills and Boon' poet echoes the fates of female poets over the preceding 300 years. Published and esteemed in their lifetimes, they lacked literary recognition and were subsequently side-lined or forgotten. In her day,

---

[3] Hill's slight was also blogged about on *Poetry News*, 1 February 2012, and on the American site *Scarriet*, September 2009.

Elizabeth Barrett Browning was suggested for laureate but passed over for Tennyson; then, after his death, Christina Rossetti was proposed but not appointed; and, rather than have a woman, there was a gap of four years. This book, therefore, aims to record the full range of verdicts on Duffy's achievements, to consolidate current readings, and to find traits that run across her entire oeuvre. Primarily, it defines what 'Duffyesque' means as an evaluative benchmark for other poets, just as Duffy is frequently compared to Philip Larkin, Seamus Heaney, or Tony Harrison. The subtitle, 'Poet for Our Times', is taken from the title to a poem discussed later that dramatizes the crossover and distance between poetry and journalism. The phrase flags the relevance of Duffy's poetry to the period in which she writes but does not mean the relevance is *only* to her lifetime. Duffy uniquely draws on the languages of both her contemporary culture and her literary heritages to probe what it means to be human, both in and beyond a specific time and place. As evidence, her date-specific 'Translating the English, 1989' (*TOC* 11) was included in a millennium anthology titled *News That Stays News* (Rae 1999), and her poems are read at ceremonies that mark the rites of passage from birth to death.

In 'Mrs Schofield's GCSE', Duffy addresses the specific issue of censoring her poem then pleads: 'Explain how poetry / pursues the human like the smitten moon / above the weeping, laughing earth; how we / make prayers of it' (*Bees* 15). Such a poem says much more than the words through the vital vehicles of image and sound. Here, her favourite symbol, the moon, is 'smitten', as if with the love and pain it sees on earth, and the assonance of the long 'oo'—in 'human' and 'moon'—stresses the magnetism between poetry and humanity. In these few lines, Duffy condenses her sense of vocation and her belief that poetry can mirror, provoke, and sacralise tears or joy: '"Poetry isn't something outside of life; it is at the centre of life. We turn to poetry to help us understand or cope with our most intense experiences. ... Whether I am writing for children or for adults, I am writing from the same impulse and for the same purpose. Poetry takes us back to the human"' (Winterson 2009). As discussed later and through the chapters, 'To be human is to reflect on being human' (Mousley 2013: 171) and this reflecting is what poetry does and produces most intensely. Duffy's poems plumb our private interiorities in which we think and feel, and which we struggle to access or verbalize. They express and explore our attempts to put into words the knotty states of love, loss, and yearning for connection—to feel at 'home in our hearts' ('Disgrace', MT 48). They pinpoint our desire to shape ourselves from within rather than according to the scripts of others, or to reach back for our child-hoods. Her poems accommodate the irrational aspects of experience that manifest in cultural myths and individual dreams. They nurture our dual sense of being unique and of wishing to identify with others; and they speak of the nourishing milk of human kindness. Collectively, they open up the full range of human experience that we can find within ourselves, in the lives of others, and in the environment.

LIFE, CAREER, AND WRITING

'Duffy likes her work to be visible but to remain herself unseen' (Ross 2012) and any 'Google' search finds a narrative about the link between her life and writing that Duffy herself has largely scripted through a handful of extensive interviews (McAllister 1988; Forbes 2002; Cooke 2009; Wroe 2014). She was born in Lennoxtown, Glasgow (23 December 1955) to Mary [aka May] (née Black) and Francis (Frank) Duffy, a fitter and sub-sequent trades union activist who stood as a Labour candidate for parliament in 1983. May's parents and Franks' grandfather were Irish, Frank and his father were Scots, and when she was six, Duffy's family moved to Stafford, England. Recalling the migration in the poem, 'Originally' (*TOC* 7), she reflects, 'I want our country, I said / but then you forget, or don't recall, or change', and this psychic dislocation reverberates in many poems. Contingently, she asserts, 'I haven't actually felt a very strong national identity, ever, ever' (*Second Shift* 1994: 20). Her lifelong enthusiasm for football, caught from her father and younger brothers, comes through in such poems as 'Munich' (*NSP* 136) or 'The Shirt' (*Bees* 18); she dedicates *Feminine Gospels* to her brothers and writes of her memories about them in 'Brothers' (*MT* 12). While professing no religious practice or belief since the age of 15, the language and iconography of Roman Catholicism, embedded from the weekly churchgoing ritual with her mother and from her convent schooling, permeate her poems and Duffy frequently talks of poetry as prayer. In 1977, she graduated in Philosophy from the University of Liverpool and the city features in several poems throughout her volumes, from 'Liverpool Echo' (*SFN* 44) to 'North-West' (*FG* 64). From 1981, she took up writer-in-residencies in East London Schools, funded by a C. Day Lewis Fellowship. Based on these experiences, 'Head of English' (*SFN* 12) jibes at the conflict between 'a real live poet' and a traditionalist English school curriculum—'We don't / want winds of change about the place'—and 'Comprehensive' (*SFN* 8) refers to the state system of schools for all, marking and interrogating its ideals of class and racial harmony. In 1996, Duffy moved to Manchester where she still resides. She was appointed Lecturer then Professor of Contemporary Poetry at Manchester Metropolitan University and subsequently became Creative Director of its Writing School.

Duffy insists that it is 'emotional truth' rather than autobiographical fact that informs the poems. Primarily, she is the rare order of professional poet: "'Yes, it is a vocation, to give your life, your imagination, to language; to offer up your experience of being human'" (Cooke 2009). Her writing began in Year 5 (aged 10) at St Austin's RC Primary School. She recalls the glow of proud detachment when the teacher, commemorated in 'In Mrs Tilscher's Class' (*TOC* 8), typed up six of her poems and tied them together with a shoelace. At St Joseph's Convent [Secondary] School, she was further inspired by June Scriven, the subject of 'Death of a Teacher' (*NSP* 134), who helped Duffy publish her first pamphlet, *Fleshweathercock and Other Poems,* in 1973, and then by Jim Walker at Stafford Girls' High School. A subsequent influence was Adrian Henri (1932–2000) whom she met in 1972, and with whom she was in relationship for nearly ten years and collaborated on a poetry pamphlet, *Beauty and the Beast* (1977). Henri was a painter, musician, and member of The Liverpool Scene, a poetry-rock group that took poetry to pubs and clubs during the 1960s. Along with Brian Patten and Roger McGough, he contributed to the best-selling anthology *The Mersey Sound* (1967) which was an antidote to the situation famously sketched by Adrian Mitchell in 1964: 'Most people ignore poetry because poetry ignores most people' (Mitchell 1964: Preface). Duffy continues these poets' left-wing perspective, strong elements of performance, rhythm, humour, and symbolism, particularly the surrealist disjunctions that Henri loved. She dedicated to him her pamphlet, *William and the Ex-Prime Minister* (1992), that had a limited print run of one hundred and that includes a sequence of satirical 'prayers' from her earlier pamphlet, *Thrown Voices* (1986).

In Liverpool, Duffy knew working-class playwrights, Willy Russell and Alan Bleasdale, and her two plays, *Take my Husband* (1982) and *Cavern of Dreams* (1984), were performed at the Liverpool Playhouse. Her radio play, *Loss,* was a BBC broadcast in July 1986; *Little Women, Big Boys* was produced at the Almeida Theatre, London in 1986, and *Grimm Tales* was performed at the Young Vic in November 1994. Among subsequent adaptations are *Casanova* (West Yorkshire Playhouse 2007), *Rapunzel,* for the balletLORENT dance version (2013), and *Everyman* at the National

Theatre, London (2015), also published by Faber. Not surprisingly, then, she excels at the dramatic monologue, evincing 'the most valuable skills of the playwright: dramatic timing and characterization' (Donaghy 1991: 244). Her skill in writing lyrics was also budding and the title of her 1982 pamphlet, *Fifth Last Song: Twenty-One Love Poems,* links to sequences by Pablo Neruda and Adrienne Rich. Looking back on these formative years, Duffy states:

> Poetry now is much more part of the fabric of people's lives than it was, say, thirty years ago. There weren't any women poets around then. The best thing that made poetry less Oxbridge, I think, was the Liverpool poets. They had quite a lot of hostility and snobbery to deal with from the Oxbridge mafia, who fortunately now don't have as much power. As a teenager, I went to poetry readings like pop concerts: I heard Norman MacCaig, Peter Porter, Adrian Mitchell, when I was 15, 16. It was wonderful. That all these poets should be alive and talking in the language I thought in. (Duffy, Viner 1999)

When Duffy won the National Poetry Competition in 1983 for 'Whoever She Was' (*SFN* 35), responses were mixed and getting her first volume published was not a given: 'I'd been to every major publisher in England before Anvil took it [*Standing Female Nude*] and they'd all turned it down' (*Second Shift* 1994: 22). Through the late 1980s and early 1990s, however, Duffy 'became one of the busiest poets on the circuit. She took residencies, gave readings, visited schools, encouraged younger poets on Arvon Foundation courses and was *The Guardian*'s poetry critic 1988–9' (Forbes 2002: 22). In 1991, Duffy met Scottish-Nigerian poet, Jackie Kay, her partner for over ten years. However, it was the birth of Duffy's daughter, Ella, in 1995, that self-confessedly became her central consciousness: 'so I changed, I learned, / turned inside out—or that's / how it felt when the child burst out' ('Thetis', *WW* 5–6). This reorientation glistens in her poems for children and in the intensified reflections on Duffy's own mother, particularly following her death in 2005: '"I remember going to see her in one of those frightening chapels of rest. And there was a silence so deafening that it did deafen me. It was four years before I could write about it, and then eventually a poem ['Premonitions'] did come"' (Preston 2010). This personal lyricism continued during her laureate years when she also resuscitated the craft of public poetry, earning praise for 'her indefatigable record in responding to public events over the five years of her tenure as poet laureate' (Wilkinson 2014).

Poetry Volumes and the Critics

Duffy made an impressive entry to the British poetry arena when reviewers applauded her first volumes. As she became a serious contender in the ring, however, some critics felt the need to knock her out and, as already illustrated, she is still not without detractors. Robert Nye's 1986 review of *Standing Female Nude* (1985) is often cited: 'A clarity, a mixture of charm and truthfulness which breaks the windows of perception in new ways altogether ... a book that marks the debut of a genuine and original poet'. Reviewing her next book, *Selling Manhattan* (1987), Vernon Scannell noted the stylistic spread, from the tender 'Warming Her Pearls' to the disturbing 'Psychopath', and judged it 'one of the most satisfying new volumes of poetry to come my way in the past couple of years ... The world that is reflected and explored in these poems is almost entirely urban and more or less darkened by poverty, violence, fear, resentment and frustration. ... [Duffy's] intelligence, wit and verbal resourcefulness treat these realities in ways that are not depressing' (1987/8). In interview, Duffy explained: '*Selling Manhattan* is mainly about loss. The poems explore the loss of contact with true values and there's an ecological theme that ties in with that although I wasn't really aware of it at the time. I suppose I'm trying to shape through language things which are outside of it; to give a voice to those whom we've denied a voice, attempts at pre-language' (Buckley 1989). In his effusive review of *The Other Country* (1990) Dennis O'Driscoll noticed these ambitious raids on the inarticulate: 'Duffy's poetry concerns itself, too, with the limits of language, with the white spaces on which words leave no imprint. She is aware of how often words veil what they signify, how difficult it can be to match language to feeling. She strives to express the ineffable, to recover lost time, to give a hearing to the body language of lovers and the "wordless barefaced truths" of strangers, to catch the "phrases of light" and "the colour thought is / before language"' (1990: 65). He approved a discernible shift towards 'more personal territory'.

Mean Time (1993) caused a cascade of praise, typically, 'one of the best and most intelligent collections to have been published by a younger poet in recent years' (Harris 1993), and Sean O'Brien's oft-cited prophecy: 'she could well become the representative poet of the present day' (1993). It was the book promoted through the New Generation Poets in 1994 and first set for A Level. *Mean Time* ends with 'Prayer', voted the 'second most popular poem in the language' in 2003, trumped only by Philip Larkin's 'The Whitsun Weddings' (Ezard 2003). In *The Poetry Book Society Bulletin*, where it was the recommended choice, Duffy explains the title:

> The poems are about the different ways in which time brings about change or loss. In the collection, I mean to write about time. The effects of time can be mean. Mean can mean average. The events in the poems can happen to the average woman or man. The dwindling of childhood. Ageing. The distance of history. The tricks of memory and the renewal of language. The end of love. Divorce. New love. Luck. And so on. ... Lastly, I have tried to order the poems in *Mean Time* in such a way that the collection shares the coherence of a record album; that it reads with some kind of emotional, not literal, narrative. Opening with Manfred Mann's 'Do Wah Diddy Diddy' and closing with the quieter place names of the shipping forecast familiar from the radio—*Mean Time* tries to record the brief words we hear and speak under the clock. In that effort, at least, I hope it is optimistic. (PBS 1993)

Duffy's role in a renaissance of love poetry was considered brave: 'At a time when coolness and cleverness are at a premium among poets of her generation, Carol Ann Duffy's passion and compassion are unfashionable virtues' (O'Driscoll 1990: 66). With the publication of *Selected Poems* (1994), critics rehearsed previous verdicts and interviewers rehearsed the stock questions about class, feminism, and sexuality whereas Duffy aired her sense of becoming more steadily autobiographical and also more confidently experimental, trying longer poems, for example. In terms of perspective, she saw beyond 'isms': 'I think I've been interested in the failures of our lives—inarticulacy and the feeling people have that they have talent and energy, but that they haven't been given any opportunity to develop it' (*Second Shift* 1994: 22). The *Selected Poems* printed new monologues that anticipated *The World's Wife* and that might explain the misogynistic bias of some reviews. *The Pamphlet* (1998) also included three of the 'wife' monologues, and it took a female critic, Helen Dunmore, to pen a spectacular article that addressed the tendency for 'biography' rather than 'form' to dominate reviews:

> Poets have been much in the public eye this past year or so. But if their personalities have been analysed in the broadsheets, or blazoned across the tabloids, poems themselves have stayed in the shadows. ... Most people prefer gossip to poetry.

Carol Ann Duffy, however, is a genuinely popular poet. Her work sells, is widely read, discussed, enjoyed, imitated. ... Few poets ever manage to make their readers feel, again and again, that strange pang of mingled recognition and excitement that Duffy can evoke with such poems as 'Plainsong', 'Warming Her Pearls', 'Small Female Skull' or 'The Way My Mother Speaks'. Her ear is fine, her tone beautifully poised, her language makes an appeal which seems to be naked but is really clothed in art. (Dunmore 1999: 80)

The World's Wife (1999) is the volume that decidedly broadened Duffy's audience, due to becoming a set text in schools and to its entertainment value, as Katharine Viner records:

In the world of British poetry, Carol Ann Duffy is a superstar. Highbrow and lowbrow, readers love her: from critics such as Sean O'Brien, who calls her 'the representative poet of her day', to students who study *Mean Time*, her majestic 1993 collection, as an A-level set text. Her poems are accessible and entertaining, yet her form is classical, her technique razor-sharp. She is read by people who don't really read poetry, yet she maintains the respect of her peers. Reviewers praise her touching, sensitive, witty evocations of love, loss, dislocation, nostalgia; fans talk of greeting her at readings 'with claps and cheers that would not sound out of place at a pop concert'. (Viner 1999)

Viner's inviting summary outlines the book's varied sources: '*The World's Wife* is a joyous, exuberant book of poems about women usually excluded from myth and history: wives, such as Mrs Pilate, Mrs Aesop, Mrs Darwin, Mrs Faust, Frau Freud, Mrs Quasimodo; women usually defined by their men—Delilah, Anne Hathaway, Eurydice; and re-tellings of old stories in which the lead changes sex—Queen Kong, the Kray Sisters and Elvis's twin sister, the nun' (1999). For Duffy, the monologues—drawing on the Bible stories from her Catholic upbringing, the history lessons at school, and the pop music and films she imbibed—are costumes for 'naked' emotions and insights:

I think the poems are looking for the missing truth, rather than accepting the way we've been taught. ... So it's looking for missing or hidden or unspoken truths in old stories. It wouldn't have worked if you'd just gone through a list of favourite tales and revised them. You had to find something hard and truthful in the story. That's why it took so long to write. Each poem had to be personally honest, and have some kind of autobiographical element in it, whether it had happened to me or whether it was an emotional or intellectual truth. (Duffy, Viner 1999)

On the subject of the book's feminism, Forbes sees 'The harrowing personal note of *The Other Country* and *Mean Time* replaced by a roistering, wickedly spiced burlesque' and although 'A few men think the poems are a bit too anti-men', he defends, 'It is hard for anyone, male or female, to resist the book's best jokes' (2002: 23).

Feminine Gospels (2002) is to date the most undervalued volume, perhaps because several poems demand more commitment from the reader, due to their longer length and densely de-familiarizing symbolism. Also, the title belies the book's scope and some critics simply made links with the use of myth in *The World's Wife* (Burt 2002). Duffy describes the book's junction of public and personal references:

> Perhaps because I've been writing a lot for children—poems and fairy tales mostly—many of the poems have a dark fairy tale, or myth-like quality. A woman grows taller and taller and taller. Another gets louder. The Map Woman's Skin is an A to Z of her home town. A girl searches in the forest for her lost umbilical cord. There are many tall stories here, circling female experience, and told as gospel truth. The poems exist in an uncertain landscape where history crumbles in the distance and the women in these gospels walk towards us out of the dust of the words. Who was beautiful? Who went shopping? Who dieted? Who was the substitute?

> ... The collection closes with poems that are more prayer than gospel and more obviously personal. I wanted the collection to move in this way—from the larger 'public' statement of the gospel to the smaller, more intimate address of the poem as prayer, in love or parenthood or bereavement. (*PBS* 2002)

Jane Draycott writes of the collection: 'Transformation and transmutation are at the heart of these poems. Like Jack's beanstalk, narratives extend supernaturally through the kaleidoscopic material, historical and imaginative worlds of female experience' (2004). Forbes reads 'The Laughter of Stafford Girls' High', that takes up twenty pages, as an allegory of the rise of feminism, 'sweeping away dowdy post-war austerity and buttoned-up emotional sterility' (2002). For Duffy, it is 'a comic elegy of the sort of schools I went to—a convent and then a girls' grammar school—and for a certain kind of woman teacher' (*PBS* 2002). Novelist Charlotte Mendelson advocates Duffy's skill with narrative: 'A brilliant tale of a school transformed by a giggling epidemic, it sings because of her language (sky "like Quink", the "passionate cold / of the snow"), her humour and, most of all, her ability to pin down a lifetime in half a line and, in a few more [poems], tell

private, dramatic, dazzling stories on which others would lavish a novel'
(Mendelson 2002). Duffy's shape-shifting in 'The Long Queen' or 'The
Woman Who Shopped' playfully scrutinizes female psychology. In 'The
Diet', a girl grows and shrinks but her abnormal relationship with food
is horribly grotesque, as Elaine Feinstein comments: 'An anorexic shriv-
els like Alice until she is blown away as a seed, to nestle at length in the
stomach of a gloriously self-indulgent eater. She has become literally that
thin woman notoriously found inside every fat one, except in this version,
she has no wish to get out' (Feinstein 2002). *Feminine Gospels* also has
poems on ageing, the commodification of feminine beauty, the war in
Afghanistan, the bombing of New York's twin towers, the struggles of a
single parent, and the challenge of love. These would unsettle the stron-
gest constitution, as Feinstein concludes:

> For the moment Duffy prefers to wear a tougher face, and to keep her voice
> jaunty. She moves through the lives she invents with a kind of casual confi-
> dence, which her characters sometimes briefly share, like the shopaholic who
> 'purchased a hat with a brim / walked with a suitor under its shadow, ditched
> him'. It is hard not to find that assumption of freedom heady. Even if, in this
> particular poem, the character is hardly given Duffy's approval, that readiness
> to move on is intoxicating. It teaches an odd, contemporary post-feminist
> courage; and perhaps that is the source of Duffy's huge popularity. (2002)

If the 'post-feminism' in *Feminine Gospels* promotes female autonomy,
in *Rapture* (2005) the fifty-two lyrics surpass specific contexts, gender,
or sexuality. Arguably, the intimacy and interconnectedness are female
preoccupations, but Duffy asserts the universality of her lyrics: 'I hope
that these poems deal with matters common to us all and that they transcend the particulars of any individual life' (*PBS Bulletin* 2005). *Rapture*
restored Duffy's waning reputation within the higher echelons of literary
police without damaging her popularity. It sold out in weeks, became a
set text at A Level, and won her the T.S. Eliot Prize. As with *Mean Time*,
acclaim tumbled from the mouths of critics: 'As the latest Carol Ann Duffy
collection it is magnificent; as an examination of modern love and how it
shapes us as human beings, it is unparalleled' (Cowing 2005a); 'The affair
may be "over", but in her verse she can sing it "over" and the effect is
uplifting and thrilling. Buy it. Keep it. Give it away' (Reynolds 2006);
and, 'This book of wonderful love poems is also a love poem to poetry
itself' (Padel 2005). While one reviewer recommends reading it from start

to finish (Cowing 2005a) and another taking it in small doses (Campbell 2006), they concur on its emotional force and literary virtuosity. As these reviews and the sales register, the narrative of a relationship from start to end both whets and satiates an appetite for a love poetry that is genuine, fresh, and makes space for the reader. The poems self-reflexively verbalize without cliché the many hues and moods of love, as Reynolds astutely comments:

> *Rapture* is sad, but not bleak. It draws on tradition, but is very up to date. Duffy is a poet who surprises with images that are precisely funny. In 'Text' the speaker, anxiously looking for secret messages from the beloved, is described tending 'the mobile now / like an injured bird'. The image returns in 'Wintering' where Duffy says 'I clutch the small stiff body of my phone'. In 'Syntax'—one of the most brilliant poems in the collection— she plays with the languages of past and present: 'Because I so do—as we say now—I want to say—thee, I adore, I adore thee ...'. Some of Duffy's phrases will not let you be. Living our ordinary lives without passion, we are 'queuing for death'; speaking ordinary phrases without telling the whole truth means that 'words, / are the cauls of the unsaid'. (2006)

As I will expand later, the sense that words are the 'cauls of the unsaid' is a Duffyesque trait. Significantly, the metaphor is deeply personal for Duffy was born with a caul, a membrane helmet, to her head ('Caul', *MT* 22).

Duffy's *New Selected Poems 1984–2004* (2004) offered a valuable compendium of her work and made a few ripples: 'her imaginative vision and her versatility with form and image are truly those of a "top poet"' (Butlin 2004); '[Duffy] seems at the peak of a thoroughly assured reputation' (Thwaite 2004). Minor alterations to the *Selected Poems* (1994) indicate how individual poems might seem more or less relevant ten years on and the eleven 'Other poems' were mostly uncollected. *Love Poems* (2010), a selection from her repertoire, was a choice for *The Guardian's* Book Club around Valentine's Day in 2013 which prompted a probing review.

> When her poems ask us to recognize common experiences they are not afraid of using common combinations of words. Her poem 'Twinned', for instance, takes the comically familiar idea of town twinning—a modern municipal vanity—as a metaphor for the giddy feeling that a person in love inhabits a related, but different place from the one in which they normally live. The ordinariness of the metaphor is signalled by the first line, which

deploys a well-worn idiom. 'I have been wined and dined / in the town with which this one is twinned'. How appropriately easy is that opening cliché, which signals that the speaker has been indulged in a way that cannot last. (Mullan 2013)

Reviewers of *The Bees* (2011), her first collection as Laureate, commended the elegies, particularly 'Water', based on her mother's last word: 'Such serious simplicity [of "Water"] reminds one of "Prayer", Duffy's breathtaking incantation of loss from *Mean Time* (1993), probably the finest single poem in her oeuvre. ... Duffy's inward turn should not imply that there's no room in *The Bees* for poems befitting a laureate' (Chapman 2011).

Alan Brownjohn describes the 'smooth, eye-catching dust jacket', the pages of textual art, the four sections of fourteen poems, and, 'her gratitude for a wide range of the poetry of the past: Shakespeare, obviously, but also Gerard Manley Hopkins, Thomas Hardy and Wilfred Owen; and, summoned by bees as celebrated in an entire book of the *Georgics*, Virgil. There is a new delighted recognition that rhyme, alliteration and repetition as they occur in ballads, folk songs and nursery rhymes deserve a place in the poetry of today'. He gladly notes her 'responsibility is to poetry more than a duty to the Establishment' (2012).

Duffy humbly likens her place in the tribe of poets to a twig on a branch or a wand in a stream ('Invisible Ink', *Bees* 26) and in 'Bees' (*Bees* 3) the symbols internationalize the tribe: 'daffodil, thistle, rose, even / the golden lotus'. Her sense of being both original and bound to her peers is also mediated by shifting singular and plural pronouns: 'and know of us / how your scent pervades / my shadowed busy heart'. Although Laureate, she still writes from the heart's shadows and this personal source is a key to her success: 'Pain past bearing, poetry's price, / to know which of the harms and hurts / dealt to you, to the day, was fatal' ('Valentine's', *Bees* 75). Dominic Hale regards the book's characteristic range:

This is an excellent collection, among Duffy's best. She has always been a political poet, and a poet concerned directly with modern as well as timeless concerns, a dual focus that certainly comes across in these poems. ... This collection, as with much of Duffy's oeuvre, is filled with poems to sing into cradles, and to pore over in dusty, tome-brimming rooms. She wields this paradox like a cutlass, a mask and an invitation all at once, switching voices, perspectives and views with the ease of a writer at the peak of her art. ... We take what we want from Duffy's poems: we plunge as far into them as we deem fit. But we all take something. (2012)

For Duffy, public and private modes are two sides of the same coin; the grief at her mother's passing infused 'Last Post' (*Bees* 4–5) that marks the deaths of the two remaining veterans of World War I. Bees are cohering symbols for species endangered by technologies and consumerism that include poetry. The strong hum of environmental awareness in many poems answers Germaine Greer's journalistic epistle when Duffy was made Laureate: 'You write about people, about feelings, about our gropings in the dark towards each other, our evasions and fantasies—and I love what you do. But I wanted [Alice] Oswald because I wanted someone who could make our hearts ache for the irreplaceableness of everything we are losing, the filthiness of our sky and our poisoned sea and the silent struggles of our trees. In my distorted view, the responsibility of the national poet is to the land and its inhabitants, not to its rulers' (Greer 2009). Duffy is too much her own voice to be goaded by such a plaint, but the buzzing alertness to climate change all though *The Bees* carries on into *Ritual Lighting: The Laureate Poems* (2014) that logs the halfway point of Duffy's term. It mixes commissioned pieces with elegies to her father, but all are determinedly faithful to her principles.

In a digital age, the rich materiality of *Rapture, The Bees*, and *Ritual Lighting* are antidotes to the increasing prevalence of reading electronically and mediates the '"enduring"' quality of the book (Duffy, Lawson 2011). *Rapture* is particularly tactile: 'Its red-ribbon bookmark and sumptuous cover, a silver-gilt scene depicting some of the book's subject matter—a heron, shooting stars, a woman with arms outstretched to a crescent moon—suggest it could be an old children's book' (Laird 2005). It is also likened to a private diary—a sort of Folio Society Keepsake book that evinces times past (Oxley 2005: 106). The covers of *The Bees* and *Ritual Lighting* are flecked with gold, the pages adorned by Stephen Raw's textual art, and a gold ribbon bookmark entices the reader within. The publication of her *Collected Poems* (2015) revives pieces that had fallen by the wayside of the *Selected* and *New Selected Poems* or that resided in newspapers and other sites of their first publication. They should rightly stimulate new overviews of Duffy's long and lofty poetic journey.

Poet Laureate

In 2001, Forbes declared, 'The poet's poet in 1994, [Duffy] is quite clearly now the People's' (2001: 22) and in 2009, the top award of Poet Laureate recognized her esteem by both the poets—she won the Poetry Society's vote—and by the public who for the first time were polled for their preference by the Department for Culture, Media and Sport.[4] Congratulations came from the Labour Prime Minister, Gordon Brown, along with the literati. The position was an endorsement to carry on taking poetry into many walks of life and signalled huge advances in the status of women as poets. Judith Palmer, Director of the Poetry Society, announced, '"She writes in so many different registers, from the sardonic to the sexy, that almost everyone can find a Duffy poem that speaks personally to them. She won the National Poetry Competition in 1983, in an era when women poets were still being described condescendingly as 'poetesses'. Her work helped open up possibilities for generations of women. Her appointment is a triumph on so many levels"', and Jo Shapcott, Poetry Society President, insisted, '"Her appointment as Poet Laureate is great news for poetry. She is the first woman Laureate, which by itself is a matter of rejoicing but, just as important, is her individual and remarkable gift as a poet. She will bring twin strengths of talent and generosity to the post and make things fizz"' (Higgins 2009). Duffy's words on the post were repeated in many media outlets, from *The Times* to BBC *Woman's Hour*: '"What I want to do with my laureateship is spread poetry around—it isn't about me, it's about poetry—and so I'm going to bring in all kinds of different poets, bring them to people's attention, use the influence that comes with this appointment to commission and encourage, but most of all, to show people what we've got, because there's enough poetry out there for everyone"' (Winterson 2009). During the first half of her ten-year rule, the Duffyesque generosity is luminous: she regularly awarded the Queen's Medal for Poetry, '"because there are very good poets working now, and they should be more visible"' (Duffy, Winterson 2009), and she donated her £5750 stipend to a new annual Ted Hughes Award for New Work in Poetry—so far, winners of the award have ventured into new media and other unchartered waters. On 19 November 2013, she held an evening at Buckingham Palace to celebrate contemporary poetry,

---

[4] Duffy was earlier counted in the ten leading British poets chosen by their peers (Hilpern 2002).

recognizing unsung heroes of the industry and newcomers along with famous frontrunners. As rising star Kei Miller blogged afterwards:

> Can we therefore give credit (if not honour) where credit is due and say hats off to the poet laureate Carol Ann Duffy … for one night, she made much of the traditionally out-crowd, become the in-crowd. In Buckingham Palace there were spoken word poets, slam poets, poets in their 90s who could hardly manage the stairs, and poets in their 20s who were sprinting up and down two steps at a time; there were poets who had written enough work to have published more than one 'collected' or 'new and selected' volumes, and there were those whose first books had only recently come out, and still those who hadn't yet published any book at all. There were poets there whose work I've heard or read and thought it was cringe-worthily bad, and poets whose works humble me. There were poetry editors, poetry facilitators, retired professors who had possibly never written a poem themselves but had spent their lives inculcating a love of it in their students; there were widows and widowers and children of famous poets; there were people who weren't poets or professors of poetry at all but simply friends and ardent readers of poetry. (2013)

Here, Duffy can be seen hinging radical and conservative poetry politics, stating on BBC News: '"Poetry is all about looking at the ordinary and transforming it—the Midas touch. And the monarchy has that too. … The presence of the Queen can help heal, transform and make things magic"' ('First female Poet Laureate named' 2009). The historic nature of Duffy's appointment also aroused new interest in its genealogy and significance. Her Scottish roots underlined that the post is not exclusive to England: 'Scot is made first female laureate', proudly declared the *Scottish Herald* (Miller 2009). Half way through her reign, an exhibition at the Palace of Holyrood, Edinburgh, 'celebrates the work of the current Poet Laureate and explores the role of the Poet Laureate, and the close relationship between poet and monarch over the last three and a half centuries'.[5] Duffy typically kept her feet on the ground by requesting her 600 bottles of sherry up front while composing a label in verse ('At Jerez', *RL* 10). She constantly extends the reach of poetry by giving her name, poems, and time to low-key projects, such as anthologies in aid of charities, paintings by a Welsh artist, or Christmas pamphlets. More visibly, she is vociferous in campaigns against cuts to the provision of books for prisoners, cuts to the Arts, and cuts to public libraries. As the

[5] Poetry for the Palace: Poets Laureate from Dryden to Duffy The Queen's Gallery, 7 August–2 November 2014.

'people's poet', she can take some credit for numbers at poetry readings shooting up from around sixty people, on a good day, to hundreds. (Reynolds 2014)

POETRY AND THE TIMES: THEY ARE A-CHANGIN[6]

In 2009, Duffy reckoned, '"Poetry has changed since the days of Larkin—he's a good poet, but poetry has changed for the better. It's not a bunch of similarly educated men—it's many voices, many styles. The edge has become the centre"' (Winterson 2009). Similarly, in *Beyond the Lyric: A Map of Contemporary Poetry*, Fiona Sampson declared, 'We're enjoying a period of tremendous richness and variety' (2012: 2). This evolution of a more pluralistic scene can be traced over the three preceding decades. In 1994, Duffy had remarked: '"The poetry reading has steadily been increasing in popularity over the last decade, almost repeating the boom of the '60s in poetry. And there's a supportive network of poetry organizers and readers who help to provide this life for poetry. And book sales, of course, are up, so I think people are now actually buying poems"' (*Second Shift* 1994: 22). In retrospect, Duffy can be seen as a major component in this continuing expansion. Along with Simon Armitage, she dominated the 1994 New Generation Promotion that consisted of twenty poets under forty who gave live readings around the country and on the media. In his editorial to a special 'New Gen' *Poetry Review*, Forbes linked literary with social pluralization: 'In England especially, the '80s was a time of social atomization—after all, it was official government policy. The centre could not hold in anything. Private worlds, subcults, proliferated. The central channels of literary culture, the BBC, Oxbridge, Penguin books, Faber & Faber, the *New Statesman* and *Listener*, all had to adapt to being just one player amongst several. … The independent poet who broke with the old tradition and established poetic independence as a viable option was Carol Ann Duffy' (Forbes 1994: 6). In 1995, however, in his survey, 'Why The New Popular Poetry Makes More Sense', Forbes tended to separate the literary from the cultural. He noted two lines of poets: the postmoderns for whom 'the relationship between language and the world is held to be intrinsically unreliable' and who reach a small number of readers; and the 'famously popular poets', which is where he put Duffy. He detects that 'popular poets'

---

[6] *The Times They are A-Changin* (1964), album with title track by Bob Dylan.

write in 'New Plain Style' that has a 'grab you by the lapels directness' and usually 'a speaking voice', but warns: 'Many poets have brilliantly exploited low-key conversational diction but it has to be played off against *something*: the rhythmic expectation of formal metre, as in Robert Frost, for instance. … If poetry has a role now and a future, it has to be as something other than a regurgitator of received ideas and platitudes clothed in language identical to that of everyday spoken and journalistic discourse' (Forbes 1995: 47).

As if in response, although published before his article, Duffy's parodic 'Poet for Our Times' (*TOC* 15) explores the overlap and gap between the poet and the tabloid journalist. The monologue is in the voice of an editor who composes headlines for a generic 'Daily Paper'. He brags that his job is not to educate but sell: 'Cheers. Thing is, you've got to grab attention / with just one phrase as punters rush on by.' Placing him in a pub, the jovial 'Cheers' indicates his lack of scruples concerning the accuracy or sensitivity of his reporting—'just bang the words down like they're screaming *Fire!*'—for he has to compete with other media: 'what with the box / et cet'. As here, Duffy demonstrates how his abuse of language is antithetical to a poet's: he uses colloquialisms and abbreviations; he turns a noun into a verb—'to headline that, mate'; and his lines, 'I like to think that I'm a sort of poet / for our times', are followed by the very unpoetic, 'My shout, Know what I mean?' The last lines, 'The poems of the decade … *Stuff 'em! Gotcha!* / The instant tits and bottom line of art', refer to the controversially demeaning photographs of topless women on page three in a certain tabloid, designed to boost sales, and allegorize his desecration of language. Thus, Duffy implicitly distances the literary poet from the shallow values and vulgar vernacular of the commercial editor, and also from readers who crave sensationalism above justice or rich language. When Thatcher's government decided to make war on the Falklands, 'Gotcha' was a famous headline in *The Sun* (4 May 1982) with the equally gloating sub-line: 'Our lads sink gunboat and hole cruiser'. Its relish in the victory of British forces over the naval ship, ARA *General Belgrano*, in which 323 Argentinian crew members were killed, typically fuelled the readers' crude nationalist tendencies.

Characteristically, 'Poet for our Times' is both period specific and enduringly relevant. In 1981, media magnate Rupert Murdoch bought the UK broadsheet, *The Times*, to which Duffy may also be referring in the poem's title. From 1969, Murdoch had owned the popular British tabloid papers, *News of the World* and *The Sun*. In 2011, Murdoch's industry was investigated for phone hackings that broke laws of privacy and moral codes of decency. In her bias against the assumptions of power-hungry capitalists, Duffy ruptures what Bakhtin calls the 'centralizing tendencies' of mono-lithic discourse in favour of 'dialogized heteroglossia' that intervenes in the 'struggle among socio-linguistic points of view' (Bakhtin 1981: 273). Duffy's 'dialogized heteroglossia' consists in the speech of the editor, the evoked voice of his drinking companion, the headlines, the stories behind them, the presumed appetites and attitudes of the paper's readers, and the implicit censure of the poet. Moreover, Duffy hits Forbes' benchmark of value by playing off the egotistical clichés of the journalist—'Make that a scotch, ta'—and the crude headlines—'GREEN PARTY WOMAN IS A NIGHTCLUB TART'—against rhythmic formal metre. The poem's five rhyming sestets accentuate how the speaker's colloquialisms and tabloi-dese impoverish thought along with language. Thus, we see in 'Poet for Our Times', Duffy's sharp use of slang to create a character and culture, her feminist lens, and her insistence on the place of poetry to reflect, comment on, and challenge dominant discourses. Thereby, she also challenges the impact of these discourses on the shared concept of decent humanity. As Mousley puts it: 'The human condition is complicated then, but not *so* complicated as to prohibit impassioned criticism of societies that run roughshod over our humanity, or accommodate only bits of it' (2013: 171).

Conversely, Duffy wants poetry to enhance the quality of life, 'to make alive the areas of existence that aren't encouraged, that aren't useful for jobs, that don't make money. It's to make all that alive' (BBC 1989). In contrast to the smutty tabloid, the broadsheet paper makes a better bedfel-low for such poetry. From 1999, Ruth Padel ran a hugely popular series, 'The Sunday Poem', comprising of an introduction to a poet along with a close reading, in the *Independent on Sunday* that found 'hungry read-ers' (Padel 2002: 3) for modern poems and Duffy's 'Prayer' inaugurated the series. In January 2000, *The Guardian* started 'The Saturday Poem', which continues to this day. Padel claims the success of these initiatives contributed to a 'Poetry renaissance' tracked back to the 1970s (2002: 1–3). Duffy reiterates, 'There are so many more voices: other cultures, women, performance poets. You know, people away from London and Oxbridge have made ... this rich kind of broth"' (Edemariam 2009). This rich broth consists of new poets and, pertinently, new dialects. As Padel observes: 'Standard English is only one version among many. That what-ever Standard English now is, to write in it is to make a deliberate choice of tradition, allegiance and voice' (2002: 34). Forbes notes Duffy's pio-neering influence here: 'Her technique is absolutely distinctive and has been much copied. Using lashings of slang ("dough", "stash", "readies") and a buttonholing style ("squire"), it grabs the attention' (2002). The prevalent vernacular did, however, risk her literary credibility, as in Mark Reid's review of *Mean Time*: 'Carol Ann Duffy has been described as the foremost of the twenty New Generation Poets. ... In this array of ventriloquist voices she reproduces and is reproduced by the cacophony of multimedia, multilingual, late twentieth-century Britain. ... Duffy typifies the seductive dangers of so much contemporary poetry' (Reid 1992/3: 34). Aware of the gender bias and elitism in such reviews, Rumens stated, 'Poetry's vital energies derive from the way we speak and it perhaps takes special courage for women poets to write in a way that stresses this relationship, rather than seek approval by flaunting their more academic literary credentials' (1990: 15).

Women and Poetry

On BBC Radio 4 in 2014, Peggy Reynolds was able to claim, 'the word "poet" in the twenty-first century so obviously includes women now' (Reynolds 2014). Leading up to this pinnacle, Duffy's career began when 'women's poetry' was a pejorative term. In her Preface to *Sylvia Plath: Poems chosen by Carol Ann Duffy*, she notes Plath's posthumous fame, 'not least as a heroine to the feminist movement of the 1960s and '70s. Here was a uniquely radical, stylized poetic voice which claimed for its subject something that had not previously appeared in "the canon"—the experience of being a woman' (Plath 2014). Into the 1980s, special 'women poet' numbers of *Poetry Wales* (1987), *Aquarius* (1987), *Women: A Cultural Review* (1990), *Poetry Review* (1996), and *Feminist Review* (1999), along with academic conferences and critical books, captured and stimulated conversations about the desirability and viability of a specifically female aesthetic. Since the early 1990s, editors preface anthologies with the regrettable necessity of segregating women: 'Ghettoising and separatism are not options I willingly court' (France 1993: 14); 'Given the space—and a more perfect world—these poets should appear alongside their male counterparts' (Salzman 2008: 7). However, they aver the need for proper critical responses: 'The best women's poetry may be still unrecognized if, as I suspect, we have not yet understood how to read it' (Greer 2001: x); 'While publishing has opened up, criticism has not, and the work of some of our best women poets continues to be neglected or ignored in the current critical climate' (Colette Bryce, Rees-Jones 2010: 402). In 1989,

Duffy was a self-proclaimed feminist (BBC 1989) but in 1990 lamented: 'I hate that expression, "woman poet". It's as though we were a separate section. ... We are reviewed together in the newspapers, while the men are treated individually. As I see it, any poet is writing about their experience of being alive. Gender informs that experience, but that is all. Feminist poetry did play a very useful role in the seventies, but we've moved beyond that' (*Options* 1990).

As she specifies here, it was the reviewing that prevented poets moving 'beyond that'. One reviewer of Duffy's *Selected Poems*, in which six of the early 'Wife' monologues first appeared, complained: 'One wants more from poetry than whinges ... The personae here are too many, I would contend, and indicate a dissipation of personality, a loss of focus on moral concerns, a loss of responsibility. ... Composition is to be found in Carol Ann Duffy's poetry ... but it is infrequent. What we have more often in its place are poetic *moments* ... unsustained by finished craft or diligence' (Milne 1995). The patronizing tone, in what reads like a school report, smacks of resistance in the gut rather than impartial engagement with the work. It complains of 'bleakness', as if it never had a place in good poetry, and queries Duffy's morality, authenticity, and skill. A reviewer in the prestigious *Times Literary Supplement*, who conceded she was 'hailed as our best British poet, the voice of a generation', described Duffy's use of italics to construct a demotic idiom as 'lean[ing] towards the demonstrative and the hysterical' (Sansom 1995). In 2002, Padel reports, 'testosterone bias is often unconscious, but women poets are aware of it all the time. ... the keener on controlling traditional patterns of rhyme and metre, the more damning [the male reviewer] can be, in unguarded moments, of women's poems. ... Form and technique still carry for many people an unspoken charge of masculine supremacy' (2002: 38–9).

In 1994, Duffy claimed the label 'woman poet' as a 'self-evident strength' rather than a category' (*Second Shift* 1994: 22) but recorded prejudice in the industry: '"Most of the publishing houses have male editors. There's one female poetry editor in Britain. Most of the reviewers are male; most of the anthologists are too. There is a two-tier thing but this is changing at the grass roots level and has yet to filter through to the boys"' (Armstrong 1993: 5). Correspondingly, 'Mrs Eurydice' laments, 'But the Gods are like publishers, / usually male' (*WW* 59). In 'Anon' (*FG* 33–4), Duffy lightheartedly alludes to all the female writers who masqueraded as 'Anonymous' but more gravely to women who became a 'nurse, nanny, or nun' and never wrote at all: 'A woman I knew / kept her skull / on a shelf in a room—/ Anon's—/ and swore that one day / as she worked at her desk / it cleared its throat / as though it had something / to get off its chest' (*FG* 33). Anon hands down the baton, the pen, urging younger women to write while the 'hey nonny no' mimics a careless indifference on the part of those who stand in her way. Duffy makes visible many women whose stories never got off their chests in *The World's Wife* monologues, 'Dorothy Wordsworth is Dead' (*Bees* 53), and 'Dorothy Wordsworth's Christmas Birthday' (2014).

The World's Wife opens with 'Little Redcap' (3–4) that charts Duffy's journey from trying to write like a man to finding her own voice: '"Little Red Cap is a version of me. The first verse describes the landscape of Stafford—houses, playing fields, factories, the allotment near the railway. These are all literal details of the geography of my home town. … But it also looks at the idea of women in poetry being dominated by the male tradition"' (Duffy, Wood 2005). The ten years of captivity to the wolf is an allegory of her writing career: 'He stood in a clearing, reading his verse out loud / In his wolfy drawl, a paperback in his hairy paw, / Red wine staining his bearded jaw.' When the heroine conquers this beast, she achieves a linguistic freedom that contingently transforms the world around. She also discovers her ancestry, 'the glistening virgin white of my grandmother's bones', as Duffy explains: '"In a sense, in the poem, the grandmothers' bones are the silent women who aren't present in English Literature"' (Wood 2005). Nevertheless, we cannot tidily reduce her reworking of the fairy tale to literal realism and the female empowerment occurs in a space between the recognizable and the fantastic. The final line, 'Out of the forest I come with my flowers, singing, all alone', leads distinctly female but also distinctly independent creativity into the next millennium.

Early in Duffy's career, Forbes noted that Duffy had 'spawned many disciples' (1994: 6). She certainly models female collegiality. Following her appointment as Laureate, *The Guardian* published a two-page spread, in which Duffy paid tribute to U.A. Fanthorpe, who had died the day before, and printed one poem each by several contemporaries, stating, 'It is a historic day for women and for poets in Britain. We celebrate and share that here—from the magnificent Welsh national poet, Gillian Clarke, to Scotland's greatest performer of poetry, Liz Lochhead, to the astonishing English lyric genius of Alice Oswald and the deep humanity of Jackie Kay. I am so proud to number myself among them' (Duffy, 'Sisters in Poetry' 2009). Putting her energy where her principle is, in 2010 Duffy initiated the biennial Dorothy Wordsworth Festival, a three-day showcase of women's poetry. In 2012, the lead names, Gillian Clarke, Liz Lochhead, and Duffy, were the National Poets of Wales, Scotland, and the UK respectively. As Duffy wrote in her warm Foreword to Lochhead's *Selected Poems*, her first volume, *Memo for Spring*, had 'blossomed out into the very male landscape of Scottish poetry and somehow managed to make that landscape female' (Lochhead 2011: ix). In 2014, there were two more female national appointments, Sinead Morrissey as first poet laureate for Belfast and Paula Meehan as the Ireland Professor of Poetry, and on the eve of International Women's Day, all five performed together at London's South Bank Centre. Duffy also admires Pakistani-British Imtiaz Dharker, whom she tags 'poet laureate for the world' (Lawson 2011). Duffy promotes established and new poets, proving that good poetry can centre women's experiences and also that a good female poet is not confined to them. In 2012, she was a judge for the T.S. Eliot prize that went to Sharon Olds, known for her confessional writing, a genre more respected in the United States than in Britain where it had been relegated to the inferior practices of amateurs and sentimental women (Pollard 2001).

Certain events indicate more steps forward than back and interviewed in 2014, Duffy perceives huge strides towards gender equality but still '"a way to go"' (Reynolds 2014). She now takes her place in a respected and dynamic genealogy of women poets: whereas in 1997, she was placed after Emily Bronte, Emily Dickinson, Plath, and Elizabeth Jennings (Gurr and de Piro 1997), in 2005, she was among one hundred American and British 'Modern Women Poets' (Rees-Jones 2005). In 2005, Fiona Sampson became the first individual female editor of *Poetry Review* since Muriel Spark in the 1940s and Ruth Padel was made the first woman Chair of Poetry at the University of Oxford in 2009 but withdrew due to allegations of a smear campaign. The first four Ted Hughes' Awards were won by women, and in the list of Next Generation Poets 2014, women outnumbered men by twelve to eight. Duffy's work and status also synchronize with the UK's gradual openness towards different sexualities. In 1999, media coverage of the laureateship spread rumours that Prime Minister Tony Blair thought her sexuality would disqualify her, which led Duffy to state: '"I think gay, straight, whatever, relationships are just a banal fact of life. They're just straight facts. I was very surprised: it made me see that the country I thought I lived in wasn't the one I lived in. It was appalling that sexuality could be written about in that kind of way. I think that gay people should be proud and relaxed and celebratory of their lives, in the same way that straight people are"' (Viner 1999). In 2004, civil partnerships were established and in 2014 gay marriage was legalized in England. Duffy's pronouns are usually open to any orientation of sex and gender but she writes of sexual ambivalence and same-sex love in such poems as 'from Mrs Tiresias' while lesbian eroticism is freighted in 'The Laughter of Stafford Girls' High' (*FG* 35–54), 'Girlfriends' (*TOC* 43), and 'Oppenheim's Cup and Saucer' (*SFN* 48)—'eight lines of smouldering lust' (Goring 2004).

In summary, Duffy's uniquely hybrid technique adds inertia to the continuing crosscurrents of linguistically formal and avant-garde practices and prohibits fixing her in any one stream. A poet with an ear to a growing polyphony in British culture since the 1980s, Duffy leads some dominant trends that extend the imaginative and linguistic boundaries of the art. She rejuvenates the lyric, centres the language and perspectives of marginal groups, and restores poetry's function as public utterance. At the same time, her poetry delves shared, often taboo or extreme, human experience that traverses time, place, or personhood.

READING THE DUFFYESQUE

Duffy's unique crafting of emotional truth into literary forms that are woven from colloquial speech patterns, disruptive syntax, de-familiarizing symbols, and captivating sound effects constitute the 'poetic independence' gleaned by Forbes. When Forbes coined the epithet, 'Duffyesque', it was undefined but implicitly gendered and urban: 'There are poets who write in Duffyesque but the ones she has supported are originals, none more so than Alice Oswald, whose poems offer a defiantly rural counterpoint to Duffy's city muse' (Forbes 2002: 22). This section surveys the critical apparatus that surrounds Duffy's work then posits a broader yet also more precise set of principles by which we might identify and apply the Duffyesque in her own terms: as 'the music of being human'.

Since three titles, *Standing Female Nude*, *The World's Wife*, and *Feminine Gospels*, are explicitly female centric, and the poems in other volumes often centre a female speaker, Duffy invites feminist and gender criticism. They feature explicitly in five chapters of the staple text by Angelica Michelis and Antony Rowland (2003) but as part of a broader canvas: Jeffrey Wainwright on 'female metamorphoses'; Rowland on 'Love and Masculinity'; Michelis on 'gender and national identity'; Avril Horner on 'patriarchy and philosophy'; and Jane Thomas on 'gender as linguistic act'. Increasingly, Duffy avoids separatism while maintaining sex and gender as valid yet fluid categories. In *Hand in Hand: An Anthology of Love Poetry* (2001), she invited men and women poets to write a love poem to put next to one by a writer of the opposite sex. Increasingly, too, she is placed in mixed company: in Lesley Jeffries and Peter Sansom's collection of style-centred approaches, Duffy is the sole subject of one chapter on 'Point of View' but discussed along with Ian McMillan and Geoff Hattersley in another on 'caricatural effects' (2000). Sarah Broom's chapter: 'Gender, Sex, and embodiment', even-handedly concentrates on Duffy, Simon Armitage, and Grace Nichols (2006). Most usefully, then, Bertram includes Duffy in advocating a feminist discourse that avoids essentializing a '"feminist" poem, poetic or aesthetic' (Bertram 2004: 283).

Duffy is rightly placed within, at the cutting edge of, and beyond the distinctly 'English' tradition that excluded women and other nations until the new canons of the late twentieth century. A dialogue with other poets pervades her work. In the Foreword to her anthology, *Answering Back: Living Poets Reply to Poetry of the Past* (2007), she writes of 'a sense of coherence and community between the living and the dead poets' and that poets believe 'in the triumph of language over time'. Similarly, in her Preface to U.A. Fanthorpe's *New and Collected Poems*, Duffy notes how she 'understood the reimagining our traditions. She knew the importance of the energy between the past and the present, particularly in poetry' (Fanthorpe 2010). In his article, 'The Larkin-Duffy Line', Justin Quinn persuades: 'When one reads Larkin and Duffy together it becomes clear that far from being a radical break with the past, Duffy is the latest exponent of the tradition which in the twentieth century goes from Hardy to Thomas to Larkin.' At the same time, he recognizes, 'it is precisely because Duffy has caught much of the energy of recent social change in her poetry that she is so important' (Quinn 2000: 4). Duffy's dramatic lyrical voice and sly formalism undoubtedly position her after Eliot, Auden, and Larkin but her range and linguistic hybridization in every poem exceed one literary parameter. As Quinn continues, 'aspects of Duffy's Britishness would have made Larkin foam at the mouth' (2000: 4). With typical wit and seriousness, Duffy asserts, '"As anyone who has the slightest knowledge of my work knows, I have little in common with Larkin, who was tall, taciturn and thin-on-top, and unlike him I laugh, nay, sneer, in the face of death. I will concede one point: we are both lesbian poets"' (Forbes 2002: 20). Forbes adds, 'She is, of course, in many ways Larkin's antithesis, but they do occupy the same niche in their respective eras. Duffy is the poet of the multicultural noughties as Larkin was the bicycle-clipped representative of the dowdy, repressed fifties' (2002). Quinn similarly observes: 'Whereas Larkin would end poems with an elegiac panning shot, Duffy will often end with an imperative to action or vision, so that she seems to participate in, if not actually in some way to activate, social change. A large part of her rhetorical power draws from the increased political power of groups that were previously marginalized by the very social hierarchy that was so dear to Larkin' (2000: 4).

When it comes to influences, Duffy states that her early fare of 'Neruda, Prévert, Aimé Césaire' from *The Penguin Modern Poets* series nourished her writing more than the English poets she studied at school (Forbes 2002). However, the liberal outlook and word-play of Shakespeare suffuse her literary consciousness: 'love's will, our heart's iambic beat, brother / through time: full-rhyme to us' ('Shakespeare', *RL* 31). Additionally, she enjoyed the Welsh poetry of Dylan Thomas, says that Anglo-American, T.S. Eliot, 'devastated me and made me shiver' (McAllister 1988: 73), and the Scots, 'Norman MacCaig, Edwin Morgan, Liz Lochhead, Tom Leonard', are among her favourite poets (Duffy, *Second Shift* 1994: 20). She is compared to the Scottish modernist W.S. Graham, and in *Dream State: New Scottish Poets*, Daniel O'Rourke compares Duffy to John Burnside in that 'Scotland, clinging tenaciously as ever, has not left them' (O'Rourke 2002: ix). Her work is discussed in *Contemporary Scottish Women Writers* (Christianson and Lumsden 2000) and she was a contributor to *Addressing the Bard: Twelve Contemporary Poets Respond to Robert Burns* (Gifford 2009). Her *Selected Poems* was listed in *The Scotsman* as one of the twenty 'must-read' Scottish books—'Passed over for Poet Laureate a few years back, Ms. Duffy is nonetheless Scotland's foremost poet'—although she was deemed 'a cheerier, modern-day Ms. Sylvia Plath' (Cowing 2005b).

As the comparison to Anglo-American-Plath indicates, while her Scottish roots place her in a 'Scottish literature', it is more difficult to read Duffy's poems as distinctly Scottish literary practice—identifiable by allusions to its weather, translating Gaelic words, and expressing a sense of nationhood (Crawford and Imlah 2000). In *The Faber Book of Twentieth-Century Scottish Poetry*, Douglas Dunn says the younger poets, such as Lochhead and Duffy, show an 'unclenched nationalism, or refusal of any kind of nationalism on a poem's surface' (1992: xiv). Christopher Whyte comments that while Duffy indicates a willingness to be labelled a Scottish writer, her Scottishness is 'problematic': 'If her poetry breathes any landscape, it is that of Midlands England … Duffy's poetry pushes further and further away from charted territories' (2004: 221). O'Rourke dissects 'what like it is' from Duffy's 'The Way My Mother Speaks' (*TOC* 54) as a 'Scottish phrase' (2002: xx) whereas Stan Smith presumes it is her mother's Irish idiom. Poignantly, Smith points out the triangulation of Duffy's linguistic drifts—from her mother's Irish tongue, her father's Scots, and the unfamiliar dialects when the family uprooted to England (2008: 102). Reading her poems, we can easily connect Duffy's orientation towards the conditions of migrancy and exile with these dislocations in her childhood. For O'Rourke, Duffy is 'one of the most supple and compelling voices in the poetry of the Dis-United Kingdom' (2002: xx) while Linda Kinnahan pertinently observes how she 'traverses ideological and discursive constructions of nationalism' (2000: 209). Certainly, Duffy eschews any partisan stance and in her later volumes tends to mediate between conflicting factions, such as the Crown and anti-monarchists. She prefers to problematize politics with love and after Scotland's failed bid for independence in 2014, wrote a searingly affective tribute from a guilty but glad England: 'Aye, here's to you, / cousins, sisters, brothers, / In your brave, bold, brilliant land' ('September 2014').

Duffy's most politically specific poems pertain to the Thatcherite years when right-wing policies stoked elitism, materialism, and racism. In her section, 'Regionalism, Thatcherism', Padel reviews the cultural and economic robbery to which poets such as Duffy could not but respond (2002: 20–2). John Redmond's chapter on 'Lyric Adaptations' reductively cites Fenton, Raine, and Reid as Martians, with allegiances to Thatcherism, while Armitage and Duffy represent the New Generation and synonymously New Labour (2007). More accurately, she exposes power corruption irrespective of national or party politics, as in her laureate poems, 'Democracy' (*Guardian* 7 May 2010) or 'Politics' (*Bees* 12). As has been well established (Gregson 1996; Rees-Jones 1999; Dowson and Entwistle 2005), Duffy's treatment of fictionalized voices chimes with Mikhail Bakhtin's theories of dialogism that analyse an author's artistic orchestration of social speech types and hidden intentions (Bakhtin 1981: 262–3, 324). Accordingly, Greenlaw moots, 'A Duffy poem looks you straight in the eye, holds your gaze, takes it where it wants you to go' (Greenlaw 2009). More specifically, O'Rourke calls Duffy's verse 'a surveillance camera trained on the greedy and the seedy' (2002: xx).

The lens of social justice can be hard to fit with the language-based spectacles of post-structuralist critics, but they have nevertheless found Duffy's poems particularly photogenic. Horner labels Duffy 'a feminist postmodernist writer' (2003: 99) and Thomas teases out her frequent tussle with yearning for a pre- or supra-linguistic realm while unable to conceive a self outside language, especially in her earlier work (2003: 122). Duffy consistently proves that poetic language is more than its words and it exploits non-verbal signifying processes to reconstruct identities through rearranging language norms. Michelis and Rowland dub her a 'naughty poet' (2003: 1) for her confident cheeky rhymes and Brian Caraher parallels the literary transgressions of Duffy and Medbh McGuckian in their rejuvenation of the lyric 'line' (2011). Kinnahan outlines how 'Duffy's seemingly non-experimental adherence to poetic conventions both reaches an audience and enacts deeply unsettling linguistic experiments. ... Her poetry leads me to ask whether it is possible or valuable to rethink the operations of linguistically traditional (on the surface) syntax and form that enacts a process of self-deconstruction' (1996: 246–8). Peter Barry's list of neo-modernist traits also suits Duffy's work: '"disjunctive" elements, such as bizarrely mixed linguistic registers—slang, street-talk juxtaposed with highly technical abstract or "learned" language"' (Barry 2006: 142). However, as these critics indicate collectively, Duffy's blend of expressive and self-reflexive methods bypasses the 'poetry wars', between an alleged conservative mainstream and the politicized neo-modernists (Barry 2006). Avoiding the polarities of linguistic self-consciousness or deconstruction and political statement, Rumens situates Duffy's traits in 'the emergence of a kind of late twentieth-century urban dialect, a montage that reverberates with the noise, colour, slanginess, jargonizing and information-glut of daily life' (1990: 15). In *Contemporary British Poetry and the City,* Barry looks more broadly at how such urban contexts, language, and imagery are rare but crucial to reaching new readers (Barry 2000: 3–6). However, Duffy can never be pigeon holed, for although her muse is frequently urban, she is also inspired by nature, and humanity's abuse of the environment is a drumbeat through her twenty-first century writing.

'The Music of Being Human'

Whether harnessing a Duffy poem to theories of identity, literary tradition, genre, place, or the politics of language, a critic always defaults to her foundational concern with what poetry, uniquely, can do. If her success were just about democratization in terms of social inclusion, it would neither resound nor endure so forcibly. It is the emotional vim and authenticity, inextricable from Duffy's artistic skill, that reviewers and readers relish: 'Duffy's most persuasive gifts are her unashamedly lyrical voice and her distinctively intellectual attention to repetition and wordplay' (Reynolds 2006); 'The poems [in *Rapture*]—electric, searing, agonized glimpses of love found and lost—read as if they were ripped out of her heart' (Paterson 2009). Much of her poetry deals with how loss—of childhood, a parent, or dreams—afflicts the psyche. The fragility of love or belonging often manifests in capturing and communicating 'moods pitched between the expectant and the retrospective' (O'Driscoll 1990: 65). Duffy's speakers never self-congratulate but voice and validate unhappy feelings, nostalgia, regret, grief, heartache, for, as she jibes, 'Happiness writes badly' (Write about *Happiness, William*, n.p.). In 'Contemporary poetry: What Good Does it Do?', David Constantine eloquently clarifies that poetic democracy is not synonymous with the much bandied term, 'accessibility', but with pinning the common stuff of human experience in fresh language:

> Poetry is an intrinsically democratic art because the stuff of it, what it is *about*, is common—common in a dual sense: occurring frequently, and common to humankind. People love, hate, do good, do ill, they rejoice, they grieve, they die. Always have, always will, in vastly changing material circumstances which poetry must, of course, always take full account of. ...
>
> The language of poetry, the means by which its common stuff is realized, is not common. At times the language of poetry has been very far removed from common speech; at present, most often, it may approximate to it. But it never was and never will be common speech. It is other, and has to be. (2004)

In the Preface to her anthology, *Out of Fashion*, in which she invited fifty contemporaries to choose a poem from another time that concerns itself with dress or fashion to put alongside one of their own, Duffy gives her rather similar, if rather unfashionable, view of poetry: 'A poem if you like, is the attire of feeling: the literary form where words seem tailor-made for memory or desire. ... However fashionably we dress ourselves up, we are all, in our common humanity, the same under the skin' (2004: xi–xii). The insistence on what it means to be human was observed by Michael Schmidt quite early in Duffy's career: 'It is in relatively conventional poems like "Prayer", "Miles Away", "Small Female Skull", "The Grammar of Light", that an unusual directness and transparent passion for the human emerge: desire, aloneness, love, the physicality of existence, the hungry libido of imagination.' He comments on how she 'works with voice, metre and rhyme, with metaphor to make us "strangers in our familiar world", finding in the experience of the poems' voices new experience in ourselves' (Schmidt 1998: 849). So, as Schmidt intimates, 'being human' involves recognizing a common humanity while guarding a sense that this humanity is dynamic and always eludes our entire grasp or expression.

Thus, Duffy's poetry accords with 'new literary humanism', a critical discourse that 'rescues for the academic study of literature, literature's human significance, interest and appeal ... but also rescues talk of a text's "human power" or relevance from vagueness' (Mousley 2013: 2). Significantly, reviewers and readers are struck by her word-play but mostly by her heartfelt treatment of love: 'Duffy is superb at love and its erotic moods, be it new-love, dying-love, lost-love. These poems seem to come from the voice closest to her heart: as clever as her overtly political, historical or fantastical poems, and in many cases more memorable' (Goring 2004). When Duffy says, 'The poem tells the truth but it is not a documentary ... [it] is a way of being near something' (Winterson 2009), she means exactly that—that it rescues talk and thought from flabby language in favour of the precise: 'Poetry, like love, depends on a kind of recognition. So often with Duffy does the reader say, "Yes, that's it exactly" (O'Brien 1993). Richard Eldridge also impresses what poetry particularly does: 'Unlike theoretical representations that present phenomena that exist "on their own", such as the melting point of lead or the composition of the atmosphere of Jupiter, poetic imitations present scenes, incidents, actions, and thoughts and feelings about them all, in relation to how they matter to and for human life. In poetry, scene (as object of attention and reflection), incident, action, thought and feeling all exist for a responding intelligence' (Eldridge 2010: 386). Duffy certainly models feeling, response, and 'how things matter to us'; and, on the other side of the coin, she models how *poetry* matters to climate change, sport, national celebrations, global disasters, prisoners, and cancer patients. She models how poetry can talk *precisely* about the varied and mixed feelings to do with loss, passion, ageing, abortion, space exploration, or death: '"Part of my vocational sense about poetry is to do with asserting the space that poetry can have. It's as important as anything else," she adds matter-of-factly, "because it's the music of being human"' (Paterson 2009).

At the same time, the strange *music* of 'being human' often forbids exact translation into words. As Stan Smith points out, Duffy's idea of being human does not 'presume a naïve philosophical realism, predicated on the direct correspondence of word and thing. The ubiquity of translation in all language acts is a central preoccupation of her work, as is that fretting over the non- or pre-linguistic, which can only be gestured towards in the inadequate metaphors of an "almost" music, an "almost" shape, which is really "something in between"'(Smith 2008: 104). Paradoxically, it is the precise exposure of this slippage between sensation and articulation that we find so recognizable. She persistently invokes an 'in-between' realm before and beyond language. The newborn baby in 'Dies Natalis' (*SM* 10) confides, 'I talk / to myself in shapes', 'they are trying to label me / translate me into the right word'. Similarly, in 'The Dolphins' (*SFN* 58), the water signifies learned language in which the dolphins are captive—'we have found no truth in these waters'—and in which they lose their being—'our mind knows we will die here'. As many e-discussions elaborate, it is through language that Duffy expresses the mammals' captivity, also a metaphor for any group or individual that feels confined: 'There is a man / and there are hoops.' In this simple sentence, Duffy makes familiar objects, 'man' and 'hoops', seem strange, almost sinister. Yet, it is with this sense of something 'unreal' that we identify. A reviewer of *Mean Time* spotted the 'renewing power of language' that lies in the accuracy of 'oddly complex lines like "the small deaths of lightbulbs pining all day"—one hears "pinging" but "pining" is the very opposite, drawn out and tense' (Thorpe 1993). Thus, the unpredictable or disconnected phrases mark 'the displacements of translation' that for Duffy 'are at the heart of the human, the guarantee perhaps of a common humanity at the very moment that they testify to human divisions' (Smith, 2008: 115). As Smith further argues, 'If words give a name to things, they also estrange those things, make them strange' (2008: 122). The precision that gives voice to common human experience is therefore one that accommodates the ineffable—the difficult-to-express—as part of that experience. Thus, expressed in language that gestures beyond itself, Duffy's frequently occurring 'something', 'somewhere' and 'somewhen' contribute to the shared human sense of displacement, of not being at home (Smith 2008: 118–9).

The search to be 'at home', is, according to Duffy, '"the most important thing to me"' (Reynolds 2014) and often manifests through imagining an 'intercalated "otherwhere"' (Smith 2008: 101). 'It must be dreams that make us different, must be / private cells inside a common skull', reflects the speaker in 'I remember me' (*SFN* 16). Dreamstate has a vividness that casts a hue on waking events, corresponding to André Breton's principle in the *Surrealist Manifesto* (1924): 'I have always been amazed at the way an ordinary observer lends so much more credence and attaches so much more importance to waking events than to those occurring in dreams'

(1972: 11). The sleeping speaker in 'Only Dreaming' (*SM* 56) is discon-
certed when an erotic fantasy of a ghostly lover seems more vivid than
waking consciousness: 'This is the real thing.' However, Breton argues
that Freud reclaimed the vital importance of mental activity that occurs
outside logic: 'Can't the dream also be used in solving the fundamental
questions of life? Are these questions the same in one case as in the other
and, in the dream, do these questions already exist?' (Breton 1972: 12).
In some poems, the dream implicitly compensates for the knowable mundane: in 'Dreaming of Somewhere Else' (*SFN* 37), the daydreamer escapes
the bleakness of a Liverpool in recession; in 'Dear Norman' (*SFN* 41), a
woman's fantasies expose her latent desires and the pleasure of fantasy is
paramount; and 'A Dreaming Week' (*FG* 55–6) corresponds to Breton's
belief, 'The mind of the man who dreams is fully satisfied by what happens
to him' (1972: 13). In each of the seven verses, the speaker repeats that
they are unavailable each night of the week, starting from 'tonight', due
to the pull of dreams:

> Not the following evening, I'm dreaming
>
> in the monocle of the moon, a sleeping *S* on the page of a bed
>
> in the tome of a dim room, the rain
>
> on the roof, rhyming there,
>
> like the typed words of a poem.

Here, Duffy explicitly equates the act of dreaming with poetry, for both
express and value the irrational; and the irrational generates a heightened
awareness that Breton calls the surreal: 'I believe in the future resolu-
tion of these two states, dream and reality, which are seemingly so con-
tradictory, into a kind of absolute reality, a *surreality*, if one may so speak'
(1972: 14). In 'Strange Language in Night Fog' (*SFN* 17), Duffy min-
gles the recognizable—some friends make their way in the dark when a
mist comes down—with the strange—animals and nature take on human
qualities. In this bizarre space, cows, the moon, a bush, and a tree teas-
ingly appear then disappear: 'But it was a strange language, / spoken only
yards away, / which turned the night into a dream.' Rees-Jones expounds
how Duffy's impulses towards and away from realism 'culminated in an
aesthetic which seeks to problematize notions of truth and the desire to
mediate an "authentic" experience, while relentlessly searching for new

ways in which to explore and examine them' (Rees-Jones 1999: 2). To mediate 'authentic' experience in new ways, Duffy draws on the non-verbal effects of rhythm, rhyme, alliteration, and assonance. She comments, '"My rhythms are dictated by my internal ear, not necessarily the ear that you use to hear things spoken. Also, I like a poem to have a form and strong imagery. I think it is a visual thing as well"' (Duffy, Armstrong 1993: 5). In a characteristically potent phrase, 'My marriage / howled like a dog / on its chain' ('How', *Pamphlet* 20–1), it is image and sound that depict the unspeakable agony of feeling you have wasted your life in a bad relationship and a vapid job.

Duffy says of her method, '"it isn't a technique"', it is trying to '"get the sound of a non-linguistic sort of music. I can have the rhythm of a whole poem in my head and no words. And it isn't music and it isn't language, it's something in between"' (McAllister 1988: 75). As previously mentioned, this 'something in between' effects an evasive referentiality that paradoxically touches the yearning for elsewhere at our heart's core. Duffy may have defended the Facebook generation in acknowledging that a text or tweet might have a role in poetry but her 'non-linguistic sort of music' is incompatible with these phenomena. As James Lawless notes, 'Text' (*Rapture* 2), 'posits the irony of isolation in the midst of a surfeit of technological communication: "Nothing my thumbs press / will ever be heard"' (Lawless 2009: 116). Whereas social communication needs to be direct and unambiguous, Duffy's 'Text' enjoyably details the fun and insecurity of sending and receiving phone messages but also throws up the impossibility of saying what we feel. During her degree, Duffy studied Ludwig Wittgenstein's (1889–1951) theories on the relationship between thought and language, stating: '"[Wittgenstein]'s ideas about language were particularly fascinating as in what it could and couldn't say and the idea of the privacy of language"' (Bray 2005). The 'idea of the privacy of language' is palpable in such arresting lines as: 'The country in her heart babbled a language / she couldn't explain' ('Free Will', *SFN* 25) or 'I had a voice once, but it's broken / and cannot recall the unspoken word' ('A Clear Note', *SFN* 27). However, Duffy would separate creativity from philosophy: '"I'm aware of the limits of language, how it barely stretches to hold whatever one wants to say. But the kinds of philosophical questions about it hover round the poet like a vulture, and would kill the creation of a poem"' (Stabler 1991: 127). As she warns in 'The Professor of Philosophy Attempts Prayer' (*William*, n.p.), 'I'll die / well off but with nothing of value to leave.' For Duffy, 'It's people and use that I'm interested in' (McAllister 1988: 70). Instead of the muckraking editor in 'Poet for Our Times', she describes poetry as 'explaining the world to myself. Part intellectual and part emotional' (*Options* 1990: 61). Thus, her poetry values the vital circularity of feeling and reflecting (Mousley 2013: 46) and provokes 'a responding intelligence'. It emphatically flows from and to the imagination as 'a time machine by which we can travel to who we were and to whom we will become' (Duffy, 29 September 2012).

'Word-music'

If given a poem blind, how might we know it were by Duffy? It would most likely be a sonnet, 'the little black dress of poetry' (*Out of Fashion* 2004: xii), quatrains, sestets, or other such form. 'Terza Rima SW 19' (*SFN* 20), for example, models the form of its title in relation to observing a couple from the perspective of a kestrel; 'The Kissing Gate' (*TOC* 46) is in two equal parts of seven lines with a gap in between, and in 'Talent' (*SFN* 42), the line, 'there is no word *net*', is placed in mid-air like the tightrope it describes. However, she is never about form for form's sake and parodies a budding poet's pride in over-worked formalism ('Dear Writer-in-Residence', 'Fuckinelle', *William* n.p.). Other ocular elements would derive from symbols and images, most frequently a moon, often wine, gambling, or a filmic reference—'the mind's mad films' ('Debt', *SFN* 33), 'see lines and lines of British boys rewind / back to their trenches' ('Last Post', *Bees* 4). There would be rhyme, largely internal: '"I quite like having rhyme snaking through a poem. I think that's more authentic. ... I like echoes and assonance"' (McAllister 76). Reviewing Duffy's work in 2015, Winterson celebrates:

> Her poetry is a practical proof of rhyme as expressive, flexible, purposefully baited. Dangle a rhyme at the end of a line and the mind-fish bites. Not only end-rhymes, but off-rhymes, hidden rhymes, half-rhymes, ghost rhymes, deliberate near-misses that hit the mark:
>
> I was wind, I was gas
> I was all hot air, trailed
> Clouds for hair.
> I scrawled my name with a hurricane,
> When out of the blue
> Roared a fighter plane. ('Thetis') (Winterson 2015)

As here, the poem's diction would be colloquial and enjamb the lines: 'Do you think they cried, the children / who followed the Piper, when the rock / closed behind them forever; or cried never, / happy to dance to his tune, lost / in the music?' ('Music', *Bees* 67). The cliché, 'dance to his tune', is reanimated by its literal context, as Duffy intends, '"Often the most tragic or joyous moments are expressed in cliché,"' so she will use italics or put a cliché next to something else to nudge the reader into seeing it freshly (McAllister 1988: 75).

Duffy's penchant for 'stops and starts, volleys of monosyllabic words and single-word sentences' (O'Driscoll 1990: 65) was unkindly parodied by some early critics. In 'Recognition' (*SM* 24–5), the one word sentences—'Quiche'. 'Claret.' 'Years.'—are parts of a pattern whereby the speaker reviews her life and the poem ends with the pitiful repetition: 'I'm sorry, sorry, sorry.' Kellaway notes:

> Carol Ann Duffy knows the power of a repeated trio of words—like Larkin's 'Begin afresh, afresh, afresh' (from 'The Trees') or Shakespeare's 'Never, never, never' in *King Lear*. In 'Hour' she writes: 'Time hates love, wants love poor, / but love spins gold, gold, gold from straw'. And in 'Spring' she writes of 'rain's mantra: reprieve, reprieve, reprieve'. This mantra belongs to more than the rain. There is nothing lost in love that can't be found again in poetry—if the poet is good enough. And Carol Ann Duffy is. (Kellaway 2005)

Duffy believes repetitions resemble the haunting refrains in sacred or pop music—'I like Gregorian chants. The Beatles' (Stabler 1991: 127). The soothing repetition of sounds is what she poetically termed, 'the chant / of magic words repeatedly' ('Whoever she Was', *SFN* 35), and we note the perfect iambics here.

Whether in a lyrical, fictional, or public register, there may be inner talk, as described by W.B. Yeats: 'I wanted to write in whatever language comes most naturally when we soliloquize, as I do all day long, upon the events of our own lives or of any life where we can see ourselves for the moment' (Yeats 2008: 386). The pronoun might be 'I', 'we', or the inclusive 'you': 'Through the high window of the hall / clouds obfuscate the sun / and you sit, exhaling grey smoke / into purpling, religious light / trying to remember everything' ('M-M-Memory', *TOC* 36). Here, the lyric subject is gender neutral or it would be female unless the speech of a man in dramatic monologue. Often, the pronouns float and shift to mystify any definite context. In 'Losers', that 'speaks of the absurdity and mystery of time' (Aitchison 1990), the 'we' can be the characters in the poem or the poet speaking to the reader:

> Look at the time. There will be more but there is always less.
>
> Place your bets. Mostly we do not notice our latest loss
>
> under the rigged clocks. Remember the night we won! The times
>
> it hurts are when we grab the moment for ourselves, nearly –
>
> the corniest sunset, taste of a lover's tears, a fistful of snow –
>
> and the bankrupt feeling we have as it disappears. (*TOC* 35)

'Look at the time' is followed by an enigmatic comment on how time fizzles out and is ghosted by 'Hurry up, please, it's time', from T.S. Eliot's *The Waste Land* (1922), accentuating the chilling sense of both a barren internal terrain and a collapsing culture. 'Place your bets' indicates the fear of a controlling Fate that at best is indifferent and at worst 'rigs' things against us. If we follow the syntax, in Duffyesque fashion the 'nearly–' operates both at the end of one line and also at the start of the next to undercut the fulfilment of the good moment while also confronting its fleeting temporality. This tantalizing lack of completeness is frequently expressed, as in 'half-smiling' ('Terza Rima SW 19') or 'half-believ[ing]' ('Never Go Back', *MT* 30). Whilst being a strong storyteller, Duffy often withholds the total interpretative context and this indeterminacy creates 'a strange tension between universalising empathy and a deadpan narration which will not open to the reader' (Smith 2008: 107). This withholding, however, is the 'perfect pitch' referred to by Fiona Sampson: 'Duffy has a fine sense for what is exactly enough' (2012: 121).

Rumens observes how Duffy, like Plath, enjoys 'splicing literary and vernacular idioms' (Rumens 1999/2000: 34). However, a typical hybrid, 'Every other word's a lie / ain't no rainbow in the sky' ('Alphabet for Auden', *SFN* 10–11), is more than a fun exercise, although prompted by Auden's challenge to new poets to invent a form (McAllister 72). The literary echo of William Wordsworth's, 'My heart leaps up when I behold / A rainbow in the sky', makes the negation—'ain't no rainbow'—painfully bleak but we do not know who is speaking or why. Two further lines—'Four o'clock is time for tea / I'll be Mother. Who'll be me?'—are redolent of middle-class vernacular and Rupert Brooke's famous lines, 'Stands the Church clock at ten to three? /

And is there honey still for tea?' ('The Old Vicarage, Grantchester', 1912). Subsequently, Duffy's neat metre and rhyme evoke a poetic past that asks very human questions about the consolations of memory and the fictiveness of that memory. Further permutations possible in 'I'll be Mother. Who'll be me?' include a woman's role versus her subjectivity, as in Duffy's 'Whoever She Was' (*SFN* 35), or how gender roles work in homosexual relationship. Thus, the echoes produced by these fragments resonate with possibilities, all the more so because they lack a backstory.

While richly literary in her intertextuality, Duffy is also brave in the orality of her verse, not least in her famed lists, since oral cultures carry the stigma of low intelligence: 'Duffy is not afraid to use techniques familiar from nursery rhymes and ballads: repetitions, choruses, full rhymes. But these [*Rapture*'s] are adult poems' (Laird 2005). Walter Ong intricately reasons how the earliest written poetry necessarily mimicked oral performances, yet later, highly literate cultures devalued the same oral devices (Ong 2002: 26). Similarly, in his searching discussion of how word-play, that initially derived from oral communities, is vital to human civilization but endangered by utilitarian views of language, Robert DiNapoli argues:

> It may well be that the endless varieties of play between sound and sense, and the numberless ways in which we create and re-create meaning from the literal facts of our experience, are fundamental to human psychology and consciousness. The raw stuff of anything we would recognize as 'thought' is the same raw stuff from which poets distil their patterns of word and sound. Across the whole run of history, human communities have possessed a bewildering variety of customs, social structures, religions and technologies. All have generated some form of poetry, and it comes well early in the day, long before letters, literacy or literature. It is only relatively recently that we have learned to do without it. (2014: 36)

Duffy proves again and again that we cannot do without it and how poetry can 'break up the boxes we ordinarily think in' (Allnutt et al. 1988: 77).

References

1977 *Beauty and the beast*, with Adrian Henri (Liverpool: Glasshouse Press).
1985 *Standing female nude* (London: Anvil).
1986. *Thrown voices* (London: Turret Books).

1987 *Selling Manhattan* (London: Anvil).
1990 *The other country* (London: Anvil).
1992 *William and the ex-prime minister* (London: Anvil).
1993 *Mean time* (London: Anvil).
1994 *Selected poems* (Harmondsworth: Penguin).
1998 *The Pamphlet* (London: Anvil).
1999 *The world's wife* (London: Anvil).
2002 *Feminine gospels* (London: Picador).
2004 *New selected poems 1984–2004* (London: Picador).
2005 *Rapture* (London: Picador).
2011 *The bees* (London: Picador).
2014 *Ritual lighting: Laureate poems,* artwork by Stephen Raw (London: Picador).
2014 *Dorothy Wordsworth's Christmas birthday* (London: Picador).
2015 *Everyman* (London: Faber and Faber).
2015 *Collected poems* (forthcoming).
1995 *Anvil New Poets No. 2* (London: Anvil).
1999 *Time's tidings: Greeting the 21st century* (London: Anvil).
2001 *Hand in hand: An anthology of love poetry* (London: Picador).
2004 *Out of fashion: An anthology of poems* (London: Faber and Faber).
2007 *Answering back: Living poets reply to the poetry of the past* (London: Picador).
2009 *To the moon: An anthology of lunar poetry* (London: Picador).
2012 *Jubilee lines: 60 poets for 60 years* (London: Faber and Faber).
2013 *1914: Poetry remembers* (London: Faber and Faber).
'September 2014: *Tha gaol agam ort'* (2014) *Guardian,* 23 September.
1989 Interview for BBC English File (http://www.bbc.co.uk/poetryseason/poets/carol_ann_duffy.shtml).
1990 'Carol Ann Duffy', Interview, *Options,* June: 61.
1993 Poet's Comment on *Mean Time, Poetry Book Society Bulletin,* Summer: 8.
1994 'A Place of Escape', Interview, *Second Shift* 4: 20–2.
2009 'Sisters in Poetry', *Guardian,* 2 May.
Addley, Esther. 2008. Poet's rhyming riposte leaves Mrs Schofield "gobsmacked". *Guardian,* September 6.
Aitchison, James. 1990. Nightmare of our times. Review of *The Other Country, Glasgow Herald,* September 15.
Allnutt, Gillian, Fred D'Aguiar, Ken Edwards, and Eric Motram (eds.). 1988. *The new British poetry 1968–88.* Colorado: Paladin.
Armstrong, Amanda. 1993. Potent poetry. Interview with Carol Ann Duffy. *Writers' Monthly,* October.
Bakhtin, M.M. 1981. In *The dialogic imagination: Four essays,* ed. Michael Holquist. Austin: University of Texas Press.
Barry, Peter. 2000. *Contemporary British poetry and the city.* Manchester: Manchester University Press.

Barry, Peter. 2006. *Poetry Wars: British poetry of the 1970s and the Battle over Earls Court*. Cambridge: Salt Publishing.

Bertram, Vicki. 2004. *Gendering poetry: Contemporary women and men poets*. London: Rivers Oram/Pandora Press.

Boland, Eavan. 1993. Between me and the mass. Review of *Mean Time*, *Independent on Sunday*, July 25.

Bray, Elisa. 2005. The five minute interview with Carol Ann Duffy. *Independent*, August 13.

Breton, André. 1972. *Manifestoes of surrealism*. Michigan: Ann Arbor Press.

Brownjohn, Alan. 2012. Waggledance and whisky. Review of *The Bees*, *Times Literary Supplement*, February 10.

Buckley, Marian. 1989. Interview with Carol Ann Duffy. *City Life Magazine*, June 15.

Burt, Stephen. 2002. Repetitive strains. *Times Literary Supplement*, September 27.

Butlin, Robert. 2004. Review of *New Selected Poems* and *Out of Fashion*, *Scottish Review of Books* 1.1.

Campbell, Siobhan. 2006. In search of rapture. *Poetry Ireland Review* 85: 87–89.

Caraher, Brian. 2011. *Carol Ann Duffy, Medbh McGuckian and ruptures in the lines of communication*, 179–195. Dowson.

Chapman, Danielle. 2011. Review of *The Bees*, *Financial Times*, October 14.

Christianson, Aileen, and Alison Lumsden (eds.). 2000. *Contemporary Scottish women writers*. Edinburgh: Edinburgh University Press.

Constantine, David. 2004. Aspects of the Contemporary (i): What good does it do? *Magma* 29, Summer.

Cooke, Rachel. 2009. I still haven't written the best I can. Interview with Carol Ann Duffy. *Observer*, May 3.

Cowing, Emma. 2005a. Love in the dock. Review *of Rapture*, *The Scotsman*, September 17.

Cowing, Emma. 2005b. The 20 Scottish books everyone should read. *The Scotsman*, December 28.

Crawford, Robert, and Mick Imlah (eds.). 2000. *The new Penguin book of Scottish verse*. London: Allen Lane.

DiNapoli, Robert. 2014. The play's the thing: Word-play and poetry. *P.N. Review* 40(4): 34–38.

Donaghy, Michael. 1991. Carol Ann Duffy. In *Contemporary poetry*, 244. London: St James Press.

Dowson, Jane, and Alice Entwistle. 2005. *A history of twentieth-century British women's poetry*. Cambridge: Cambridge University Press.

Draycott, Jane. 2004. Review of *Feminine Gospels*, *Poetry London* 47, Spring: 28.

Dunmore, Helen. 1999. Waiting for the world's wife. *Poetry Review* 89(2): 80–81.

Dunn, Douglas (ed.). 1992. *The Faber book of twentieth-century Scottish poetry*. London: Faber and Faber.

Edemariam, Aida. 2009. Carol Ann Duffy: "I don't have ambassadorial talents". *Guardian*, May 26.

Eldridge, Richard. 2010. Truth in poetry: Particulars and universals. In *A companion to the philosophy of literature*, ed. G.L. Hagberg and W. Jost, 385–398. Oxford: Wiley-Blackwell.

Ezard, John. 2003. Poet's poll crowns Larkin king of verse. *Guardian*, October 15.

Fanthorpe, U.A. 2010. *New and collected poems*, Preface by Carol Ann Duffy. London: Enitharmon.

Feinstein, Elaine. 2002. A casual kind of confidence. *Guardian*, September 14.

Flood, Alison. 2009. Carol Ann Duffy becomes first female poet laureate. *Guardian*, May 1.

Flood, Alison. 2012. Carol Ann Duffy is "wrong" about poetry says Sir Geoffrey Hill. *Guardian*, January 31.

Forbes, Peter. 1994. Talking about the new generation, Carol Ann Duffy. *Poetry Review* 84(1): 4–6, 111.

Forbes, Peter. 1995. Why the new popular poetry makes more sense. *Poetry Review* 85(3): 46–47.

Forbes, Peter. 2001. Seven years on, Carol Ann Duffy. *Poetry Review: A New Generation Retrospective* 91(1): 3, 22.

Forbes, Peter. 2002. Winning lines. *Guardian*, August 31.

France, Linda (ed.). 1993. *Sixty women poets*. Newcastle-upon-Tyne: Bloodaxe.

Gayle, Damien. 2012. Poet Laureate compared to Mills & Boon romance writers in stinging attack by rival. *Daily Mail*, January 31.

Gifford, Douglas. 2009. *Addressing the bard: Twelve contemporary poets respond to Robert Burns*. Edinburgh: Scottish Poetry Library.

Goring, Rosemary. 2004. Review of *New Selected Poems*. *The Herald*, October 23.

Greenlaw, Lavinia. 2009. The public poet. *Granta*, May 5.

Greer, Germaine (ed.). 2001. *101 poems by 101 women*. London: Faber and Faber.

Greer, Germaine. 2009. I'd be happy if the new laureate blew all her money on the horses or invested in fetish gear. *Guardian*, May 11.

Gregson, Ian. 1996. *Contemporary poetry and postmodernism: Dialogue and estrangement*. Basingstoke: Macmillan.

Gurr, Libby, and Celia De Piro (eds.). 1997. *19th and 20th century women poets*. Oxford: Oxford University Press.

Harris, T.J.G. 1993. WOW!. Review of *Mean Time*, *PN Review* 20, November/December 2, 58.

Higgins, Charlotte. 2009. Carol Ann Duffy becomes first woman laureate. *Guardian*, May 1.

Hilpern, Kate. 2002. The Top Brass: The ten leading poets in Britain as chosen by their peers. *Independent*, October 7.

Horner, Avril. 2003. "Small female skull": Patriarchy and philosophy in the poetry of Carol Ann Duffy, 99–120. Michelis and Rowland.

Kellaway, Kate. 2005. I am in heaven, I am in hell. Review of *Rapture, Observer,* October 9.

Kinnahan, Linda. 1996. "Look for the doing words": Carol Ann Duffy and questions of convention, 245–268. Acheson and Huk.

Kinnahan, Linda A. 2000. Now I am Alien: Immigration and the discourse of nation in the poetry of Carol Ann Duffy, 208–225. Mark and Rees-Jones.

Laird, Nick. 2005. The secret is to walk evading nothing. *Daily Telegraph,* November 13.

Lawless, James. 2009. *Clearing the tangled wood: Poetry as a way of seeing the world.* Palo Alto: Academic Press.

Lawson, Mark. 2011. Poet laureate Carol Ann Duffy. Interview, *Front Row,* BBC Radio 4, September 30. http://www.bbc.co.uk/programmes/b0151xt6

Lochhead, Liz. 2011. *A choosing: The selected poems of Liz Lochhead,* Foreword by Carol Ann Duffy. Edinburgh: Polygon Books.

McAllister, Andrew. 1988. Carol Ann Duffy. *Bête Noir* 6, 69–77.

Mendelson, Charlotte. 2002. The gospel truth. Review of *Feminine Gospels, Observer,* October 12.

Michelis, Angelica, and Antony Rowland (eds.). 2003. *The poetry of Carol Ann Duffy: 'Choosing tough words'.* Manchester: Manchester University Press.

Miller, Phil. 2009. Scot is made first female Laureate. *The Herald,* May 2.

Miller, Kei. 2013. Not everyone was invited to the party. Blog, November 20. http://underthesaltireflag.com/2013/11/20/not-everyone-was-invited-to-the-party/

Milne, W.S. 1995. Review of *Selected Poems, Outposts* 180/181, Spring/Summer: 157–158.

Mitchell, Adrian. 1964. *Poems.* London: Jonathan Cape.

Mousley, Andy. 2013. *Literature and the human.* Abingdon: Routledge.

Mullan, John. 2013. Love poems by Carol Ann Duffy. *Guardian,* January 18.

O'Brien, Sean. 1993. Illuminating manuscripts. *Sunday Times,* July 18.

O'Driscoll. 1990. The day and ever. *Poetry Review* 80(3): 65–66.

O'Rourke, Daniel (ed.). 2002. *Dream state: The new Scottish poets* [1994]. Edinburgh: Polygon.

Ong, Walter. 2002. *Orality and literacy: The technologizing of the word.* London: Routledge.

Oxley, William. 2005. Love's virtuoso. *Acumen* 53: 105–106.

Padel, Ruth. 2002. *52 ways of looking at a poem.* London: Chatto and Windus.

Padel, Ruth. 2005. Review of *Rapture, Independent,* September 16.

Paterson, Christina. 2009. Carol Ann Duffy: "I was told to get a proper job": The Big Interview. *Independent,* July 10.

Plath, Sylvia. 2014. *Poems,* chosen by Carol Ann Duffy. London: Faber and Faber

Pollard, Clare. 2001. Getting poetry to confess. *Magma* 21: 41–44.

Preston, John. 2010. Carol Ann Duffy interview. *Daily Telegraph,* May 11.

Quinn, Justin. 2000. The Larkin-Duffy line. *Poetry Review* 90(3): 4–8.

Rae, Simon (ed.). 1999. *News that stays news: The twentieth century in poems*. London: Faber and Faber.

Redmond, John. 2007. Lyric adaptations: James Fenton, Craig Raine, Christopher Reid, Simon Armitage, Carol Ann Duffy. In *The Cambridge companion to twentieth-century English poetry*, ed. Neil Corcoran, 245–258. Cambridge: Cambridge University Press.

Rees Jones, Deryn. 1999. *Carol Ann Duffy*. Plymouth: Northcote House.

Rees-Jones, Deryn. 2005. *Consorting with angels: Essays on modern women poets*. Tarset: Bloodaxe.

Rees-Jones, Deryn (ed.). 2010. *Modern women poets*. Tarset: Bloodaxe.

Reid, Mark. 1992/1993. Near misses are best. *Orbis* 1992/3: 34–38.

Reynolds, Margaret. 2006. The end of the affair. *Guardian*, January 7.

Reynolds, Peggy (host). 2014. *Four women poets today*, produced by Beauty Rubens, BBC Radio 4, September 20.

Ross, Peter. 2012. Interview with Carol Ann Duffy. *The Scotsman*, December 2.

Rumens, Carole (ed.). 1990. *New women poets*. Newcastle-upon-Tyne: Bloodaxe.

Rumens, Carole. 1999/2000. Trouble and strife. Review of *The World's Wife*, *Poetry Review* 89(4): 33–34.

Salzman, Eva, and Amy Wack (eds.). 2008. *Women's work: Modern women poets writing in English*. Bridgend: Seren.

Sampson, Fiona. 2012. *Beyond the lyric: A map of contemporary British poetry*. London: Chatto & Windus.

Sansom, Ian. 1995. Wayne's world. Review of *Selected Poems*, *London Review of Books*, July 6, 20.

Schmidt, Michael. 1998. *The lives of the poets*. London: Weidenfeld and Nicolson.

Sissay, Lemn. 2012. Carol Ann Duffy and Geoffrey Hill: Truly poetic heavyweights. *Guardian*, January 31.

Smith, Stan. 2008. *Poetry and displacement*. Liverpool: Liverpool University Press.

Stabler, Jane. 1991. Interview with Carol Ann Duffy. *Verse* 8(2): 124–128.

Thomas, Jane. 2003. "The chant of magic words repeatedly": Gender as linguistic act in the poetry of Carol Ann Duffy, 121–142. Michelis and Rowland.

Thorpe, Adam. 1993. Light-bulbs and dangling sun. Review of *Mean Time*, *Observer*, November 21.

Thwaite, Anthony. 2004. Anglo-Irish accords. Review of *New Selected Poems*, *Sunday Telegraph*, October 17.

Viner, Katharine. 1999. Metre Maid. Interview with Carol Ann Duffy, *Guardian*, September 25.

Wainwright, Jeffrey. 2003. Female metamorphoses: Carol Ann Duffy's Ovid, 47–55. Michelis and Rowland.

Whyte, Christopher. 2004. *Modern Scottish poetry*. Edinburgh: Edinburgh University Press.

Wilkinson, Kate. 2014. Carol Ann Duffy: A great public poet who deserves her public honour. *Guardian*, December 31.

Winterson, Jeanette. 2009. Can you move diagonally? Interview with the Poet Laureate, Carol Ann Duffy. *Times*, August 29.

Winterson, Jeanette. 2015. On the poetry of Carol Ann Duffy—Of course it's political. *Guardian*, January 17.

Wood, Barry. 2005. Carol Ann Duffy: *The World's Wife*. Conversation with Carol Ann Duffy.http://www.sheerpoetry.co.uk/advanced/interviews/carol-ann-duffy-the-world-s-wife

Wroe, Nicholas. 2014. Carol Ann Duffy on five years as poet laureate: "It has been a joy". *Guardian*, September 27.

Yeats, W.B. 2008. A general introduction for my work. In *The major works by W.B. Yeats*, ed. Edward Larissy. Oxford: Oxford University Press.

Shakespeare, William. 1993. *The complete works*, ed. Jeremy Hylton. http://shakespeare.mit.edu

CHAPTER 2

Lyrics of Love, Loss, and Longing

Poetry, like love, depends on a kind of recognition. So often with Duffy does the reader say, 'Yes, that's it exactly'. (O'Brien 1993)

'LIKE THIS'

Rapture (2005) was acclaimed for its lyric inventiveness, range, and power, yet Duffy has written fresh lyrics of 'desire, devotion and despair' (Tonkin 2010) from her first volume, *Standing Female Nude* (1985), to her most recent, *Ritual Lighting* (2014). She plumbs emotional depths that defy easy access or utterance, 'the things that words give a name to' ('Away and See', *MT* 23). This oft-quoted line encapsulates her skill in illuminating deep feeling while stressing how it cannot be fully verbalized: 'For I am in love with you and this // is what it is like or what it is like in words' ('Words, Wide Night', *TOC* 47). Here, the line space marks the gap between the 'this' and the words and between the words and the communication of 'this'; finally, 'this' is best presented by non-verbal sounds, 'la lala la'. Yet, the Duffyesque lyric pins precisely 'what it is like' across an extraordinary gamut of sentience, concerning romantic, erotic, or familial love, concerning the loss of childhood or loved ones, and concerning the lack of, yet search for, faith. Profoundly, Duffy taps into an underlying 'this', the human tendency towards 'elsewhere', symptomatic of the heart's search for a home: 'What country do we come from? This one?' ('Homesick', *SM* 19); 'The other country, is it anticipated or half-remembered? / Its language is muffled by the rain' ('In Your Mind',

J. Dowson, *Carol Ann Duffy*,
DOI 10.1057/978-1-137-41563-9_2

TOC 55). Through the mind's journeys that poetry recreates, we touch the elsewheres of memory and desire, albeit temporarily: 'For a moment / you are there, in the other country, knowing its name' ('In Your Mind'); 'The past is the future waiting for dreams / and will find itself there' ('Caul', *MT* 22); 'I pine for the future / alone, down by the river by the Brine Baths / longing to get out' ('Hometown', *TOC* 10). This yearning for an 'otherwhere' that can only be named a 'something', 'an ache', 'that small familiar pain', or '*Like this*', is what, paradoxically, constitutes Duffy's talent for 'expressing it how it is' (Cowing 2005).

Although the speakers can only name a muffled feeling as 'this' or 'something', they constantly avow, 'this is real', 'this is not a fiction', thus dissolving an either/or between post-structuralist and realist readings. Duffy's lines absorb the former's principles, that words produce experience—'When the words have gone away / There is nothing left to say'—and also reinforce how psychic states pre-exist words: the baby's fear, 'I will lose my memory, learn words / which barely stretch to cover what remains unsaid' ('Dies Natalis', *SM* 12), is almost verbatim the mother's lament in 'A Clear Note' (*SFN* 30): 'Listening / as language barely stretched to cover / what remained unsaid'. However, sometimes it is impossible to determine whether feeling or expression comes first: 'Love holds words to itself, repeats them / till they're smooth, sit silent on the tongue' ('The Kissing Gate', *TOC* 46). It may be 'generally accepted by commentators on her work that Carol Ann Duffy's poetry is concerned with the nature of human identity and its construction in, and by, language' (Thomas 2003: 121) yet, as Rees-Jones asserts, 'In her desire to return to an Imaginary state, Duffy values experience over the failure of telling that experience' (1999: 49). Duffy is self-confessedly '"writing *for* language"' (Kellaway 1993) but insists, 'Poetry, above all, is a series of intense moments—its power is not in narrative. I'm not dealing with facts, I'm dealing with emotion' (Winterson 2005). Duffy exacts precise human emotions through potent symbols that both renounce and rely on words: 'something like a cat claws from my head, spiteful' ('The Suicide', *MT* 41) or the train 'pulls you away, rewinding the city like a film' ('Never go Back', *MT* 30), and most of all, the omnipresent moon that 'has always been, and always will be, the supremely prized image for poets—a mirror to reflect the poetic imagination; language's human smile against death's darkness' (Duffy, *To the Moon* 1999: xvii). In 'The Suicide', 'the bitter moon' 'gleams with resentment' (*MT* 41); someone in grim lodgings looks out at a 'giftless moon' ('Room', *MT* 50) and, for dolphins, displaced from their proper environment, 'the moon has disappeared' ('The Dolphins', *SFN* 58). Often, the disorientating juxtaposition of familiar symbols—'Under the giggling stars, / The sly moon. My cool apple' ('Lovesick', *SM* 54)— produces what Breton terms an 'absolute reality, a *surreality*' (1972: 14). Breton and his associates looked to dreams to release hidden desires, irrational love, the delirium of obsession, and madness. Lines like, 'New fruits sing in the flipside of night in the market / of language' ('Away and See', *MT* 23), limn the 'absolute reality' of irrational but truthful emotions that cannot be pinned to one specific canvas. Referring to 'I Remember Me' (*SFN* 16), Antony Rowland identifies Duffy's surrealist collages as attempts to 'disrupt any possibility of a fixed reading' (2003: 62). Lack of fixity does not, however, equate to lack of meaning, for the symbols give shape to complex and elusive impulses; they 'Let in the new, the vivid / horror and pity, passion' ('Away and See'). Typically, the vivid and the horrible co-exist: 'The ghost is devoted, stares into your eyes behind the lids. / This is the real thing' ('Only Dreaming', *SM* 54).

Since lyric conventions subsume universality into the speaking persona's experience, cultural critics have denounced and contemporary poets eschewed the attendant erosion of minority identities into a predominantly male, archaic, and Western mould of humanity. Nevertheless, the lyric has remained for many critics and theorists a significant mode imbued with the power to counter de-personalization. Like Theodor Adorno in his influential 'Poetry and Society, Jonathan Culler, in 'Poetics of the Lyric', politicize how lyrics afford personal witness: 'Poetry lies at the centre of the literary experience because it is the form that most clearly asserts the specificity of literature, its difference from ordinary discourse by an empirical individual about the world' (1975: 162). Similarly, Duffy's contemporary Sarah Maguire argues: 'It's precisely because the poem can render the most intimate and elusive of subjective experiences in language that it's able to bear witness to what's excluded from dominant discourses' (2000: 250). The universality towards which the lyric simultaneously reaches is not straightforward, however. In outlining a new literary humanism, Andy Mousley points out that 'a particular that *resonates* with universal meaning is not the same as a particular that straightforwardly unequivocally instantiates a universal'. Citing F.R. Leavis, he coins the term 'poetic universal' for 'the allusive evocation or intimation of a "felt significance" to life' (Mousley 2013: 83). Duffy's line, 'I write and write and write your name' ('Spell', *Bees* 56), encapsulates her 'poetic universals' in its cleverly impersonal expression of a deeply personal source, 'anonymous yet—

texted from heart / to lips' ('Invisible Ink', *Bees* 26). The Duffyesque repetitions, invigorating symbolism, and resonant rhythms effect an intensity that is contiguous with the tight literary forms she calls, 'the attire of feeling', expounding that poetry is 'the literary form where words seem tailor-made for memory or desire. Good poems have their origins in intensely lived days or nights, yet continue to exist independently of these beginnings. Birth, work, love and death are, in themselves, messy events; but poetry is the place where they all scrub-up well' (*Out of Fashion* 2004: xi–xii). She frequently sports the sonnet, adorned with the idioms of contemporary British culture. This vital blend of literary and colloquial registers initially split Duffy's fans from her detractors but has now won almost unanimous respect. Writing in the Scottish *Herald*, Lesley Duncan praises her formidable range of love poems that are 'at once specific and universal', radiating 'a palpable humanity' (1999). Duffy also merges individual with collective experience through the inclusive second person pronoun—'The words you have for things die / in your heart' ('Plainsong', *SM* 60)— or first person plural, 'Some days, although we cannot pray' ('Prayer', *MT* 52). Dramatizing subjectivity as a process rather than a fixed essential entity, a speaker's internal dialogue frequently invokes a significant Other, such as her mother in the moving elegy 'Water'—'The times I'd call as a child / for a drink' (*Bees* 33)—or an absent lover—'I want you and you are not here' ('Miles Away', *SM* 61).

Freed from cultural and contextual specificity, the lyric best depicts and, crucially, feeds the imagination, for life without dreams is a 'tuneless, flat bell / marking the time' ('Hometown', *TOC* 10). The dolphins, removed from their deep waters, are as good as dead—'And now we are no longer blessed, for the world will not deepen to dream in', and for a baby ripped from its originating home, 'sleep / is dreamless' ('Dies Natalis', *SM* 12). Dreams include the faltering reach of memory, 'a handful of years like old-fashioned sweets / you can't find anymore', and fantasy, 'Wherever I went then, I was / still there; fretting for something else, someone else / somewhere else. Or else, I thought, I shall die' ('Hometown'). It is poetry that vitalizes these essential dreams, for 'The dreams we have / no phrases for slip through our fingers into smoke' ('Saying Something', *SFN* 18) and 'She feels she is somewhere else, intensely, simply because / of words' ('River', *TOC* 53). With reference to the late-Romantic to late-Victorian periods, Isobel Armstrong and Virginia Blain rehabilitate the 'affective', meaning literature of 'excess' that conjures what language cannot contain, arguing: 'To want more than the minimal experiences which keep us alive is perhaps to be fully human. Certainly this is not a private experience, for to know about wanting is to understand the social importance of desire, which is one of the vectors of change' (1999: 28). However painful, it is these reflective moments and moods that poetry uniquely shapes and that make us 'Alive-alive-oh' ('Lessons In the Orchard', *RL* 40). As Robert DiNapoli urges: 'Without poetry to reinvigorate our language, we will in the end find ourselves in a kind of linguistic hell, very unlike Dante's, in which we will be left speaking with all the verve, freedom and inspiration of the instructions on the back of a soup-tin' (2014: 37).

'Hard to Say' (*TOC* 45) enacts how poetry provides the fresh metaphors and music that love needs to survive. As if confiding in the reader, it starts, 'I asked him to give me an image for Love', since the tired phrase 'I love you' is 'grubby confetti'. Then finding their own dynamic images—'like a peacock flashing wide its hundred eyes, or a boy's voice / flinging top G to the roof of an empty church, or a bottle / of French perfume knocked off the shelf, spilling into the steamy bath'—the speaker awakens 'the very shock of love' in the lovers, and potentially in the reader too. Thus, while 'as readers we are most likely to turn to poetry when we are in love, or troubled by love, or wish to mark its anniversaries, or its private significances' (Duffy, *Daily Telegraph* 2010), poetry is also intrinsic to *having* these intense moments. Poetry gives a local habitation and a name to our private formless feelings:[1] 'a baby / crying in the night like a new sound flailing for a shape', Duffy writes in the wistful 'Brothers' (*MT* 12). Her poems give shape to a vast repertoire of conditions that are hard to say: passion, grief, and unquenchable longings, all underpinned by a primordial quest to feel at home: 'When we love, when we tell ourselves we do, / we are pining for first love, somewhen, / before we thought of wanting it.' These haunting lines from 'Homesick' (*SM* 19) point to a homing desire that prefigures language and is half-remembered. They also allow some indeterminacy—the 'somewhen' and 'when we tell ourselves we do'—that paradoxically adds to the emotional precision, uniqueness, and authenticity. Thus, verbal expression is all the more credible for being self-consciously inadequate: 'wordless at last meeting love at last, dry /

---

[1] 'The poet's eye, in fine frenzy rolling, / Doth glance from heaven to Earth, from Earth to heaven. / And as imagination bodies forth / The forms of things unknown, the poet's pen / Turns them to shapes and gives to airy nothing / A local habitation and a name' (Theseus, Shakespeare, *A Midsummer Night's Dream*, Act 5: 1).

from travelling so long' ('River', *Rapture* 5). The metaphor and breathless lack of punctuation here speak louder than the words.

LOVE: 'SAYING SOMETHING'

For Duffy, 'Poetry is what love speaks in. Longing, desire, delirium, fulfilment, fidelity, betrayal, absence, estrangement, regret, loss, despair, remembrance—every aspect of love has been celebrated or mourned, praised and preserved in poetry. ... Our poets suffer no more than the rest of us in love. They don't feel more deeply or make better lovers. But they are, the best of them, able, as Auden said, to tell us "the truth about love" in the hard-earned word-music of their poems' (*Daily Telegraph* 2010). Duffy's 'word-music' resonates with the poetic past while also making it new. Shakespeare's language particularly breathes through the poems and the preface to *Rapture* (2005), 'Now I can break my fast, dine, sup, and sleep / Upon the very naked name of Love', is taken from his romantic comedy, *Two Gentlemen of Verona* (Valentine, Act 4 Scene 2). The voice in Duffy's 'Valentine' (*MT* 34) follows the argument of Shakespeare's famous sonnet, 'My mistress' eyes are nothing like the sun', by denouncing over-worn romantic signifiers, such as the red rose or 'cute card', to assert the speaker's more genuine sentiments. However, through the unlikely image of an onion, we see Duffy 'strip bare the linguistic devices of poetic language' and 'explore some of the patterns and rhythms of everyday, non-standard English' (Rees-Jones 1999: 1). She deflates tear-jerking sentimentality with the striking metaphor of peeling away the onion's layers: 'Its platinum loops shrink to a wedding-ring, / if you like.' The verb 'shrink' casts a shadow over the lovers peeling away their defences to find some essential core and rather suggests that marriage diminishes them. Additionally, the casual vernacular of 'if you like' might imply a comfortable amiable closeness but also a disconcerting indifference, or even obligation. The Duffyesque one-word line, 'Lethal.', denies the reader any lingering illusions of happiness-ever-after. In the concluding line, 'Its scent will cling to your fingers, cling to your knife', 'Its' refers back to the onion, the lover's gift that signifies 'the careful undressing of love' but also intimates that vulnerability is subject to violence: syntactically, 'your knife' can belong to the speaker, their lover, or the reader. Thus, Duffy unveils the knife edge between intimacy and isolation, security and betrayal, mutuality and power play. One of three with 'valentine' in the title, this 'brutal' (Cowing 2005) poem is oddly popular, joint eighth with Sylvia Plath's 'Daddy' in a readers' poll of 2003.[2] Speaking of Plath's *Collected Poems* that she was given when she was 25, Duffy reflects: 'I felt, then as now, as though I were reading a superior contemporary', and '"Valentine" has a DNA link to Plath's "Cut"' (*Guardian* 2012). Like Plath, Duffy's bizarre, sometimes macabre, evocations of unconscious drives investigate the shifting sands of hope, disappointment, and fear to transcend differences in identity or context and to challenge any off-the-peg interpretative logic.

The popularity of lyrics like 'Valentine' documents contemporary concerns about intimacy, as registered by the number of books and studies on the subject. The poems are not, however, about how to conquer Western culture's increasing isolation due to ruptured family life, geographical mobility, and social networking (Griffin 2010); they are about the conflicted nature of desire and about how attempts to connect through relationship also magnify our core sense of exile. In *Rapture*, intimacy unequivocally means home, but in previous volumes, the voices speak of outsidedness and alienation, frequented by 'the ghosts of ourselves behind and before us' ('Close', *MT* 37). Love is often most harmonious when a couple are geographically or chronologically distant, as in 'Telephoning Home' (*SM* 52), 'Miles Away' (*SM* 61), 'The Darling Letters' (*TOC* 48), or 'Who Loves You'. In 'Oslo' (*MT* 32), although estranged from his or her cultural environment, a traveller finds psychic coherence through knowing: 'For now, you're lucky—// across the world, someone loves you hard enough / to sieve a single star from this dark sky'. The lack of material detail reproduces surreality, the sensed strangeness of absolute reality that is paradoxically all the more authentic. Even when a lover is euphoric after a phone call with their beloved and walks out into the countryside, they reflect, 'This is not my landscape, / Though I feel at home here, in a way' ('The Kissing Gate', *TOC* 46). Without a context, the emphasis moves to the internal space and 'in a way' qualifies the feeling of being at home. Physical proximity produces more intense, problematic, and evasive feelings. 'Saying Something' (*SFN* 18) has a sketchy narrative in which a lover moves in to the speaker's home, bringing their stuff and, contingently, mixed feelings around comfort and insecurity: 'Things assume your shape; discarded clothes, a damp shroud / in the bathroom, vacant hands. This is not fiction. This is / the plain and warm material of love. My heart assumes it.' The ambiguity of 'assumes', as

---

[2] http://www.theguardian.com/uk/2003/oct/15/books.artsandhumanities

in being clothed in warm feelings but also as in taking something to be true without evidence, impresses the see-saw of hope and anxiety. The images of emptiness, 'Discarded', 'shroud', and 'vacant', and the confession, 'I dreamed I was not with you', capture the state of missing the other person while fearing one might lose them. The near end-rhymes of the sonnet's final couplet provide an aesthetic completion that jars with the casually anticlimactic statement: 'I come in / from outside: calling your name, saying something.' This ending takes a number of emotional temperatures: it can seem quite cool in its casual inconsequentiality; it can indicate lukewarm chat instead of opening up and risking vulnerability; and it can sound warmly intimate, as if the words are not as significant as the solace of reunion. Thus, it illustrates how 'emotional subtleties elude language's crude conceptual grid' (Robinson 1988: 199). 'Something' is a recurring word in Duffy's work and echoes Larkin's frequent 'something' and 'nothing', as Stan Smith elaborates (2003). However, whereas Larkin tended to nihilism, with Duffy, 'Sometimes it ["something"] is the very figure of desire, that unidentified thing which cannot be specified because the power of desire lies in its indeterminacy, in one's not knowing what it is one wants' (Smith 2003: 153).

Desire: 'a flame's fierce licks under the skin'

Crucial to Duffy's appeal and achievement is her insistent validation of desire, albeit knowable and expressible only in part: 'absence the space we yearn in, clouds / drift, cluster, east to west, north, south; / your breath in them' ('Near', *Near* 7). As Jane Thomas notes, 'Images of breath, fog and smoke occur frequently in Duffy's poems as metaphors for what cannot be expressed in verbal or written language' (2003: 134). As already indicated, the recurring ghosts and dreams are symbols for unconscious states of feeling. The speaker in 'Strange Place' (*SM* 55) watches the lover undress, half-listening to the wireless, and when they make love, she projects to the future: 'Here, later / I will feel homesick for this strange place'. The quirky opening of 'Steam' (*MT* 36)—'Not long ago so far, a lover and I / in a room of steam—' literally means 'not very long ago' yet sounds like 'Once upon a time' and evinces a teasing play between fabrication and actuality that extends all through the poem; the phrase, 'Faces blur to dreams of themselves', and the metaphor of a Life drawing that can be rubbed out, convey the precariousness of love. 'The Grammar of Light' (*MT* 32), like

'Steam' and 'Saying Something', has the Duffyesque lexicon of open or shut curtains, leaving for somewhere else, coins, bells, undressing, and wine—its romantic allusiveness increased by the candle next to it—but the contextual evasiveness is baffling. As Michael Woods comments, 'The Grammar of Light' is 'perhaps the most strikingly direct of Duffy's poems that seeks to transcend words and does this by using light as an alternative system of signification' (2003: 171). 'Echo' (*Bees* 6) invokes the myth of the nymph who fell in love with Narcissus but could only repeat his phrases so the first six lines are mirrored to visually portray an echo. Echo expresses how her delight at finding love turned to sadness when she discovered that it, like her speech, is only a copy for her loved one is not really present but is just 'the emptying air ... // the emptying air'.

Referring to Wittgenstein's picture theory of language, Woods finds 'questions that clearly preoccupy Duffy. How is language possible? How can anyone, by uttering a sequence of words, say something? And how can another person understand them?' (2003: 172). Duffy's refusal of transparent realism foregrounds these fault lines in communication and corresponds to Wittgenstein's principle: 'When we understand a statement we often have certain characteristic experiences connected with it and with the words it contains. But the meaning of a symbol in our language is not the feelings it arouses or the momentary impression it makes on us. ... Of course if the symbol were used differently there might be a different feeling, but the feeling is not what concerns us' (Ambrose 1979: 29). Duffy, however, *is* most concerned about the feelings associated with worn-out symbols and about displacing and replacing them to sharpen the precision of meaning that has been blunted by overuse. She itemizes love's moods through the 'word-music' of image and rhythm: 'The love comes, like a sudden flight of birds / from earth to heaven after rain' ('Rapture', *Rapture* 16); 'the crouched, parched heart' in love's first flush is 'like a tiger ready to kill; a flame's fierce licks under the skin' ('You', *Rapture* 1); and a killer shark is an extended metaphysical conceit for jealousy ('Jealous as Hell', *SFN* 19). In 'Row', the lovers' hearts 'were jagged stones in our fist' (*Rapture* 18) and in 'Wintering' (*Rapture* 36–7), 'I wear a shroud of cold beneath my clothes' while 'the garden tenses, lies face down, bereaved, / has wept its leaves'. When love is done, despair is 'a damp and heavy coat' ('A Disbelief', *Pamphlet* 23–4) and making a disillusioned tryst against taking any more lovers, 'this old heart of mine's / a battered purse' ('To an Unknown Lover', *Pamphlet* 45–6).

Duffy concurs with Culler and Maguire in the social implications of personal witness:

> 'The idea of love, sexual, romantic love, as being a thing that offers itself as a country, as a place of escape, a very personal place which perhaps is an alternative to the political that one experiences in public life, particularly during the eighties and nineties—the juxtaposition between the cruelty of Thatcher's policies and the tenderness that one could find in love was particularly stark for a lot of people'. (*Second Shift* 1994: 20)

Her poetry of coupling often captures the wish to carve an alternative space in which to feel complete, as in John Donne's 'Nothing else is' ('The Sunne Rising' 1977: 27). A sequence in *The Other Country*, starting with 'Two Small Poems of Desire' (42), portrays erotic intimacy as itself another country, and in *Rapture*, love *does* equal home. The protagonist meets 'the love of my life', declaring, 'I drop my past on the grass and open my arms, which ache / as though they held up this heavy sky'; free and at home, '[I] feel // my soul swoop and ease itself into my skin, like a bird threading a river' ('River', *Rapture* 5). In her bliss, she pities 'the lovers homeless / with no country to sail to' ('The Lovers', *Rapture* 24), and after a separation, reunion is 'my ship coming in / with its cargo of joy' ('Ship', *Rapture* 26).

Frequently, however, erotic activity aggravates the very isolation that Duffy's lovers seek to assuage. Narrated in the present tense, the internal monologue 'Close' (*MT* 37) disturbingly dramatizes the felt proximity of security and danger when it comes to sex. It also illustrates how 'Erotic poetry allows us to engage our imagination, to be titillated, turned on, and sometimes plain terrified' (O'Riordan 2009). The vein of mutual passion is arrested by its ambiguous narration. For a start, the title suggests both the verb 'to shut' and the adverb meaning 'near', flagging the simultaneous wish to invite and avoid close scrutiny. The opening imperative, 'Lock the door', could be threatening, excited, or regimented. The next phrase, 'In the dark journey of our night', added to the room being 'hired', hints at a clandestine encounter that is temporal, provisional, and possibly illicit. The evocative 'two childhoods stand in the corner of the bedroom' continues the ambiguity about whether the pair embark on their lovemaking with the embarrassment of innocents or the shame of naughty children. (Well into the twenty-first century, children who broke school rules were made to stand in the corner of classrooms to be shamed (Kisiel 2010).)

Duffy further illuminates how intimacy is unfathomably bound up with formative experiences and social mores when the pair's attempt to overcome their separateness is stymied by the 'suitcase crammed with secrets'. The phrase, 'we take each other to bits', resonant of the contemporary cliché to love someone 'to bits', in this context can also mean the couple destroy each other emotionally. The erotic charge intensifies as the pair make love repeatedly—'Undress.' ... 'Dress again. Undress.'—and the room trembles, as if with boisterous sexual activity. Warm intimacy is suggested by the speaker hearing their partner talk in their sleep and by the plural possessive pronouns—'our heart' and 'our mouth'—but signs of pleasure—wine, cigarette, post-coital quiet—are undercut by opposite signals: the glass and cigarette are singular and haven't been enjoyed; the bells ring with pity; the lovers' open mouth is black and 'utters its tuneless song'. The ambivalent comfort of 'you move in close till I shake, homeless' extends in the other person's 'lost accent'; their country is now 'unreadable', and 'where I live now', is somewhere else. Love 'has me where I want me, now you, you do', intensifies the inward drama and the final assertion, 'Love won't give in', sounds both grim and triumphant. In her anthology, *Hand in Hand*, Duffy chose 'Close' to put alongside 'My Errors, My loves, My unlucky star', a lament for the illusions and pains of passion by the Portuguese poet Luis Vazde Comoes (c. 1524–80).

We can weave a narrative around the couple, imagining that they are strangers or culturally different lovers. However, the poem's refusal of realism along with its blatant treatment of troublesome erotic intimacy, explains why 'Close' was considered by a sixth form student, 'the most impenetrable thing I've ever read'.[3] The impenetrability is the Duffyesque concealment of a context, the something 'at the core of the poem that the reader doesn't know, and isn't being told' (Smith 2008: 107). In 'Sleeping' (*MT* 35), the pronouns 'I' / 'You' refer to a couple so deeply joined that their emotional and sexual penetration seem symbiotic, 'You're in now, hard, / demanding'. Lacking a context, however, the tone and sense are open to interpretation, for the 'demanding' can sound either rhapsodic or unreasonable. Symbols that conceal as much as they reveal augment how 'in questioning the ways in which we are represented, [Duffy] also addresses the difficulties of knowing the self through otherness'

---

[3] UK.answers.yahoo.com, citing their teacher's caveat that it was the 'hardest one' of the Duffy poems set for the Edexcel A-Level syllabus.

(Rees-Jones 1999: 17). In 'Till our Face' (*SFN* 22) the alliteration of 'Whispers weave webs amongst thighs' and the stock imagery of roses, music, silver, gold, planets, and doves, tread a fine line between parody and genuine poetic expression and thus between aggrandizing or trivializing sexual behaviour. Frances Leviston remarks how with Duffy, 'A cliché is swiftly followed by something far more interesting, as in "I burned for you day and night; / got bits for your body wrong, bits of it right / in the huge mouth of the dark in the bite of the light" ('Rain', [*Rapture* 9]), so that the familiar phrase, by keeping better company than itself, is somehow ennobled' (2005). O'Riordan also argues that the erotic and the poetic 'help us better understand our impulses and in doing so an erotic poem becomes a place we can play out our irrational fears or indulge our deep-seated desires' (2009). Accordingly, 'This Shape', 'derived from a poem by Jean Genet', is a series of images about the interplay of fear and desire: 'My tongue thrusts, drinks at the rose's edge, / My heart uncertain. Golden hair, ghostly nape' (*SFN* 17). The state of absolute desiring while absolutely fearing is presented vividly since the assertion 'this is for real' occurs only in the speaker's dream while their partner holds on frantically, 'as if we were drowning'. The 'drowning' can be mutual abandonment but also a desperate clinging-on. Christopher Whyte comments on the poem: 'a sultry vagueness predominates, with touches of the uncanny, because the landscape of this love defies identification and, in any case, the poem takes place at a different level from daytime consciousness' (2004: 222).

Boland argues that a woman poet 'cannot make a continuum with the sexualized erotic of the male poem' (1994), as a result of being objectified in it. However, dealing with their sex-specific bodies, Duffy's speakers are remarkably gender-neutral. Mari Hughes-Edwards sees no 'great distinction between homosexual and heterosexual desire' (2006: 135) in Duffy's work and Rowland agrees that 'Two Small Poems of Desire' (*TOC* 42) 'suggest that amorous utterance somehow transcends gender difference. As in many of Duffy's love poems, the identity of subject and object remain a mystery; the phrase "these things" in the first piece refers to sexual endeavors but their exact nature persists in obscurity' (2003: 66). 'Love Birds' (*SFN* 23) presents the stages of lovemaking through sexless symbols of birds—a jay, gulls, doves, and owl. In *Rapture*, 'Elegy' (17) unashamedly enumerates a lover's body and distinctive features while 'Fall' (25) recounts making love outside on coats in Autumn but whether the lovers are male or female is immaterial. And yet, the Duffyesque repetition here—'fall and fall and fall towards you'—delicately marks the sensuous physicality of sex. 'Crush' (*MT* 29), however, relates a schoolgirl's sexual awakening through an obsession with an older girl: 'At first a secret, erotic, mute; / today a language she cannot recall.' Whyte states, 'The uncanny quality of Duffy's erotic writing destroys any potential for coyness … In "Crush", only the title identifies an emotion, a compulsion whose very poignancy consists in its avoidance of anything explicit' (222–3). This withholding is consistent with Duffy's larger aesthetic of prodding at imagination's embers. 'Only Dreaming' (*SM* 30) is a fantasy of a ghost who is a man with a woman's face and body, with whom the speaker orgasms but when the ghost departs, she or he feels 'abandoned', indicating both delight and desolation. Arguably, this device allows a lesbian poet to write of female sex and it follows 'Crush' in sequence.

Duffy, then, forges new ways of accounting for both heterosexual and same-sex eroticism. For her, poems examine, 'how we dress or undress, how we cover up or reveal, and how clothes, fashion and jewelry are both a necessary and luxurious, a practical and sensual, a liberating and repressing part of our lives' (*Out of Fashion* 2004: xi–xii). In the popular 'Warming Her Pearls', Duffy melds the lyric convention of poet-speaker with a dramatic persona. Arguably, this fictive distancing releases some poetic licence with which to express and scrutinize more taboo drives and hidden fantasies, specifically here, a female servant's lust for her mistress. In 'Girlfriends' (*TOC* 43), where one reminisces to the other about their youthful experiment with naked sex, orgasm is signalled by the 'de // da de da de da' of a siren that also suggests the alarm bell of social taboo or guilt. Duffy attributes the poem to the French love poet, Paul Verlaine (1844–96), whose pamphlet '*Les Amies*', praising lesbian love, was published secretly under a pseudonym. Her free translation follows his sonnet structure, two quatrains and two triplets, and implicitly licenses the literary representation of same-sex bliss that Verlaine celebrated covertly. 'Oppenheim's Cup and Saucer' (*SFN* 48) has been much discussed for its dynamic narration around the surrealist sculpture of fur-covered objects. Transposing visual art into lyric cross-dressed with dramatic monologue, Duffy's conversational script evolves from the image's evocation of luxurious pleasure. It starts with the scintillating, 'She asked me to luncheon in fur', playing with Breton's nickname, 'Le Déjeuner en fourrure', for Oppenheim's 'Object' (1936), but, the 'she', 'me', and the place are left to the imagination. While the fur, like the jewels in 'Warming Her Pearls', along with the high-class idiom, 'luncheon', signify wealth, to whom it belongs is unclear. We may presume that the initiator is socially superior, but the sex is certainly consensual. The seduction does not mimic patriarchal power play, for 'Far from / the loud laughter of men', it is a female-only affair in which the speaker willingly participates. The speaker's emphatically visceral pleasure partly arises from acknowledging her lesbian identity—'our secret life stirred', 'our breasts were a mirror'—and is magnified by the end rhymes ('spine' and 'mine') along with assonance ('bed', 'legs', 'neck', 'Yes'). Although the context is explicitly lesbian, the erotic potency is available to readers of both sexes and any sexual orientation. 'Swing' (*Rapture* 8) recounts 'the soft unbearable dawns of desire', a delicate generic symbol, but the liquidity of 'foam / boasted and frothed like champagne at the river's bed'—can be read as lesbian imagery. Whyte observes how Duffy achieves a 'language of the body which employs lesbian tropes while retaining a sense of hiddenness, of the unspoken and unidentified' (222); 'We lift up our skirts in the sea' ('White Writing' *FG* 57) is such a discreet signifier.

'Finding the words'

'Oppenheim's Cup and Saucer' illustrates how Duffy's ekphrastic poems put words in dialogue with alternative systems of signification (Woods 2003). David Kennedy observes:

> British poetry has been and continues to be formed by the extent to which a poet chooses to engage with cultural and linguistic polyphony. And the more a poet chooses to engage, the further he or she seems to drift from the lyric as the concentrated apprehension of an individual singing. Ekphrasis as a predominantly social mode may be, then, a consequence of a wider polyphonic turn, since art about other art is already willing to play with multiple forms and languages. (2012: 56)

As already discussed, Duffy's lyrics zoom in on the process of representation in tandem with the 'something' being represented. 'Woman Seated in the Underground, 1941: *after the drawing by Henry Moore*' (*SFN* 50) embellishes Moore's eerie watercolour of a solitary figure behind whom stretches an endless murky tunnel. Duffy imagines that the woman is pregnant and has been discarded to endure public shame: 'I have either lost my ring or I am / a loose woman.' She picks up on the woman's anxiously clasped hands to explore the suggested desertion, trauma, and amnesia:

'yet my mind / has unraveled into thin threads that lead nowhere'. The words 'somewhere', 'somebody', 'nowhere' and 'nothing' swirl around like the smoke in the background of Moore's drawing. The thread on which her sanity hangs is fabricated by her insistence that 'Someone has loved me'. Discussing this poem, Thomas concludes, 'the idea of subjectivity shifts uncertainly between a reflective and a constructive model. The speaker fails to recognize herself in the cultural and linguistic mirrors that surround her whilst at the same time discovering that the powerful defining terms that she cites compulsively—"darling", "baby"—have lost their shaping power and fail to signify any longer' (2003: 128–9). Thomas also underlines the painful narrative of the woman's desertion in the lines '*Underneath the lantern / by the barrack gate*' from 'Lili Marlene', a wartime song in which soldiers celebrated their lovers at home: 'deprived of the stabilising effect of a coherent subjectivity and a position from which to articulate herself, she begins to unravel into psychosis'. (2003: 128)

The ekphrastic and dramatic lyrics might participate in a perceived 'polyphonic turn' and illuminate deconstructive linguistic principles, but increasingly Duffy's allusive evocations 'capture the "felt significance" to life' (Mousley 2013: 83). In *Rapture* (2005), the book-length sequence carries full signifying power as Duffy refashions the lyric that Kennedy defines as 'the concentrated apprehension of an individual singing'. The singing is never, of course, mere solipsism nor sheer joy:

> It is about deep feeling. I could not feel more deeply than I have in these poems—but these are not journals or diaries or letters, they are works of art. A transformation takes place—it has to, if the feeling is to be revealed to others. Intensity of emotion is only the beginning—I have to do something with it. (Duffy, Winterson 2005)

The fifty-two lyrics tell of the bliss and ache of love from start ('You') to finish ('Over') against a backdrop that shifts from one summer to the next. As Duffy intended: 'The poems draw on a deeply familiar, almost fairytale-like, bank of images—rivers, forests, birds, moons—to map the courses that love can take from its beginnings through its stops and starts and changes' (*PBS* 2005). As Leviston says of *Rapture*: 'Duffy is operating on a different plane, ahistorical, archetypal, where "moon" and "rose" and "kiss" come clear of the abuses of tradition to be restored to the poet's lexicon, as the things of the world are restored to the lover' (2005).

Whereas Duffy's earlier love poetry depicts feelings of strangeness, the sequence in *Rapture* is about finding the words for the sheer intensity of love's seasons, from falling in love, through desire, mutual passion, mundane companionship, delight, suspicion, separation, reunions, and finally ending. Jane Griffiths applauds how the early poems in *Rapture* catch 'through litany and incantation the sheer transformative shock of falling in love. Like medieval lyrics, these poems are both particular and general: rhythm, and rhyme rather than content convey the essence of the experience' (2005). Duffy similarly comments: 'In *Rapture*, I was also interested in the love poem itself—in how much distance, if any, there is between the experience of love and the expression of it in poetic language. If love is the most powerful of emotions, is the love poem the most power-ful of poems?' (*PBS* 2005). She writes in 'Syntax' (53), 'Love's language starts, stops, starts; / the right words flowing or clotting in the heart', and 'Finding the Words' (31) is about saying the words 'I love you, I love you, I love you—/ as though they were new'. Even when reliving the most private moment, she allows the narrative to question its own veracity without losing the surreality of fairytale romance: 'we knelt in the leaves, / kissed, kissed; new words rustled nearby and we swooned // Didn't we?' ('Forest' 4). The couplets of 'Text' (2) visualize the simultaneous sense of closeness and distance in being a couple for 'the codes we send / arrive with a broken chord'. In 'The Love Poem' (59), 'a tissue of deliberate echoes' (Oxley 2005: 105) from famous love poems by women and men, who include Emily Dickinson, Elizabeth Barrett Browning, Shakespeare, Philip Sidney, Christopher Marlowe, Donne, and Percy Bysshe Shelley, Duffy 'tells the reader—in part—where all this sequence is coming from. Real experience made over into art' (Oxley 105). The poem of the vol-ume's title, 'Rapture' (16), is one of several sonnets in the book, but their language is always direct and contemporary: 'Thought of by you all day, I think of you.' The imagery and halting iambic pentameter contrive the erotic and emotional poignancy of mental replay: 'Your kiss, / recalled, unstrings, like pearls, this chain of words.'

Thus, Duffy proves how pleasure stimulates the poetic line that in turn memorializes pleasure beyond its actual shelf life. The references to mobile phones in 'Text' and 'Quickdraw' (2, 30) accord with what David Morley observes: 'Yet the poems are a kind of anti-literature ... So, while *Rapture* deserves much applause for its emotional honesty, consolation, and gen-erosity, it also deserves praise for its cunning, its impersonality, and its mercilessness, all of which virtues make the invisible work of poetry an act of concentrated ferocity' (2006). In 'Row' (18), the 'bank of images', along with the sound, metre, and uneven line lengths forcefully convey the 'concentrated ferocity' of passion. The verbs onomatopoeically express the anger and anguish of argument: 'But when we rowed, / the trees wept and threw away their leaves, / the day ripped the hours from our lives, / the sheets and pillows shredded themselves on the bed.' Such erupting passion is prized for its ferocity even while it is regretted. Like many critics, in his enlightening review of Duffy's *Love Poems*, John Mullan weighs her manipulation of language with what it is expressing: 'Language is often Duffy's subject matter in these poems, for love calls upon it to do impossible things. "Love is a look / In the eyes in any language". Not so much what words say as what we intuit from them' (2013). In 'White Writing' (*FG* 57), the finished poem contradicts her refusal to put love into words: 'No poems written to praise you, / I write them white'. 'By Heart' (*SM* 57) cleverly testifies to love's power through a voyage of the imagination in which 'I made myself imagine that I didn't love you' and 'Treasure' (*Rapture* 41) turns glints of suspicion into evidence of love that values, 'Even the fool's gold / of your lies'. The iconography of myth enlarges the deadness of a broken relationship in 'Ithaca' and 'Land' (*Rapture* 50–1): 'If we were shades, we would rather lie there // Than where we are here'.

Duffy excels at heartache: 'There's a persistent sense in her work that love involves as much suffering as it does joy. As she writes in one of the poems in *Rapture*: "Falling in love is glamorous hell"' (Preston 2010). Her preference for human failures arguably compensates for the self-congratulatory ethos of her contemporary image culture. 'At Ballynahinch' (*Bees* 72) enacts the heart's thunderstorms when love is cheated or unreturned. She paints a romantic scene—patterns of sunlight on the river at a beauty spot in Connemara—in which the speaker bemoans, 'the one / who did not love me at all, / who had never loved me, no, / who would never love me.' The light hurls down, the sun flings hammers that batter the water, and the unhappy lover repeats 'At Ballynahinch' three times, as if punching the ground. Two subsequent poems, 'New Vows' and 'Valentine's' (*Bees* 73, 75), also augment the pain of brokenness by detonating romantic motifs: 'from this day forward to unhold' (73) or 'a kick to the heart by the ghost of a mule / you thought to ride to your wedding feast' (75). Similarly, 'The Suicide' (*MT* 41), the lyrical dramatic monologue of someone riddled by resentment due to betrayal—'Kisses / on a collar. Lies. Blood'—cries, 'Who wants / a bloody valentine pumping its love hate love?' Like 'Valentine', the morbid Plathesque symbolism,

'I dress in a shroud', and 'I get out the knives', shockingly marks the intolerable pain that prompts the speaker's death wish. In 'Disgrace' (*MT* 48–9), the snapshot of sweet love turned sour depicts an arid emotional state concerning a broken self / other negotiation. The domestic images provoke 'feelings that are the more powerful for the inadequate linguistic means available' (Mullan 2013): 'Woke to the absence of grace; the still-life / of a meal, untouched, wine-bottle, empty, ashtray, / full. In our sullen kitchen, the fridge / hardened its cool heart, selfish as art, hummed.' Neil Roberts writes, '"Home" is a key word in Duffy's love poems, occurring in at least ten of them, and in a poem about a failing relationship, "Disgrace", she figures estrangement as "We had not been home in our hearts for months"' (1999: 192). 'Love makes buildings home', she writes in 'A Disbelief' (*Pamphlet* 23–4) that also distils the disorientation that follows a break-up: 'This is myself outside in the rain. / I can't speak our language. The locks / have been changed. The worst that can possibly happen will. // The worst that can possibly happen will.' The repeated phrase mimics the mind replaying the event, with quatrains, assonance and dissonance providing the background music. Helen Dunmore observes how 'The simplicity of the language works beautifully, because it is married to emotional truth.' Deeming 'A Disbelief', 'one of the best poems in *The Pamphlet*', she latches on to Duffy's evocation of 'this sudden despairing sense of exile': 'Carol Ann Duffy's poetry has always reflected a strong sense of the tension between being inside and being outside and indeed between being an insider and an outsider. Her love poetry is sharpened by a sense of fragility. At any moment, the bliss of being one of love's insiders can be destroyed. Love is a home, and the loveless are homeless, wanderers on the outside, lookers-in through windows at the magnified allurements of belonging and being welcome' (1999: 81).

Loss: 'unmendable rain'

As Dunmore perceives, Duffy's love poetry illuminates how loss, whether actual or apprehended, is inseparable from romance and passion. Grief may be 'Love's spinster twin' ('Grief', *Rapture* 49) but is always hard to bear: 'Love is a form of prayer; love lost / a disbelief' ('A Disbelief', *Pamphlet* 23–4). 'Mean Time' (*MT* 51) recreates the dead-end gloom of a broken relationship: 'The clocks slid back an hour / and stole light from my life / as I walked through the wrong part of town, / mourning our love.' The potent image of 'unmendable rain' speaks of unmitigated hopelessness and the title phrase condenses lost love's many moods, with 'mean' indicating miserly, as in feeling that life is stacked against one, or 'average', that 'life sucks', and 'meanwhile', as in trying to fill up the newly vacant days. In this commonplace but dense imagery and colloquial idiom, 'Mean Time' does all that we want from a lyric: it conjures the painfully repetitive thoughts of regret and remorse—'there are words I would never have said / nor have heard you say'; it provides catharsis through verbalizing the pain; and there is consolation in not being alone with an inner darkness. Additionally, the artifice of the quatrains, end-rhymes ('say' / 'day'), and imperfect rhymes ('life' / 'love') communicate the poet's oxymoronic rewards of what Rees-Jones calls 'momentary recreation': 'the act of articulating the loss of that which by its nature cannot be articulated acknowledges the unobtainable nature of her desires while nevertheless deriving pleasure from the momentary recreation (both through memory, and through the act of creating a poem) of the realization of that loss' (1999: 43). 'Lovesick' (*SM* 54), 'Haworth', 'Absence', and 'World' (*Rapture* 6, 10, 14) similarly encapsulate, without cliché, the sweet sorrow of 'momentary recreation' when missing the beloved: 'I'm here now where you were' ('Haworth').

Rapture's 'poetically universal' (Mousley 2013: 83) sequence on the couple's break-up is satisfyingly heart wrenching in its 'momentary recreation'. 'Unloving' (61) is a profoundly beautiful rendition of projecting emotion on to the surroundings: 'Learn from the dumbstruck garden, summer's grave / where nothing grows'. 'Midsummer Night' (47–8) has the gravitas of Donne's 'A Nocturnall upon S. Lucies Day' that starts, 'Tis the yeares midnight, and it is the dayes' (1977: 50). Duffy's version of utter void begins, 'Not there to see midsummer's midnight', and 'not there' hauntingly repeats throughout the speech to negate the list of romantic signifiers. 'Art' (60) is more self-referential about how the sparks of a broken bond 'fizzled into poems; page print / for the dried flowers of our voice'. The flat tone mediates heartache while the rhymes, right down to the closing couplet, model and query the consolations of artistic re-makes: 'and the Oscar-winning movie in your heart; / and where my soul sang, croaking art'. However, the final poem, 'Over' (62), offers the consolations of memory in its preface from Robert Browning's lines on how the thrush sings each song twice to 'recapture' 'The first fine careless rapture!' While the literary echo resonates across place and time, the private reference in 'no skelf of light', the Glaswegian word for splinter that occurs in 'Originally' (*TOC* 7), thus transposes personal to universal pain. However sad the loss, then, Duffy models the pleasures, the 'rapture', of imaginative reinvention.

'Memory's caged bird won't fly'

For healthy people, 'All the careful moments will be dreamed and dreamed again', Duffy writes in 'Dream of a Lost Friend' (*TOC* 39). Elsewhere, memory's limitations in regaining the past only accentuate the past-ness. 'Originally' dramatizes how losses in and of childhood are more long lasting than lost love. 'Moments of Grace' (*MT* 26) is a meditation on how harping back to childhood feels at once fruitful and futile. The subject recalls the excitement of their first love as they 'sit now / in a kind of sly trance' but 'sly' is an odd—yet Duffyesque—word that hints of deception. It alludes to a shaky grasp of the distinction between internal and external realities. 'I dream through a wordless, familiar place' is also ambiguous about whether the 'place' is the present in which the dream occurs or the time being remembered. The repeated 'Now' in the first stanza seems to break the spell as the dreamer returns to their current situation and lover. The italicized sentences, *'Like this.'*, *'Of course.'*, and *'Gone.'*, further register how memories appear then recede. Paradoxically, they must be unleashed or 'Memory's caged bird won't fly' and without memory, there are no 'doing words', neither life nor poetry, for, Duffy tells us, verbs are 'the secret of poems'. The speaker in 'Practising Being Dead' (*SM* 9) mentally revisits a place, autobiographically Duffy's school, where 'The trees sigh' and 'Your own ghost, you stand in dark rain / and light aches out from the windows'.[4] The narrative logic breaks down but the potency of loss is pinned: 'It is accidental and unbearable to recall that time, / neither bitter nor sweet but gone, the future / already lost as you open door after door, each one / peeling back a sepia room empty of promise.' The emotional precision renders the description uniquely personal while the archetypal symbols of a gravel drive, big oak doors, and wooden floors shift to a more mythical plane. Roberts makes a persuasive comparison between these endless corridors of memory with T.S. Eliot's imagery for what might have been—'Down the passage which we did not take'—in *Burnt Norton*. He argues for the skilfully impersonal voice of Duffy's lyric and that her 'destabilization of time, space and person ... make[s] the reader engage with what is going on in the text, rather than leaning on a facile referentiality' (2003: 43). However, like the 'didn't we?' in 'Forest', discussed earlier, the reader engages with *both* what is going on in the text

[4] The poem refers to an occasion where the girls were once allowed to pray and sprinkle Holy Water on the body of a nun who had died.

and its complex referentiality. 'I Live Here Now' (*SM* 18) again finely balances realism with self-conscious narration: 'I invented it, that wee dog barking / at the postman (a soldier with one arm, still)'. The Scottish 'wee' both recollects Duffy's early life and also sniffs of a fairy story. Even if the childish scenes were fabricated,[5] the imagination that invented them is certainly alive alive-oh. More pertinently, the emotional truth endures, especially through the unforgettable image of the child waving to the adult self who sometimes waves back, 'over the fields, the years'.

These 'momentary recreations' are the bittersweet delights of the 'other country' from where the poems come and to where they take us. Sometimes, the speaker can 'clench my eyes / till the pictures return, unfocused at first, then / almost clear, an old film / played at slow speed' ('First Love', *MT* 27). More agonizingly, in 'Beachcomber' (*MT* 20) an older person strains to play memory's films. Two competing voices enact the sense of being outside a past he or she tries to enter. One is animated by memories and the other, a sensible companion or alter ego, kills their spirit through rational argument about the impossibility of going back: 'You remember that cardigan, yes? / You remember that cardigan'. Ultimately, she cannot contact her young self and the other voice becomes unexpectedly querulous: 'and what / what would you have to say, / of all people, / to her / given the chance? / Exactly'. The 'exactly' is rhetorical and cruelly enforces the pointlessness of the exercise, as in 'what exactly would you have to say?' In similar vein, the title of 'M-M-Memory' (*TOC* 36) onomatopoeically depicts how remembering always falters. The voice recalls a scenario in which they were a child scooping spilt oil from a flagstone floor, a symbol for trying in vain to scoop up memories, 'Those unstrung beads of oil', and yet the unreachable dull mundane of childhood shines like unattainable jewels in retrospect.

The no-win conclusion is that the psyche suffers whether it tries to touch the past or whether it tries to ignore it. The seductiveness of 'Living / in and out of the past' is compared to a tide in 'All Days Lost Days' (*SM* 46). Here, the subject wastes their life in a limbo, 'between dreaming / and dreaming again and half-remembering'. The speaker in 'Survivor' (*TOC* 33) is deranged with longing: 'The gone years where I lived. I want them back', 'this is bereavement', 'It is making me ill', 'I rock / and weep for what has been stolen, lost.' She lounges around 'in the past', lamenting,

---

[5] Duffy has in mind the garden scenes constructed in boxes that children made from available items, such as a mirror for a pond.

'I have hidden myself in my heart' and 'It is like an earthquake and no one to tell'. The earthquake stands for the unutterably strong urge to reach back to an irrecoverable past that blocks the grown-up speaker from her lover who 'rises and plunges above me'. The inward disorientation is further portrayed through threading assonance—'fifteen', 'Leeds', 'bereavement', 'feel', 'weep'—with dissonance—'not knowing', 'stolen', 'lost', and 'Please.' at the end of line 13 is a *cri du coeur* to lover and reader. As Duffy comments, perhaps with this poem in mind, '"Even if you are in bed with your beloved there is a sense in which you are forever excluded from any sort of contact. That is the condition and tragedy of us as humans"' (McAllister 1988: 70). Roberts explains how in Duffy's poetry, 'outsidedness' is not a person set against a norm but 'Outsidedness *is* the norm. It is an aesthetic principle in her representation of subjectivity' (Roberts 1999: 184). Furthermore, 'either thematically or through disruptive linguistic practices, problems of language are inseparable from the outsidedness of Duffy's poetry' (1999: 191). Linguistic and self-alienation run through such lyrics as 'I Remember Me' (*SFN* 16) and in 'Whoever She Was' (*SFN* 35), Duffy pinpoints the mother's suspended identity as a pain she cannot locate or name—'where does it hurt?' Her children have leapt from babe to adult and now she longs for a skin in which to feel comfortable but the longing is grasped more by the reader than the speaker. The 'whoever' in the title phrase carries the possibility of equilibrium—as in the idiomatic '*whatever*'—but the imagery of her mind's flickering screen indicates the 'whoever' of psychic disturbance:

> They see me always as a flickering figure,
>
> on a shilling screen. Not real. My hands,
>
> still wet, sprout wooden pegs. I smell the apples
>
> burning as I hang the washing out.
>
> Mummy, say the little voices of the ghosts
>
> Of children on the telephone. Mummy.

Rees-Jones defines such a de-familiarizing conjunction of images as verbal surrealism, 'acting like a hinge between self and otherness, the private and public, the blatant and the covert, the knowable and the unknowable' (1999: 8). Here, one group of images pertain to the common acts of making paper dollies, cutting toast into 'soldiers' to eat with boiled eggs, kissing children good night, making masks from turnips for bonfire night, and shaping hands while reciting, 'Here's the church and here's the steeple, open the door and here's the people.' These remembered rituals provoke warm nostalgia but also chronic pain at leaving them behind. In parallel, symbols for domestic drudgery, the washing and cooking, accentuate the role that arguably stunted the mother's self-realization. The sense of being outside herself further presents through switching first and third person pronouns: 'She cannot be myself and yet I have a box / of dusty presents to confirm that she was here.' Michelis and Rowland view her failure to assemble a unified self as a reflection on culture's contamination of language that deprives her of the means to do so (2003: 24–5). Thomas proffers an incisive feminist reading of how the mother's platitudes—'I do not know. / Perhaps tomorrow. If we're very good'—are formulaic iterations of the socially scripted maternal role that only purport to be soothing. She persuasively sees in 'sprout wooden pegs' a veiled reference to the myth of Daphne, a beautiful nymph who was metamorphosed into an immobile tree (Thomas 2003: 129–30). Duffy describes 'Whoever She Was' (*SFN* 35) as 'a Plath-enabled piece about motherhood' and, for all its personal source in Duffy's own mother, the poem demonstrates the 'lunar detachment' that she admired in Plath: 'Plath, like all great poets, is ruthless in her pursuit of the poem. ... she had a kind of lunar detachment that ultimately sets her poems free of herself' (*Guardian* 2012).

Many readers deem Duffy at her best when most undoggedly personal, as in the elegies to her mother in *The Bees* (Kellaway 2011; Sexton 2011). Yet, with 'lunar detachment', the cohering imagery of coldness paints the wintry landscape of grief that could be any reader's: 'Decembers' (*Bees* 60) traces Christmas celebrations from childhood to the present when her mother's absence is keenly felt; and in the fourteen lines of an unrhymed sonnet, 'Cold' (*Bees* 58), compares her childhood memories of playing in the snow while her mother peeled vegetables in cold water with kissing her dead body in the Chapel of Rest, balking at the coldness of her skin. The closing couplet, in which the end rhyme of 'old' and 'cold' emphasizes the finality of death, offers the artistic completion with which elegy consoles. 'Water' (*Bees* 33) refers to her mother's last request and reminds the poet of when she was a child and her mother would bring her water, 'holding my hand, / just as we held hands now and you died'. In her turn, Duffy takes water to her own child's side: 'What a mother brings / through darkness still / to her parched daughter.' The word 'still', at the end of the line, points beyond itself to mean both motionless and continuously. The end rhyme of 'daughter' with 'water' chimes with the poem's argument—that the plastic hospice cup connects mother with daughter across the generations. As Kellaway notes, '"Water" is perfectly controlled, yet written with what could almost be mistaken for casualness. It carries its emotional weight effortlessly. It acknowledges three generations, needing one another in ordinary ways' (2011). The poem proves intensely how memory's 'momentary recreation' both fills and deepens the holes of loss. When the disillusioned speaker in 'Losers' (*TOC* 35) complains of 'The times / it hurts', the 'it' is 'the bankrupt feeling' we have as memory disappears. Nonetheless, poetry preserves and appeases what is lost by naming the unnamable, albeit as an 'it' or 'something' or as the white space between the lines.

LONGING: 'AN ACHE, *HERE*, DOCTOR'

Whereas 'Away from Home' (*TOC* 49–50) details a literal homesickness—'a blurred longing / sharpens like a headache'—and 'Moments of Grace' (*MT* 26) explores the first love that haunts every subsequent relationship, 'Homesick' (*SM* 19) manifests a more metaphysical longing for 'something' primordial and pre-linguistic, 'lost chords, wordless languages': 'We scratch in dust with sticks, / Dying of homesickness / For when, where, what.' Regarding 'Homesick', Rees-Jones draws on Freud's terminology of 'unheimlich' to describe the human longing to return to the maternal body but sees Duffy as offering a 'conjunction between the heimlich and the unheimlich, the natural and constructed' (1999: 42). In 'Nostalgia' (*MT* 10) Duffy relays an incurable homesickness—'They had an ache, *here*, Doctor'– with a narrative that is both natural and constructed, historical and fictional. She explains that the title takes its name from an illness suffered by mercenaries who lived in the mountains of Switzerland. When they went down to the lower levels to fight for money, they would become ill because of the change in altitude and this illness—'a sweet pain in the heart'—was called nostalgia because they associated it with leaving home: 'other people who lived in the mountains would be afraid to leave their villages in case they became nostalgic. But if one looks at world cinema and listens to music, that quality is coming from many different nations' (*Second Shift* 1994: 22). 'Nostalgia' resembles a tableau in which some of the mercenaries return but they and the place have changed. At a stile, marking the spot where individuals choose between home or away, stand the priest and teacher, redundant cornerstones of the now fragmented community. McCulloch comments on the poem, 'For Duffy, "outsidedness" is everywhere, from the experience of the immigrant to longing, homesickness and our simple inability to inhabit the moment. "Nostalgia", which appeared in the *TLS* in March 1992 and was later published in *Mean Time*, is about both kinds of exile—from our homes and our lives—its language a blend of narrative account and lyrical address. Here, words do not only isolate us from others, they separate us from ourselves: "It was given a name ... the word was out"' (2014). Where Duffy taps into this outsidedness and longing, she evades logical coherence for the sake of depicting the wordless state in which the ache exists, described only as 'how it hurt' and 'Stones in the belly'. At the same time, she illuminates how it is the ache that moves us to memory and dream.

In 'Dies Natalis' (*SM* 10–13), the narrating persona undergoes a sequence of reincarnations as someone else, from the cat of an Egyptian queen, perhaps Shakespeare's Cleopatra, to the albatross in Samuel Coleridge's 'The Rime of the Ancient Mariner'. The next persona is a man whose love for his wife turned to loathing but after twenty-five years of unhappy marriage, she died of cancer so he buried her in his allotment and 'what blew back in my face was grey ash, dust'. The final voice belongs to a baby, born to mixed race parents. It is best read as a poem about what is lost when translating the state of being into words, starting with the Latin words of the title, which Google translator produces as 'birthday' rather than the more rejuvenating and metaphysical 'day of birth'. The cat hears the queen 'singing // her different, frantic notes into my ear. / These were meanings I could not decipher' and the albatross views the waves 'muttering in syllables of fish' and they 'trod air, laughing'. In an eloquent reading of the poem, Woods comments, '"Dies Natalis" is linked to a preconscious sequence of selves that seek to explore the supra-linguistic realm. These metamorphosing, protean personae that none the less have to resort to forms of language ... may be viewed as the part of us all that craves some Platonic certitude of imperishable singularity' (2003: 179–80). While the human couple conformed to social expectations and 'whispered / false vows which would ruin our lives', the unique languages of the other creatures are contingent with their 'imperishable singularity': 'The cat 'purred // my one eternal note beneath the shadow of pyramids'. However, singularity has a price, for the whales sing 'bleak songs' and the albatross is alone: 'Men's voices / came over the side in scraps. I warned patiently / in my private language, weighed down with loneliness.' The baby hears 'the adults chanting my new name' and remains apart. In the baby's final words, 'And when they disappear. I cry', Woods notes the echo of Gerard Manley Hopkins's brilliant depiction of human singularity—'each mortal thing does one thing and the same / ... /, crying *What I do is Me, for that I came*' ('As Kingfishers Catch Fire', Gardner 1975: 51) (Woods 2003: 179–80). Similarly, 'Nothing's the same as anything else', Duffy writes in 'Away and See' (*MT* 23).

Smith also detects the Duffyesque desire to match words with our sensed singularity, 'for a fullness of self-presence in which sign and refer- ent, language and things, are one' (Smith 2008: 119). Accordingly, 'River' (*TOC* 53) asks the reader to enter a scene that words cannot describe—they 'stumble, fall back'—where a woman has a new language for 'cluing the bird's song' and worshipping a red flower: 'She feels she is somewhere else, intensely, simply because / of words; sings loudly in nonsense, smiling, smil- ing.' Duffy's 'because' at the end of the line reads as if the woman is sing- ing, 'simply because'—she is just being present—and also simply because of the nonsense words. She thus points to some pre-linguistic consciousness, aroused in such lines as 'Waking, with a dream of first love forming real words' or 'Tonight, a love letter out of a dream / stammers itself in my heart' ('First Love' *MT* 27). To this end, her surreal imagery defies words and corresponds to Breton's urge to mine matters that are of primary con- cern: 'We are still living under the reign of logic: this, of course, is what I have been driving at. But in this day and age logical methods are applicable only to solving problems of secondary interest' (1972: 9). Smith accords: 'In a world of simulacra, copies, echoes, we are "dying of homesickness / for when, where, what", for a lost unity of being, the quiddity and *haec- ceitas* of things, in which the self comes home to an unmediated time and place where all beyonds are incorporated in the instant, without any waste sad time stretching before and after. It is in fact a yearning straight from the mainstream of the Christian mystical tradition' (2008: 119).

Post-religious Loss: 'that small familiar pain'

The unabated longing for home, for completion, for flesh and word to chime, corresponds to what Edna Longley calls 'a post-religious sense of loss [that] gives modern poetry its persistent metaphysical dimension' (2003: 24). This late twentieth-century zeitgeist hovers over Duffy's vexed equation with formal religion. In 'Over' (*Rapture* 62), she yearns, 'What do I have // to help me, without spell or prayer, / endure this hour, endless, heartless, anonymous, / the death of love? Only the other hours—/ ... the blush of memory'. Her dramatic lyrics scrutinize religion's representatives whose speeches betray their own misuse of power, hypocrisy, and human failing. 'Pope Joan' (*WW* 68–9) is elevated to the highest place of honour, worshipped by 'fervent crowds', and speaks Latin but believes none of what she preaches. 'Mrs Pilate' (*WW* 18) reveals how she was impressed by 'the Nazarene', that her dream of Pilate stopping the crucifixion was part sexual fantasy, and how she regrets that her crowd-pleasing husband sentenced Christ to death. She attests, however: 'Was he God? Of course not.' Duffy again refers to the Christian story in 'History' (*FG* 27–8), personified as a woman watching how the claims to Christ's resurrection led to religious wars, crusades, murders, and martyrdom. History likens them to the Nazi slaughters of Jews, making the point that if humans ignore past evils, they just repeat them. More autobiographically, 'Ash Wednesday, 1984' (*SFN* 14) recalls Duffy's early experiences of Roman Catholicism—the spankings, the 'bigot's thumbprint' of ash, and the mystification of Latin, 'Dead language rises up and does them harm'. Plain speech runs across the lyric, culminating in, 'For Christ's sake, do not send your kids to Mass', an imperative that echoes Larkin's stark, 'And don't have any kids yourself' ('This be the Verse', 1990: 180). Duffy's line, 'It makes me sick', in 'Ash Wednesday, 1984' recurs as '*You make me sick*' in 'Following Francis' (*TOC* 32), an unsettling narrative by a man who left his family to be with Francis of Assisi. Whether in the man's fantasy life or for real, there are intimations of erotic relations between disciple and saint. More explicit is the priest's abuses in 'Confession' (*MT* 15) in which the 'hidden man' in a musty cell has the young Duffy recite her transgressions and his threats of damnation wheedle the small child's spirit into guilt and shame. The damaging legacy of Roman Catholic dogma on women particularly is also explored in 'Words of Absolution' (*SFN* 32) in which a mélange of phrases from the catechism, the rosary, and confession perpetuate the fearsome doctrines of sin that erode the old woman's sanity as she faces death: 'Chastity. Piety. Modesty. Longanimity. / How should you finish the day? After your night prayer what should you do?' The list of Christian virtues here, taken from the fruits of the spirit in *Catechism of the Catholic Church,* imply that these impossible ideals of self-sacrifice and sexual abstinence account for her unresolved desires and shame. 'Free Will' (*SFN* 25) ironically takes the theological phrase for believing that the individual is free to choose hell or redemption by applying it to a woman who has had an abortion, an act prohibited by the Roman Catholic Church.

It illustrates how a sense of loss is keen on such occasions when religious absolution might free a stinging conscience or assuage the woman's grief; instead, the dogma rubs salt into her wounds. In contrast, Duffy's poem offers some relief in its non-judgmental exploration of the woman's torment: 'Whatever it was she did not permit it a name', 'It was nothing yet she found herself grieving nothing'. Based on the Sanctuary of Asklepios, 'Sanctuary' (*SM* 14) points to ancient methods for treating soul sickness. It dramatizes a woman's search for healing in the site dedicated to the god of medicine where she laps up the serene surroundings: 'The months flew, that year in the Sanctuary / when you were cured'.

For Duffy, a 'post-religious' condition is seeped with nostalgia for the spiritual consolations that religion promised but failed to deliver. The emptiness of non-belief ebbs and flows through all her volumes—'But we will be dead as we know / beyond all light' ('Mean Time' *MT* 51). The first line of 'And Then What' (*SFN* 61)—'Then with their hands they would break bread'—takes its imagery from Holy Communion or Mass but what follows outlines the brevity and bleakness of the human life cycle. Hands are the cohering signifier of the inexorable progress from youth to work to love to death. A dramatic lyric that speaks of the impending nothingness beyond the grave, 'Letters from Deadmen' (*SFN* 62), neither confirms nor discounts the dubious comfort of the common placebo, 'They say we rest in peace'. Instead, the voices suggest a kind of purgatory, a limbo before complete extinction. The dead verbalize questions that exercise bereaved loved ones over whether the funeral was executed appropriately, whether to leave their possessions untouched, and how best to honour their memory. The lines in italics, '*They parted his garments, casting lots upon them / what every man should take*', copy the Biblical account of Christ's death and suggest how men argue over the deceased's spoils. 'Honeymoon' (*NSP* 135) is in the voice of a man who relays what it is like to die, be buried, and finally snuff out in the 'dark // dark' underground. 'An Old Atheist places his last Bet' (*SM* 16) personifies the angst of viewing life as a mere game of cards with no Dealer: Poker is the card game and the look on his face while images of nothingness signal the vacant space left by religious faith.

The joyless futility in 'All Days Lost Days' (*SM* 46) follows Larkin's 'Days' that captured post-war agnosticism. Duffy's speaker knows that living in the past robs the present of its vitality yet the future holds 'a line of black cars'. A procession of funeral cars in 'November' (*TOC* 51) also reminds how death 'can ruin a day' and cause a woman to cross herself superstitiously. Thus, the mystical infiltrates the mundane for the speaker had merely gone to post 'a harmless optimistic letter'. In another poem, Duffy's harmless reflections on her four younger brothers lead to thoughts of her mother's inevitable death: 'One day / I shall pay for a box and watch them shoulder it' ('Brothers', *MT* 12). These morbid moments mark a palpable absence of faith shot through with longing for spiritual connectedness: 'There must be a word for home / if they only knew it' ('Strange Language in Night Fog', *SM* 17). 'Forever dead. Say these words and let their meaning / dizzy you like the scent of innumerable petals', speaks the poet in 'Père Lachaise' (*TOC* 37), situated at the large cemetery in Paris where many great writers, artists, and musicians are buried, and who seem to plead, 'Remembrance. Do not forget'. The same equalizing but crushing finality, that is only tempered if the living remember us, comes across in 'Funeral' (*TOC* 38): 'All afternoon // we said your name, / repeated the prayers of anecdotes'. Next to 'Funeral', 'Like This' (*TOC* 40), possibly about the same friend, is composed of a single sentence that runs through the sonnet's fourteen lines as if imitating their rapid and inexorable journey to oblivion. Afterwards, the deceased only lives on in 'brief epitaphs of love, regret'. Whyte sees the contextual vagueness in such a poem as 'Dream of a Lost Friend' (*TOC* 39) as a 'potent enabler' to elegy for in the dream, 'Chronology is reversed, or turned backwards, or set leapfrogging over itself, and the resultant uncertainty gives an appropriately nightmarish quality to the poem' (223). The speaker's reverie is of meeting their friend who has died of Aids and confessing to have missed his funeral. In conscious time, they conclude: 'Awake, alive, for months I think of you / almost hopeful in a bad dream where you were long dead.' As Whyte remarks, 'However uncanny, even Gothic, the mechanics of the poem may be, it evokes more effectively than a more prosaic account could do the experience of watching a friend succumb to that illness—a sense of being trapped, relentless uncertainty, impotence and fatedness, denial, and a longing for it all to be over that cannot help resembling a betrayal' (2004: 223–4). The 'almost hopeful' marks the questionable solace of imagining but not reaching equilibrium, just as visitors to graves of the famous are 'almost comforted' 'by misquotations / or humming quietly' ('Père Lachaise'). The persistent angst of losing a faith and its contingent sense of a 'homeland' is acute in 'Plainsong' (*SM* 60) in which religious chants are overheard by an ex-believer: 'you kneel, no-one's child, absolved by late sun' and the distant church bell calls you '*Home, Home, / Home*', echoing the little brother's bawl of displacement, 'Home home', in 'Originally' (*TOC* 7).

'Prayer', first published in *Mean Time* (1993), considered 'probably the finest single poem in her oeuvre' (Chapman 2011), and consistently top of the polls (Ezard 2003), illustrates a culture 'drained of religious significance but yearning for the metaphysical and religious' (Roberts 2008). The unstoppable impulse for meaning is depicted in the arresting opening, 'Some days, although we cannot pray, a prayer / utters itself', and in the image: 'So, a woman will lift / her head from the sieve of her hands and stare / at the minim sung by a tree, a sudden gift.' The head in the hands neatly depicts despair and weariness in Duffy's 'Small Female Skull' or 'And then What' (*SFN* 61)—'Then with their tired hands slump / at a table holding their head'—but here the woman *lifts* her head in a moment's epiphany. The next stanza centres a man remembering the Latin chants of his youth: 'Some nights, although we are faithless, the truth / enters our hearts, that small familiar pain'. Sounds—'utters', 'sung', 'chanting'—put him in contact with the 'familiar pain' of nostalgia, regret, guilt, loneliness, or loss, yet also console the loss. 'Pray for us now', a fragment from 'Hail Mary', is a dreg of the Roman Catholic mass he no longer attends. The connection between Mass and train, along with the surrealist image of 'a minim sung by a tree', signify the disjointed and perturbing referents that lurk in the unconscious. It is not far-fetched to summon the words of Paul Simon's 'Train in the Distance' (1983): 'Everybody loves the sound of a train in the distance / Everybody thinks it's true / What is the point of this story / What information pertains / The thought that life could be better / Is woven indelibly / Into our hearts / And our brains.' Duffy's sequence through time—day, night, dusk, darkness—corresponds to the purposeless life of the song's Mr Average who 'thought that life could be better'. Against the grain of the popular lyrics, Duffy's sonnet is tinged with the faith of metaphysical poet George Herbert and his sonnet 'Prayer', a collage of metaphors that ends with the assertion that prayer is 'Something understood'. Duffy's final couplet on the 'radio's prayer', the shipping forecast, is contrastingly prosaic yet represents how the human antennae for 'otherwhere' is attached to the most mundane rituals. In 2002, when 'Finisterre' was dropped from the list after 53 years, listeners mourned the loss: 'Broadcast by the BBC four times a day, the shipping forecast is crucial for seafarers but its soothing, rhythmic intonation of bizarre names has gained a wider fame and turned it into a British institution' ('Shipping forecast loses household name', 2002). Finisterre means literally 'the ends of the earth' and Padel concludes that the shipping forecast signifies distant places that feel familiar yet are rarely, if ever, experienced: 'Whatever, the poem, like the radio, is now reaching out away from it into darkness trusting—like a child not knowing what will come—that the first steps out will lead somewhere good' (2002: 168). Kellaway also notes a life-affirming element:

> Indeed, in an airy definition of the word, her poetry is religious—her love poems often read as small acts of faith. She's also capable of wonderful, apparently casual, moments of spiritual uplift. "Prayer" … is moving precisely because it is domestic (that marvelous sieve!) and pedestrian and then transforms itself. (1993)

Several poems meld the 'post-religious sense of loss' with recent discourses about post-secularity, the cultural condition that both continues and shifts away from the post-religious: 'a mode of being and seeing that is at once critical of secular constructions of reality and of dogmatic religiosity' (McClure 2007: ix). In 'Nostalgia', the image of the priest 'with his head / in his hands' evinces sympathetically his lament for the lost due to their search for wealth, his inability to cure their souls, and the loss of his role. Duffy's negative allusions to the lure of 'money, dull crude coins clenched / in the teeth', correspond to the anti-materialism in post-secularist discourses: 'Today, the greatest ally of obscurantism is the spiritually empty economism of our prosperous liberal societies. If our cynics up there at the apex of power were less concerned with the Dow Jones Index there would undoubtedly be fewer devotees, down here, in the mosques and basilicas' (Debray 2008). Here, religious extremism is attributed to capitalist greed. Another facet of post-secularity rejects outdated dualisms: 'Literature, like religion, has always implied a challenge to strict boundaries—between fantasy and fact, transcendence and immanence, the spiritual and the material' (Carruthers and Tate 3). Correspondingly, Duffy often asserts that poetry is 'secular prayer' and thus to some extent takes the place of religion in a secular society (Forbes 2002). Whereas a man diagnosed with Aids utters 'frenzied prayers to Chemistry' ('Dream of a Lost Friend', *TOC* 39), Duffy's 'Space, Space' (*SM* 53) delineates how: 'The brain says *No* to the Universe. *Prove it.* / but the heart is susceptible, pining for a look, a kind word.' Here, religious practice is both enviable and maligned: 'Some are brought to their knees, // pleading in dead language at a deaf ear.' 'Pluto' (*MT* 19) is a heart-wrenching dramatic lyric in the voice of an old man in a residential home who remembers being a boy when the planet got its name in 1930 and halfpennies were still currency.[6] However, his vain attempt to touch his past parallels humanity's yearning for 'otherwhere' through space exploration: 'To think of another world out there / in the dark / unreachable'. The incompleteness of memory is expressed as 'half-hearing my father's laugh' and 'half-comforted' by what he can grasp.

Duffy certainly proves how poetry can articulate and evaluate the streams and crosscurrents of post-religion and post-secularism. For a start, her references characteristically mix myth, the Bible, literature, popular culture, folk, and fairy tale. For example, 'Before You Jump [for Mister Berryman]' (*SFN* 38) is woven with parallels to Christ's crucifixion. In her later poems, she takes the symbol of bowing the knee in worship to places where human heroism and sacrifice warrant collective reverence, such as the television image of an innocent soldier *in extremis* ('Far Be It', *NSP* 139) and the bravery of parents whose sons were victims of senseless racial murders ('Birmingham', *RL* 19; 'Stephen Lawrence', *Near* 10). 'Telling the *Bees*' (*Bees* 52) stitches a seam between the sacred and secular as Duffy refreshes the iconography of prayer by applying it to global concerns about endangered species. The terrible consequences of bees dying off, their dead bodies strewn on the ground, are likened to beads lying around from a broken rosary. The speaker remembers being a child, watching and talking to the bees in wonder as 'bees pray on their knees, sing, praise'. Thus, the verb 'tell' plays on its double meaning of counting and confiding in, the latter being redolent of the Elizabeth custom, 'the telling of the bees', whereby the family would inform the bees of significant household events, particularly deaths. On the other hand, the allusion to tea—'So how could I tell the bees? … No honey for tea', as in 'Alphabet for Auden', links to Rupert Brooke's sonnet, 'The Old Vicarage, Grantchester', and sets in motion a chain of literary and cultural associations concerning nostalgia. 'The Beauty of the Church' (*RL* 26–9), composed for the centenary of the *King James Bible*, comprises the erotic 'Song of Solomon' as if to celebrate the humanity that the sacred book chronicles, laments, and celebrates.

In a piece on contemporary poets' eschewal of God, Kathryn Simmonds notes a handful who do mesh the secular and spiritual, and asserts, 'the poem, with its big white space is the natural place to confront mystery, the natural place to question, praise or meditate' (2014).

---

[6] The poem is prescient of how Pluto was stripped of its planetary status in 2006.

Duffy's later writing introduces more catharsis or light to the mysteries of love, death, and faith, and she often states, '"I feel, like Beckett, that all poetry is prayer"' (Winterson 2005). In 'Death and the Moon' (*FG* 65) 'for Catherine Marcangeli',[7] there is no skirting round the 'silence' of death, 'I cannot say where you are. Unreachable / by prayer, even if poems are prayers. Unseeable / in the air, even if souls are stars,' but the poem at least airs the dim feelings: 'The black night / is huge, mute, and you are further forever than that.' The 'you' here is Adrian Henri, but also any addressee. Dunmore comments: 'Duffy captures the power and the powerlessness of memory, which can bring the dead before us but cannot make them respond to us' (1999: 81). In some elegies, she offers solace through acts of the imagination. 'Sung' (*Bees* 71), for example, ponders the life of a woman who 'lives' under a tombstone, dancing, kissing, and dying for love, and in 'Premonitions' (*Bees* 81–2), the poet winds backwards from her mother's death to an earlier period when she can see and hear her, as if for the first time. Mother and daughter are rejoined through these memories, 'the loving litany of who we had been'. In 'Wish' (*FG* 63), she similarly imagines a dead friend rising again and runs to embrace her. She then extends the scene to a universal heaven where: 'Nobody died. Nobody / wept. Nobody slept who couldn't be woken / by the light.' The joyful fantasy of resurrection occurs again in 'Winter's Tale' (*Bees* 61) that refers to Shakespeare's play of that name in which the statue of a wronged queen, Hermione, comes to life. Our reasoning says, 'If only' or 'In your dreams', but the heart's overflow at seeing a lost loved one again transfers to the reader: 'love where death, where harm, hope / flesh where stone'. Nature and religious imagery blend in the prayerful 'Pathway' (*RL* 32) that confronts the death of the poet's father. She pictures a garden that registers all the seasons where he 'had treaded spring and summer grasses', the childish expression accentuating Duffy's vision of her younger self following at a distance. She watches, 'like a nun', as he entered 'Autumn's cathedral', the birds sang rosaries, and Winter finally 'palmed his eyes for frozen bulbs'. 'An Unseen' (*RL* 35), the next poem in *Ritual Lighting*, is a lament for soldiers gone to war but ultimately celebrates enduring love: 'Love was here; not; missing, love was there; / each look, first last.' The halting syntax indicates a heart aching with grief and also clasping on to a love that outlasts death.

---

[7] Catherine Marcangeli was Adrian Henri's partner who cared for him after his stroke until his death.

Elsewhere, epiphany happens when someone imagines snow falling to be a shining letter from the palms of the dead that carries some immortal words to the living: 'what will you do now / with the gift of your left life?' ('Snow', *Bees* 62).

Poetry as Celebration: 'the hive is love'

Whereas her earlier poetry explored sexual love, Duffy's later work advocates love between parents and children and the milk of human kindness. The privacy and secrecy of erotic relationship is shunned for expansive collective compassion and celebration. The bees teach that we are all 'concelebrants' at the hive of love: 'hive, alive, us' ('Hive', *Bees* 31). Whereas the concept of reincarnation is rather troubled in 'Dies Natalis' (*SM* 10–13), there is more imagery of joyful rebirth in her twenty-first century books. Much relates to the very human miracle of having her daughter, as Pope Joan puts it, 'the closest I felt // to the power of God' was when 'a baby pushed out' (*WW* 68–9) and Duffy's lyrics to her child resound with love's reviving force. 'Demeter' (*WW* 76) narrates 'I sat in my cold stone room / choosing tough words', but her icy broken heart was thawed and healed when, 'She came from a long, long way, / but I saw her at last, walking, / my daughter, my girl, across the fields, // in bare feet, bringing all spring's flowers / to her mother's house'. The baby's arrival transformed the cold house to a warm home, above which shone 'the small shy mouth of a new moon'. 'The Light Gatherer' (*FG* 59–60) and 'A Child's Sleep' (*NSP* 133) stir the same sense of the numinous through the gift of new life. Duffy relates a similar epiphany when watching her daughter on holiday—'my heart makes its own small flip'. The clichéd 'flip' is excusable because it links to the fish that her now teenage daughter is excitedly filming ('Orta St Gulio', *Bees* 69).

'Music' (*Bees* 67) celebrates how music, the spirit's language, is the food of love and the poet asks rhetorically, 'Do you think it hears and heals our hearts?' Healing sounds and light permeate many poems in *The Bees* and *Ritual Lighting* to indicate that what makes us 'Alive-alive-oh' is 'the heart's impulse to cherish' ('Lessons in the Orchard', *RL* 40). Unlike the bowl of apples 'rotten to the core' in 'Disgrace', here, Duffy sees, 'This bowl life, that we fill and fill', echoing Virginia Woolf's inspiring reference to the base of life as a 'bowl that one fills and fills and fills' (Woolf 2002: 78). (The poem was fittingly written for the twenty-fifth Charleston

Festival held at the famous house of Bloomsbury artists Vanessa Bell and Duncan Grant.) 'Gesture' (*Bees* 79), written for *Soul Feathers*, on the theme of hope concerning cancer, asserts how courage and love transform suffering. Whereas in several earlier poems, hands hold a head slumped in despair, here, human touch brings healing: 'Know—your hand is a star.'

As discussed in Chap. 6, the dramatic narrative lyrics, 'The Christmas Truce', 'Wenceslas', and 'Mrs Scrooge', insist on the place of poetry to model and mediate reconciliation by recognizing our enemies or the estranged as our human family. In the Introduction to *Twelve Poems of Christmas* (2009), Duffy writes, 'many of the carols that we sing are, in fact, poems. ... In December, our streets seem alive with sung language. Poets—by their very calling, great celebrators—have always written Christmas poetry, regardless of faith or its absence.' She includes her own poem 'December' that typically blends the personal and universal, the language of religion with secular expression. December is her 'birth month' yet the sky 'lays its cheek' on the fields and 'The dusk swaddles the cattle, / their silhouettes / simple as faith', the archaic 'swaddle' echoing Biblical accounts of Christ's nativity. The imagery of wrapping and unwrapping, that denoted erotic intimacy in her earlier poems, refers here to the widespread exchange of presents during the festival. Duffy is more lighthearted in 'The Bee Carol' (*Bees* 59) although the wistful reference to the religious meaning of Christmas is still there: 'Come with me on Christmas Eve / to see the silent hive— / trembling stars cloistered above— / and then believe, / bless the winter cluster of the bees.' This Christmas Eve pageant is reminiscent of Hardy's 'The Oxen' that ends with the Duffyesque half-belief, 'Hoping it might be so' (Hardy 1993: 110). 'The Bee Carol' was printed in the *Guardian* as one of several 'new carols' introduced by Duffy (18 December 2010). 'A Rare Bee' (*Bees* 83–4) wholly appropriates the language of religion to the art of poetry. The poet visits a hermit and seeks honey from a rare specimen of bees for allegedly, 'when pressed to the pout of a poet / it made her profound.' Duffy's pilgrimage is a post-secular combination of East with West: 'So I came to kneel at the hermit's hive—a little church, a tiny mosque—in a mute glade / where the loner mouthed and prayed'. Foremost, her search is artistic and she asks the bee to '*bless my tongue with rhyme, poetry, song*'. When the bee stings her it dies, presumably meaning that the bee has sacrificed its life to pass on the gift of poetry in a natural sequence of death and reincarnation.

Ultimately, as Duffy intends, her lyrics are about and for intense moments. The first poem in *The Bees*, 'Bees' (3), introduces the reader to 'my poet bees', the sources, inspirations, and experiences whose 'honey is art'. 'Bees' is dense with symbolism and alliteration—'so glide, / gilded, glad, golden'—that reviewers have readily condemned for being over-done: 'She has far too many word combinations designed to prove her attentiveness to the way their sounds interknit with each other!' (Sexton 2011). The fact that Duffy is a mature, experienced, and versatile word-smith makes us pause on why these heavily alliterative lines are still one of her trademarks. The poem was partly inspired by eleventh century Sanskrit verse (Khan 2010), echoes Anglo-Saxon alliterative verse, and also sounds like poet Hopkins, as in his paean, 'Pied Beauty' (Gardner 1975: 30–1): 'Fresh-firecoal chestnut-falls; finches' wings; / Landscape plotted and pieced—fold, fallow, and plough'. For Hopkins, the litany of sounds was the result of his 'deep long looking' and an attempt to find and present the inscape, the singularity, of each created thing, that for Duffy is the core and unique 'bee-ness' of bees or essence of love. In this way, her 'bees, / brazen, blurs on paper, / besotted; buzzwords, dancing' tell of the daring, mystery, and joy of the poet in forging language to express and provoke complex emotional power. The line also evokes the endangered species of tongue twisters, like 'round the rugged rocks, the ragged rascals ran', passed down from generation to generation, where the sense is more in sound than logic. As critics like Rees-Jones and Morley discern, these devices, like her startlingly surrealist images, refuse to fix the meaning that the realist backdrops invite. As Liz Lochhead observes: 'the lists and litanies, and, above all, the lovely lyrics of longing and loneliness and sorrow [are] laced with ephemeral moments of almost-acceptance, lightness and grace' (2011). The 'almost-acceptance' is the Duffyesque refusal to pretend the human appetite for something more, for elsewhere, can or should be satiated; rather, it is vitally stimulated by fresh poetic evocations.

REFERENCES

1985 *Standing female nude* (London: Anvil).
1993 *Mean time* (London: Anvil).
2005 *Rapture* (London: Picador).
2014 *Ritual lighting: Laureate poems,* artwork by Stephen Raw (London: Picador).
2004 *Out of fashion: An anthology of poems* (London: Faber and Faber).
1994 'A Place of Escape', Interview, *Second Shift* 4: 20–2.
2010 'As Tempting as Chocolates', *Daily Telegraph,* 13 February: *Saturday Review*: 20
2012 'Choosing Sylvia's Poems', *Guardian,* 2 November.

Ambrose, Alice (ed.). 1979. *Wittgenstein's lectures 1932–35.* Oxford: Blackwell.

Armstrong, Isobel, and Virginia Blain (eds.). 1999. *Women's poetry: Late Romantic to late Victorian: Gender and genre, 1830–1900.* Basingstoke: Macmillan.

Boland, Eavan. 1994. Making the difference: Eroticism and ageing in the work of the woman poet. *P.N. Review* 20(4): 13–21.

Breton, André. 1972. *Manifestoes of surrealism.* Michigan: Ann Arbor Press.

Carruthers, Jo, and Andrew Tate (eds.). 2010. *Spiritual identities: Literature and the post-secular imagination.* Bern: Peter Lang.

Chapman, Danielle. 2011. Review of *The Bees, Financial Times,* October 14.

Cowing, Emma. 2005. Love in the dock. Review *of Rapture, The Scotsman,* September 17.

Culler, Jonathan. 1975. Poetics of the lyric. In *Structuralist poetics: Structuralism, linguistics and the study of literature,* 161–188. London: Routledge.

Debray, Régis. 2008. God and the political planet. *New Perspectives Quarterly* 25(4): 33–35.

DiNapoli, Robert. 2014. The play's the thing: Word-play and poetry. *P.N. Review* 40(4): 34–38.

Donne, John. 1977. In *Selected poems,* ed. John Hayward. Harmondsworth: Penguin.

Duncan, Lesley. 1999. A Lady to take charge of toad odes. *The Herald,* April 26.

Dunmore, Helen. 1999. Waiting for the world's wife. *Poetry Review* 89(2): 80–81.

Ezard, John. 2003. Poet's poll crowns Larkin king of verse. *Guardian,* October 15.

Gardner, Helen (ed.). 1975. *Gerard Manley Hopkins: Poems and prose.* Harmondsworth: Penguin.

Griffin, Jo. 2010. *The lonely society.* London: Mental Health Foundation.

Griffiths, Jane. 2005. Words for love. *Times Literary Supplement,* November 18.

Hardy, Thomas. 1993. *Selected poems.* Harmondsworth: Penguin.

Hughes-Edwards, Mari. 2006. "The house … has cancer": The representation of domestic space in the poetry of Carol Ann Duffy. In *Our house: The representation of domestic space in modern culture,* ed. Gerry Smyth and Jo. Croft, 121–140. Amsterdam/New York: Rodopi.

Kellaway, Kate. 1993. When the moon is an onion and the tree sings minims. *Observer,* June 20.

Kellaway, Kate. 2011. Review of *The Bees, Observer,* November 6.

Kennedy, David. 2012. *The ekphrastic encounter in contemporary British poetry and elsewhere.* Farnham/Burlington: Ashgate.

Khan, Urmee. 2010. Inspiration behind laureate's passion for romantic poetry. *Daily Telegraph,* February 13.

Kisiel, Ryan. 2010. Dunce's Corner Banned. *Daily Mail,* January 5.

Larkin, Philip. 1990. In *Collected poems,* ed. Anthony Thwaite. London: Faber and Faber.

Leviston, Frances. 2005. Review of *Rapture, Tower Poetry.* http://www.towerpoetry.org.uk/poetry-matters/poetry/poetry-archive/169-frances-leviston-reviews-rapture-by-carol-ann-duffy

Lochhead, Liz. 2011. Review of *The Bees*, *Guardian*, November 4.

Longley, Edna (ed.). 2003. *The Bloodaxe book of twentieth-century poetry*. Tarset: Bloodaxe.

Maguire, Sarah. 2000. Poetry makes nothing happen. In *Strong words: Modern poets on modern poetry*, ed. W.N. Herbert and Matthew Hollis, 248–251. Tarset: Bloodaxe.

McAllister, Andrew. 1988. Carol Ann Duffy. *Bête Noir* 6, 69–77.

McClure, John A. 2007. *Partial faiths: Postsecular fiction in the age of Pynchon and Morrison*. Athens: University of Georgia Press.

McCulloch, Andrew. 2014. Nostalgia. *Times Literary Supplement*, December 2.

Michelis, Angelica, and Antony Rowland (eds.). 2003. *The poetry of Carol Ann Duffy: 'Choosing tough words'*. Manchester: Manchester University Press.

Mousley, Andy. 2013. *Literature and the human*. Abingdon: Routledge.

Mullan, John. 2013. Love poems by Carol Ann Duffy. *Guardian*, January 18.

O'Brien, Sean. 1993. Illuminating manuscripts. *Sunday Times*, July 18.

O'Riordan, Adam. 2009. The uses of erotic poetry. *Guardian*, September 16.

Oxley, William. 2005. Love's virtuoso. *Acumen* 53: 105–106.

Padel, Ruth. 2002. *52 ways of looking at a poem*. London: Chatto and Windus.

Preston, John. 2010. Carol Ann Duffy interview. *Daily Telegraph*, May 11.

Rees Jones, Deryn. 1999. *Carol Ann Duffy*. Plymouth: Northcote House.

Roberts, Neil. 1999. Carol Ann Duffy: Outsidedness and Nostalgia. In *Narrative and voice in postwar poetry*, 184–194. Essex: Longman.

Roberts, Neil. 2003. Duffy, Eliot and impersonality, 33–46. Michelis and Rowland.

Roberts, Michael Symonns. 2008. Poetry in a post-secular age. *Poetry Review* 98(4): 69–75.

Robinson, Alan. 1988. *Instabilities in contemporary British poetry*. Basingstoke: Palgrave.

Rowland, Anthony. 2003. Love and masculinity in the poetry of Carol Ann Duffy, 56–76. Michelis and Rowland.

Sexton, David. 2011. Review of *The Bees*, *London Evening Standard*, September 22.

Simmonds, Kathryn. 2014. The God allusion. In *Poetry News*, 5. London: The Poetry Society.

Simon, Paul. 1983. Train in the distance. *Hearts and bones*. Warner Bros, Burbank, California.

Smith, Stan. 2003. "What like is it?": Duffy's *différance*, 143–168. Michelis and Rowland.

Smith, Stan. 2008. *Poetry and displacement*. Liverpool: Liverpool University Press.

Thomas, Jane. 2003. "The chant of magic words repeatedly": Gender as linguistic act in the poetry of Carol Ann Duffy, 121–142. Michelis and Rowland.

Tonkin, Boyd. 2010. A valentine strictly for grown ups. Review of *Love Poems*, *Independent*, February 8.

To the Moon: An Anthology of Lunar Poems, London: Picador. 2009.

Whyte, Christopher. 2004. *Modern Scottish poetry*. Edinburgh: Edinburgh University Press.

Winterson, Jeanette. 2005. Interview with Carol Ann Duffy. *Times*, September 10. http://www.jeanettewinterson.com/journalism/carol-ann-duffy/

Woods, Michael. 2003. "What it is like in words": Translation, reflection and refraction in the poetry of Carol Ann Duffy, 169–185. Anglelis and Rowland.

Woolf, Virginia. 2002. *Moments of being: Autobiographical writings*. London: Pimlico.

First female Poet Laureate named' (2009) *BBC News*, May 1. http://news.bbc.co.uk/1/hi/entertainment/8027767.stm

CHAPTER 3

Voices from the 1980s and After

[Duffy] is a poet of society and history, with an eye to the dispossessed. ... The books she published during the late Eighties and early Nineties were an extraordinary articulation of the broken-down state of Thatcher's Britain. This poet of dislocation (social, sexual, psychological, linguistic, political) met her subject in those bankrupt, disjunctive times. (Greenlaw 2009)

'JUST TEACH ME / THE RIGHT WORDS'

Duffy's first four volumes and bold red pamphlet, *William and the Ex-Prime Minister*, register the events, zeitgeists, and legacies of 1980s Britain. References to telephone boxes and the wireless evoke the pre-digital age before mobile phones, personal computers, and the World Wide Web. Margaret Thatcher, who was elected Prime Minister in 1979, 1983, and 1987, looms over portrayals of the displaced, whether due to economic disadvantage, social marginalization, or just seeking meaning in a decade that would retrospectively be called the 'selfish' Eighties. This book's Chap. 4 attends to specifically female perspectives, Chap. 5 to Duffy's direct treatment of shared public concerns, and this chapter to the 'thrown voices' of fictional characters.[1] The dramatic monologue was a self-confessed means to extend the reach of the poet's subjective

---

[1] *Thrown Voices* is the title to her early pamphlet (1986).

J. Dowson, *Carol Ann Duffy*,
DOI 10.1057/978-1-137-41563-9_3

87

experience and became a Duffy trademark. As Charles Simic writes in 'Notes on Poetry and History': 'The poet like anyone else is part of history, but he or she ought to be the conscious part. That's the ideal' (1985: 126). He commends the poet's skill in bringing distant matters close to the reader through the 'fury of the imagination': 'If history, as it comes through the historian, retains, analyses, and connects significant events, in contrast, what poets insist on is the history of "Unimportant" events' (126). Accordingly, the contexts of Duffy's poems are often rights and causes that may not feature in the period's grand narratives, as Ruth Padel reflects:

> Fashion commentators may look back at the eighties as a time when every-one made money and wore gold. Poets saw a different eighties. Unsalaried, travelling to underpaid readings in unfunded poetry societies, teaching in increasingly run-down schools with plastic buckets put out to catch leaks from the roof, poets saw in action year by year, the giving up on the welfare state. As the divide between rich and poor was knowingly increased, poems increasingly spoke of the inner effects of Thatcherism: economic, educa-tional, and social oppression and depression, unemployment, miserable and underfunded care homes, corruption, pollution of the environment, extinc-tion of animal species, and eventually a war played out on our own TV screens, which enabled us to exalt in the new technologies of mass killing while glazing over the gruesome details. (2002: 21–2)

Rather than 'glazing over' unwelcome realities, Duffy's monologues have a lyrical intensity that resuscitates the readers' sensibilities. Her speakers demand our attention and require a response.

In 1994, Daniel O'Rourke chose Duffy amongst other poets who, pro-pelled by the public's disillusionment with the Thatcher government, 'felt a need to acknowledge the moment': 'It seemed that the poets, more confidently than the politicians, were dreaming a new state' (O'Rourke 2002: xvii). It is dashed dreams, however, that her poems' speakers often articulate. They reflect how unemployment rose to three million in 1983, with more job losses in Britain's industrial north. Some speak out of, or to, a multicultural Britain during a time when the immigration flow was stemmed but race riots broke out, significantly in Brixton, Manchester, and the Midlands. Others blur the line between a sane, mad, or criminal mind, connecting with debates around 'Making a Reality of Community Care' (1983), a report that recommended patients in mental hospitals be supported at home. The 'Nancy and Ron' mocked in 'The Act of

Imagination' (*TOC* 25) refers to Ronald Reagan, president of the USA from 1981 to 1989, and 'The B Movie' (*SFN* 57) harps back to when Reagan featured with Shirley Temple in a derisory flop, 'That Hagen Girl' (1947). Additionally, 'The B Movie' makes implicit reference to the Cold War period 1985–91: 'we need a Kleenex the size of Russia here' but 'there ain't no final reel'. Other poems register dissatisfaction over The Falklands conflict as well as campaigns for nuclear disarmament (CND). 'Space, Space' (*SM* 53) links to several launches and orbital voyages in a decade that saw the first American woman in space (Sally Ride in 1983) and a disaster in January 1986 when Space Shuttle Challenger exploded just after takeoff. 'A Healthy Meal' (*SFN* 60) makes meat-eating sound indecent—'Capped teeth chatter to a kidney or at the breast / of something which once flew'—and it was during the 1980s that vegetarianism became a mainstream choice.[2] One trigger was the BSE epidemic in 1986, resulting from cattle being fed animal by-products, hormones, and pesticides. Anita Roddick, who founded the successful Body Shop chain in 1976, and Linda McCartney promoted animal rights. 'The Dolphins', on a literal level, speaks in the voice of mammals lamenting their captivity and Peter Forbes calls 'The Legend' (*TOC* 21) 'one of the few really effective green poems in existence; it does what only a poem can do, make you see afresh' (1994: 111). Duffy does this by characteristically balancing realism with 'the fury of the imagination'. The repeated phrase, 'some say', sets up a mythical framework around the commentator's description of a creature resembling an extinct mammoth: 'Huge feet. Some say if it rained you could fish in a footprint, / fruit fell when it passed. It moved, food happened, simple. / You think of a warm, inky cave and you got its mouth all right.' The colloquial language and familiar signifiers bring a fantastical beast up close while the past tense brings home the possibility that it could be any contemporary elephant species threatened by extinction due to an unscrupulous ivory trade.

The 1980s saw the discovery of the Aids virus and Duffy's elegy 'Dream of a Lost Friend' (*TOC* 39) expresses and provokes sympathy for a sufferer and their loved ones in the face of scaremongering about how it starts and spreads: 'Some of our best friends nurture a virus'. Homosexuals in the 1980s no longer risked criminal conviction but were subject to prejudice that the disease only inflamed. Duffy invites compassion for an

[2] Megan Lane, 'Is the veggie boom over?', BBC News, 27 November 2002, http://news.bbc.co.uk/1/hi/uk/2516305.stm

old woman who confesses the 'Sin of Sodom' and is wracked by fear of damnation ('Words of Absolution', *SFN* 32), for two men who embrace furtively by Piaf's grave in the Parisian cemetery where Oscar Wilde is buried ('Père Lachaise', *TOC* 37), and in 'Café Royal' (*MT* 28) for a young man seeking a lover, ghosted by Lord Alfred Douglas and Wilde whose affair led to the imprisonment of the 'Lord of Language'. 'Someone Else's Daughter' (*SFN* 59) is a drug addict who turns to prostitution and shoplifting. The voices painfully present the young woman's self-harm that leads to 'Herpes and hepatitis' and the suffering of her parents as they watch her downward spiral. They grieve their unrecognizable child whose over-indulgence on Easter eggs now manifests as a self-destructive craving over which she has no control: 'This is your last chance. *I know.* / Why do you do this? *I don't know.*' The young woman smokes 'a trembling chain of cancer cells', that, like the line, 'clouds are the colour of smokers' lungs' ('Room', *TOC* 50), registers the decade's anti-smoking campaigns and legislation.[3] 'Free Will' (*SFN* 25) probes a woman's state of mind in the context of a rise in legal abortions following The Abortion Act of 1967. The 1980s was a decade when domestic abuse started to be taken seriously by the police and Duffy's portrayal in 'Alliance' (*SFN* 26)—'She smiles / at his bullying'—alludes to such cruelty in marriage where it was most commonly experienced and most often unreported. The free indirect discourse accentuates how the woman's interiority has been snuffed out: 'She is word perfect. Over the years he has inflated / with best bitter till she has no room.'

In 'The Dummy' (*SM* 20), the ventriloquist's stooge is a provocative metaphor for any oppressed individual or group: 'you keep / me at it' sounds like a woman physically or emotionally assaulted, a child sexually abused, or workers condemned to intolerable conditions and low pay. The dummy exposes and reverses the power situation, humiliating the ventriloquist in the actions and phrases he uses to mock the dummy, such as trying to sing, dance, or speak when drunk. Furthermore, the dummy threatens to retaliate: 'Why do you / keep me in that black box? I can ask questions too, / you know. I can see that worries you. Tough.' This rebellion resonates with the colonized native, Caliban, in Shakespeare's *The Tempest*

---

[3] In 1978, the Independent Broadcasting Authority published a Code of Advertising Standards that pronounced cigarettes and cigarette tobacco 'unacceptable products' and regulated all TV and radio commercials.

who can only plead for his freedom in the language allotted to him by the magician, Prospero, whom he curses, 'for learning me your language!' (Act 1: 2). Likewise, the dummy can be a contemporary immigrant disempowered because their first language is not English: 'Just teach me / the right words'. The dummy can also be the projected voice of the ventriloquist facing his own sense of failure, for if he could dance, he wouldn't be 'doing this' and surely, 'You can do getter than that?' The voice, then, is whatever a person or human society suppresses which, referring back to Simic, may be 'gruesome' but which the poem makes conscious.

Objecting to the proliferation of colloquial speech in Duffy's poems, one reviewer complained: 'There is often a felt need to reproduce common cultural experience which can bypass both feeling and intelligence, and can end up merely as babble and mimicry' (Reid 1992/3: 36). On the contrary, Duffy's dramatic voices flatten the hierarchal sway of writing over speech in a predominantly print culture. As Walter Ong observed,

> Print created a new sense of the private ownership of words. Persons in a primary oral culture can entertain some sense of proprietary rights to a poem, but such a sense is rare and ordinarily enfeebled by the common share of lore, formulas, and themes on which everyone draws. ... Typography had made the word into a commodity. The old communal oral world had split up into privately claimed freeholdings. (2002: 128–9)

Thus, in bringing characters and their speaking modes into print, Duffy broadens the 'proprietary rights' to poetry and, by association, to elitist social spheres. In 'The Dummy', she typically runs colloquial language across the sonnet form—four unrhymed quatrains and a couplet—drawing attention to how literary conventions can be hybridized with speech patterns. In 'Yes, Officer' (*SM* 31), the police convict a man unable to defend himself, but who reveals his unspoken narrative to the reader: 'Without my own language, I am a blind man / in the wrong house'. In a police cell, threatened by violence, he takes on the words attributed to him by the intimidating officer: 'uttering empty vowels until // they have their truth'. However, Duffy constructs the speaker against the grain of their typecast for he is capable of appreciating nature, of intelligent thought, poetic vocabulary—'a skein of geese', of love, compassion, and upright civil acts, for we glean that he rescued a woman in danger and is now being scapegoated for someone else's crime. Duffy explains, '"I come from a working-class background which, in many areas, was inarticulate.

Not politically, but on those levels where one speaks of the personal, the feelings, the private inner life"' (Stabler 1991: 127). Thus, her speakers often reveal an interiority that they themselves barely grasp or understand but which pushes to be made conscious.

As we pass through the perceptions of the speaker, we have to negotiate their draw on our sympathy (Sinfield 1977: 6): the convicted man tells the reader that his truth is not what the officers think; the dummy cries out against being someone else's impersonation of him or her, 'listening / to the voice you gave me croaking for truth'. Other voices draw attention to the 'gutter press', 'paperback fiction', movies, or an abstract 'they say' that would tell them who they are. Deryn Rees-Jones begins her chapter 'Masquerades' with: 'Knowing who we are, and finding a way to tell ourselves, are two of Duffy's central concerns. In questioning the ways in which we are represented, she also addresses the difficulties of knowing the self through otherness' (1999: 17). Similarly, Sean O'Brien points out that Duffy's speakers are 'prisoners of socially acquired representations of themselves'; they depict a 'sense of homelessness' specific to their condition but which can also be more broadly representative of any individual who strives in vain to find a satisfactory subject position' (1998: 166). In *Marxism and the Philosophy of Language*, V.N. Vološinov, sets out how: 'a psychic phenomenon becomes explainable solely in terms of the social factors that shape the concrete life of the individual in the conditions of his social environment'; furthermore, this 'psychic phenomenon' consists in signs that represent how inner speech is 'in close dependence on the historical conditions of the social situation and the whole pragmatic run of life' (Vološinov 1994: 56). Duffy frequently exposes to the reader how the languages of others, the media, education, or an elusive 'them', shape a speaker's identity and conflict with their sensed interiority. Some monologues, usually narrated by an observer, have vivid naturalistic detail, such as the stages of drug addiction, while others disorientate the reader's grip on a coherent reality. Consequently, while the premise of this chapter is to situate poems in their historical moment, it also opens them to continuing interpretation and relevance. As Jane Thomas concludes: '[Duffy's] work suggests that because poetry derives its force from ambiguity, association and multiplicity of meaning, in addition to its defamiliarizing potential, it has the power to reconstitute the world in differently meaningful ways' (2003: 135). Thus, these poems affirm, enlarge, and reconstitute what 'being human' means.

'POWERAN MONEYAN FAME'

Through her speaker's revelations, Duffy typically strips away status, bravado, and bluff to expose hubris, vulnerability, and error. The epigraph of 'Weasel Words' (TOC 14), 'words empty of meaning like an egg that had had its contents sucked out by a weasel', refers to Sir Robert Armstrong, secretary to Thatcher's cabinet (1979–87), who notoriously coined the phrase 'economical with the truth' during the trial over the banning of *Spycatcher* in 1986. The poem's speech mimics politicians' defensive protestations and schoolboy fun—the 'hear hear', cheers, and laughter of the House of Commons that shocked the public when its proceedings were first broadcast on television in November 1989. The egg allusion also relates to the Conservative Health Minister's unwarranted scare over salmonella in 1988. The MPs' denial of bias is contradicted by their accusations towards 'the Ferrets opposite'. 'The Literature Act' (*TOC* 52), prompted by the fatwa on Salman Rushdie in 1989, is a fantasy of being married to a right-wing 'yob' who lives in 'a high-rise flat' that symbolizes his frustrated ambitions. He protests against a book written by 'a blasphemer or a lesbian' 'for the benefit of the gutter press', whose crude language merges with his. The speaker wishes him to be arrested and reformed by learning the poem by heart. In 'Poet for our Times' (*TOC* 15), as discussed in Chap. 1, Duffy clearly distances herself from commercially driven media that feed aspirations to money, power, and fame, and her hypothetical headlines are not random. The 'CECIL–KEAYS ROW' refers to the revelation in 1983 that Cecil Parkinson was having an extra-marital affair with his secretary Sarah Keays and that she was bearing their child. He subsequently resigned as a Conservative minister and the 'row' was a dispute over his reluctance to pay child maintenance and also over the media's exposure of their daughter. Thus, this reference incorporates how the media can hold the powerful to account but also damage the vulnerable. In interview, Duffy admits, '"I'm often either annoyed or irritated or amused by hypocrisy, and certainly Britain, or England, is known for sexual hypocrisy. There's a huge tabloid industry that works on that alone"' (Dunmore 1999: 81). The mass market's predilection for sexual scandal is reinforced in the poem's other headlines that put the escapades of an MP, a rock star, a diplomat, and a character in the working-class soap opera *EastEnders*, on the same rung. So, too, are the readers who take pleasure in the 'gigantic' breasts on the newspaper's page three. 'Kinnock-basher' refers to the Prime Minister, Thatcher, engaging in cheap conflict politics with Neil Kinnock, leader of the Labour Party, 1983–92. In other headlines, the editor fuels xenophobia, by using *argot* stereotyping for Italians ('eyetie') and the French ('frog'), and the inflammatory racist metaphor, 'immigrants flood in'.

Britain in the late 1980s and early 1990s, 'is represented as a consumer society where commercialization has become the major denominator of national culture' (Michelis and Rowland 2003: 20) and its legacy continues. Critics of Thatcherism point to policies that encouraged a free market and economic self-sufficiency that contingently promoted unrealistic expectations of betterment, often involving hire purchase. In Duffy's 'Debt' (*SFN* 33), a man who was once happy to buy his sweetheart a bar of fruit-and-nut chocolate is overtaken by the desire for more money. He dreams of winning the pools to give pearls to his wife and ponies to the children so he buys goods on credit and is sleepless with worry over repayments he cannot afford. The poem is written in free indirect discourse whereby the man's thoughts are in the third person—'There was nothing he would not do'—as he reveals losing his possessions, health, and sanity: 'the mind's mad films' have replaced his over-reaching fantasies. 'Making Money' (*TOC* 17) is set when 'the economy booms / like cannon far out at sea on a lone ship'. The boom can only be enjoyed by a minority yet across the globe people go to any length to acquire wealth. The names for money denote several currencies and classes, from stockbrokers to collectors of disused bombs. 'Fraud' (*MT* 43–4), the monologue of a man who took a false identity in order 'to change from a bum / to a billionaire', dramatizes how money leads to corruption. Politicians, military men, or spies are all liable to con people for 'Mo-ney. Po-wer. Fame' because 'poverty's dumb': 'They're all the same, / turning their wide blind eyes to crime'. The implications are generic but also specific in the coded references to publishing magnate Robert Maxwell (1923–91) who had also been a Labour MP. Each line of the poem ends with an 'M' sound and the speaker, like Maxwell, was Jewish, rose from poverty, squandered his wealth, misappropriated funds (from the *Mirror* paper that Maxwell owned), and was found dead in the ocean. He confesses: 'Mine was a scam / involving pensions, papers, politicians in-and-out of their pram. / And I am to blame.' Padel notes:

> As a new generation of British became newly aware of being lied to, and ads became an image for the mismatch between public political promises and inner reality, poets began raiding the pacey wit, irony and allusiveness of ads

and the increasingly dominant media. "Do you fancy me, lady? Really?" asks the speaker of Carol Ann Duffy's "Money Talks". "Don't let my oily manner bother you. Sir." (2002: 22)

'Money Talks' (*SM* 33), personifies Money as an indiscriminate seducer of men and women with a god-like status. Echoing St Paul's phrase, 'the love of money is the root of all evil', Money's 'one commandment' is 'Love me'; additionally, 'See me pass through the eye of a needle!', challenges Christ's edict that it is easier for a camel to pass through the eye of a needle than for a rich man to enter the kingdom of God (*The Bible*, 1 Timothy 6: 10; Mark 10: 25). Furthermore, 'I am a jealous God' (*The Bible*, Exodus 20: 5) indicates how Money demands exclusive worship from its followers. In the final stanza, money can buy limousines but more chillingly, 'the big bombs'. The mention of 'it's raining dollar bills', '$-sounds', and '$-stammering' links to the eight-lined '$' (*SFN* 43), composed of the sounds of exultant music and dancing, 'boogie woogie chou chou cha cha chatta', 'yeah yeah yeah', to denote the money-driven popular music industry. Significantly, it is the dollar sign that produces the wordless revelry for during the 1980s the dollar climbed steadily against all other currencies.

In 'Money Talks', Money mentions the myth of Midas who wishes that all he touches be turned to gold but when it comes true he regrets his wish and asks for it to be reversed. Duffy returns to the story in 'Mrs Midas' (*WW* 11–13), in which his wife narrates her distress when the Midas touch stripped them of personal freedom and physical contact. Similarly, 'Mrs Faust' (*WW* 23–7) depicts a Thatcherite, self-made couple who 'met as students', lived together, got a mortgage, and then Mr Faust becomes wedded to riches and power. He tells his wife that the Devil owns him—'*For all these years of / gagging for it, / going for it. / rolling in it, / I've sold my soul*', but she scathingly concludes, 'he didn't have a soul to sell'. 'Selling Manhattan' (*SM* 34) re-enacts the historical myth that Dutch explorers exploited Native Americans by purchasing the island for $24 worth of beads and trinkets. There is evidence of this in the Dutch archives although contemporary commentators argue that the 60 gilders paid for New York's Manhattan Island were worth more like one thousand dollars in 1626. The brutally superior yet vulgar voice of the Christian colonizer who praises the Lord but plays god—'Now get your red ass out of here'—contrasts to the pantheistic spirituality of the gentle man he boots out: 'I will live in the ghost of a grasshopper'. Thus, Duffy gives the high poetic lines to this unmaterialistic native: 'I have learned the solemn laws of joy and sorrow, in the distance / between morning's frost and firefly's flash at night'. The man's rich interior life and language illuminate how capitalist materialism kills both art and the human spirit. 'Talent Contest' (*TOC* 19) is the interior monologue of a contestant in an amateur show who comes to despise his own pointless ambitions: 'Poweran moneyan fame you say to yourself / like a blessing'. Elsewhere, imagery of cash marks this same sense of futility and search for meaning: 'Each day / is a new game, sucker, with mornings and midnights / raked in by the dealer. Did you think you could keep those cards?' Here, in 'Losers' (*TOC* 35), the lexis of gambling depicts how humans conceive loss and gain in monetary terms: 'One saves up for a lifelong dream, another / spends all she has on a summer decades ago.'[4] The Duffyesque emphasis on the vitality of the imagination, that paradoxically and tragically also leads to perpetual disappointment, is condensed in the sentence: 'We are the fools who dwell in time / outside of time.' Similarly, the voice in 'The Windows' (*MT* 47) seems to belong to a passer-by looking in on what they imagine are enviable lives. In reality, the inhabitants' daily rituals of meals and work are unexceptional and Duffy's evocation of the 1946 American film, *It's A Wonderful Life*, introduces the same paradox that dreams both quicken and deaden us. When the film's hero loses the quotidian events and people of the confined world against which he chafes, he comes to value love, family, and friendship over his vain aspirations to money, power, and fame. *It's A Wonderful Life*'s moral also haunts Duffy's 2008 Christmas poem 'Mrs Scrooge' in which the eponymous widow watches the stressed shoppers make purchases 'all done on credit cards' and campaigns against consumerism. Then she has a reverie during which she is shown her family and friends celebrating her death and pronouncing, '"She really had a wonderful life!"' With Duffy, counting one's blessings is integral to 'submit[ting] to the lyrical imagination' (Wilkinson 2014).

'LIKE A JOB'

The title poem, 'William and the Ex Prime Minister' (*William*, n.p.), refers to 'only Grantham's daughter', denoting Margaret Thatcher's humble origins in a grocer's family in Lincolnshire from which she proudly

---

[4] Duffy has a sequence of poems on gambling on the Sheer Poetry Website: http://www.sheerpoetry.co.uk/general-reader/carol-ann-duffy/carol-ann-duffy-archive

rose. Her premiership ended in 1990 leaving two million unemployed. The voice is that of William Brown, the eponymous protagonist of the books by Richmal Crompton that started in 1922 with *Just William*. The tales span five decades and record the changes to a typical English village. Their topicality is sustained through the Just William Society, a fan club, and frequent television remakes. Therefore, Duffy—a fan of the books— might reasonably assume the reader's knowledge of the stories in which the mischievous but loveable eleven-year-old schoolboy leads his gang, the Outlaws, into various scrapes. Making a mouthpiece out of a young rascal whose literacy is weak and morals dubious rubs against any claims to accuracy: 'William stood upon a soapbox, / said *She is a norful sort. / Half the country reckons hope's lost. / Jolly well resign, she ought.*' Yet, how-ever discreditable the character, the voice of the unemployed is here— '*But there's thousands jobless! Millions! / Thanks to that narsy ole witch*', and addresses the reader along with William's disenfranchised gang. True to Crompton's characters, they lock the Prime Minister in the barn, their gathering place, and Duffy gives her the lisping voice of *Just William*'s Violet Elizabeth Bott, the spoiled daughter of a nouveau riche millionaire who would threaten: 'I'll thcream an' thcream an' thcream till I'm thick'. Duffy's drama ends with William beating up his rival, Hubert Lane, an act of empowerment in the absence of any social purpose.

William's vernacular is what Bakhtin calls 'a heteroglossia consciously opposed to literary language. It was parodic, and aimed sharply and polemically against the official languages of its given time' (1981: 273). Similarly, in 'Politico' (*SM* 35), the names and dialect of 'McShane' and 'Wee Frank' sketch the sense of solidarity in the Upper Clyde shipbuilders who fought against liquidation by staging a work-in to prove their worth. (Frank can refer to Duffy's grandfather who was a strong trade unionist.) The image of them launching a boat that would put them out of a job is testimony to a bygone heroism and principle. They stubbornly opposed the tides of capitalism and their spirits might look regretfully on as 'These days' socialism is a 'tree that never grew' and 'the bird that never flew', resonant of Glasgow's Coat of Arms. In 1988, Duffy commented, '"Well we don't now have a Labour Party. As we speak they're in Blackpool trying to rewrite what socialism is. [Thatcher's] done it hasn't she?"' (McAllister 1988: 71). In 'The Tory Candidate On the Eve of the General Election Gets Down on His Knees' (*William* n.p.), Duffy parodies the smugness of the politician, who beseeches Christ to 'pull a few strings', through echoes of the Scottish dialect poem, 'Holy Willie's Prayer' by Robert Burns.

Burns's satirical monologue reveals the hypocrisy of the 'holier than thou' Calvinist whose prayer denigrates other churchmen: 'O Lord, Thou kens what zeal I bear, / When drinkers drink, an' swearers swear'. Duffy yokes her contemporary politician with 'Holy Willie' through the same colloquialisms and rhyming quatrains: 'I blame the Unemployed. The idle sods / won't do a thing to help themselves. A spell / of National Service is the answer, I can tell. / Short socks, smart uniforms and healthy bods.' In the sonnet's final tercets, the Tory candidate drops his hubristic rhetoric as he realizes that Christ was 'a bit of a pinko', a very human communist who shared food among the masses. The reader has the pleasure of seeing him thus condemn himself and his Party's godless self-seeking.

Many monologues present a 'humanized engagement[s] with history' as they 'reveal, explore and communicate the full extent of the devastated interiorities of individuals' (Mousley 2013: 44, 67). The devastating stagnation of being unemployed is aired by speakers who cannot fully apprehend it themselves. 'Like Earning a Living' (*MT* 17) signals how the purposelessness that William expressed through his punch up with Lane defies verbalization: 'There just aren't the words for it' and 'She dunno'. Instead, this speaker's psyche consists in signs—'Video. Big Mac. Lager. Lager'—of attempts to fill up empty days: 'Ambition. Rage. Boredom. Spite. How / do they taste, smell, sound?' Neil Roberts applies Bakhtin's principle of 'sympathetic co-experiencing' to such places—where Duffy draws attention to the reader's remoteness from the speaker but also corrects it: '"A sympathetically co-experienced life is given form not in the category of the *I* but in the category of the *other*, as the life of *another* human being, another *I* ... essentially experienced from *outside*"' (2003: 185). In 'Stealing' (*SM* 38), the first rhetorical question, 'The most unusual thing I ever stole?', draws in the reader as eavesdropper or addressee of the speaker's amusing anecdote of stealing a snowman. Their narration hints at an aching void: 'Mostly I'm so bored I could eat myself'. He or she is 'Sick of the world' and knows 'Life's tough'. However, the unsettling interrogative with which the speech ends, 'You don't understand a word I'm saying, do you?', maintains the gap between speaker and reader. As Roberts explains, 'The co-operative tone in which the anonymous speaker has coaxed the reader into the act of "sympathetic co-experiencing" gives way to one almost of impatience, as when the words "imagine that" ['Foreign' (*SM* 47)] are used to imply that the addressee is precisely incapable of imagining it' (1999: 186). Similarly, 'Education for Leisure' (*SFN* 15) is in the voice of a youth who, as the title suggests, has no prospects: 'I squash a fly against the window with my thumb. / We did that at school. Shakespeare. It was in / another language and now the fly is in another language.' The metaphor evokes the tragic sense of powerlessness uttered by Shakespeare's Gloucester—'As flies to wanton boys are we to the gods. / They kill us for their sport' (*King Lear* Act 4: 1)—and takes the youth's predicament to an existentially human level. Boredom produces one violent act that leads to another: fed up with destroying creatures in the home, the protagonist steps outside where the pavements 'glitter', but not with gold, and threatens violence. As in 'Stealing', the closing sentence, 'I touch your arm', is at once a gesture of approach and a hostile marker of difference.

Various references document the deadening requirement for job seek-ers to present at an unemployment office. The speaker in 'Education for Leisure' walks 'the two miles into town / for signing on' [the dole] 'once a fortnight'; a dole queue in Liverpool features in 'Scraps' (*SM* 36–7) in which, as in 'Brothers' (*MT* 12), Duffy refers to 'UB40s', named after the form issued by the Department for Health and Social Security [DHSS] (1968–88) to those claiming benefit: 'UB40. Giro. / Words had died a death. / DHSS.' As here, the 'scraps' in the poem refer to the reduction of language to acronyms, to strangers trying to converse in the 'drizzling chain' to collect their payout, to the litter swirling round their shoes, and to the individuals' dregs of self-worth. The unemployed are likened to both the seagulls overhead and the scraps off which the gulls live: 'Nowhere to go, nothing to do / but circle the city's black grooves, / repeating its past like a scratched L.P.' The sound of the gulls as 'the bleak farewell to the old ships' explains why so many are out of work. The redundant boat build-ers and dockers also feature in 'Job Creation' (*TOC* 16) that illustrates its title through a sequence of images rather than narrative logic. Gulliver's Land, a theme park near Warrington, was built in 1989 and thus made jobs for local people. Building a giant statue of Gulliver, the speaker cor-responds to a tiny inhabitant of Lilliput in Jonathan Swift's satirical novel *Gulliver's Travels* (1726) and the ropes that restricted Gulliver are the restraints of economic measures on the individual and a community. The local people of this Merseyside town had to adapt their skills to a mind-numbing theme park and the concluding image, 'darkness settled on his shoulders / like a job', ambivalently combines the comfort of putting on a familiar coat with the sense that this work stuns the spirit. In 'Never Go Back' (*MT* 30), the line, 'cheap tricks / in a theme park with no theme', indicates Duffy's scepticism towards the commercially driven simulacrum that a theme park embodies. This postmodern 'simulacrum', in the terms of Jean Baudrillard, is where representations of reality feed off themselves: 'never again exchanging for what is real, but exchanging in itself, in an uninterrupted circuit without reference or circumference' (1988: 170). In 'Translation' (*SM* 39), Duffy's symbol of the fruit machine, in which fruit mean cash, more sordidly signifies the commodification of culture that indirectly deprives men and women of authentic self-fulfilment.

THE 'BRUISED INDUSTRIAL SKY'

In *Contemporary British Poetry and the City*, Peter Barry poses that 'contemporary poetry is in trouble', largely due to ignoring the urban worlds inhabited by the majority of potential readers brought up in a television age. He argues that during the 1970s and 1980s, decades of post-industrial decline, 'the realization that the cityscape which had seemed so immutable was actually just like stage scenery and could be swept away when finished with, did much to stimulate my sense of the city as a place of peculiarly fraught interaction between the person, the social and the political' (2000: 9). Duffy's cityscapes tend to be both descriptive and figurative: 'a bruised industrial sky' is the back drop to feelings of alienation in 'Away from Home' (*TOC* 49–50); 'a dirty industrial town' is the context for an ignorant 'yob' who needs to be civilized by poetry ('The Literature Act', *TOC* 52); and Liverpool's managed economic decline is painted by 'Long dark streets of black eternal rain / leading to nowhere' ('Dreaming of Somewhere Else', *SFN* 37). 'Every Good Boy' (*SM* 30) is the monologue of a composer who makes music as 'the inner cities / riot in my ear' and 'the smash of broken glass is turned / into a new motif', but the critics condemn his work as '*Discord*'. The title cleverly stems from the lines of the treble clef, EGBDF, which some piano students remember by the mnemonic Every Good Boy Deserves Favour. *Every Good Boy Deserves Favour* is also the title of the seventh album by the Moody Blues, released in 1971. Thus, the poem questions whether or not the bad boy mugger or hooligan merits any favours or could inspire music. In 'Never Go Back' (*MT* 30), the 'flick imagery' (Barry 2000: 56) of smoky mirrors, a jukebox, conversation, and card games sketch out 'the bar where the living dead drink all day'. Personifications of the seedy surroundings accentuate the speaker's alienation from a place they once frequented: 'Outside, the streets tear litter in their thin hands, / a tired wind whistles through the blackened stumps of houses / at a limping dog.'⁵ 'Room' (*MT* 50) describes the psychic temporality of rented accommodation—'£90'pw is written in the manner of a newspaper advert—in which lodgers stare out at one another's lights: 'the roofs of terraced houses stretch from / here to how many months' // ... 'Then what.' Ironically, the city's individuals share the tragic feelings of isolation that separate them.

Liverpool

As already discussed, Duffy presents Liverpool's sense of itself when its leisure, education, and 'culture' industries drive the employment economy as coal, steel, shipbuilding and railways once did (Barry 2000: 10). The voice in 'Scraps' (*SM* 36-7) mourns 'Nobody's famous / here and now' but their reference to someone playing *Help* on a harmonica, albeit a rusty one, sustains the memory of The Beatles and the poem puts the city's Renshaw Street on the map. The typography mimics the ragged line queuing for the dole and also the ragged collective mind that describes itself as 'a B movie'. 'Dreaming of Somewhere Else' (*SFN* 37) blends Liverpool's proud landmarks, history, people, and dialect with the reflections of a heightened consciousness that seeks something better. The poem alludes to the stone birds on the two towers of the Royal Liver Buildings, the two grand cathedrals, the pier, the Philharmonic orchestra, and Titanic that had strong links with Liverpool where it was registered and from where many engineers and crew originated. Duffy's extended imagery of the ship's famous disaster in 1912 unpacks a mood of impending doom tied to the city's social disintegration. There is a recession in which people cannot pay their mortgages so they take to drugs, drink, and violence: 'The cat is off its cake' and 'Even the river is too pissed / to go anywhere'. The phrase, 'Et in Arcadia Ego', that translates as 'And I am in Arden', signifies the wish for 'somewhere else', whether memories of Liverpool's past or dreams of a utopian future. The unfulfilled yearning, however, drives people to distraction: 'the wind screams up from the Pier Head / dragging desolation, memory; as the orchestra / plays on for the last dancers bouncing off the walls'. Against the sophisticated language of inner wishful thinking, the words spoken out loud flounder to communicate: '*Know what I mean like?*' and finally, '*You wha*'?' We see here how 'these *total*

⁵ The allusion to the burned homes might allude to the terrorist bombing of a plane that crashed in Lockerbie, Scotland, 21 December 1988, killing several civilians.

impressions of utterances' are joined with one another 'not according to the laws of grammar or logic but according to the laws of *evaluative* (emotive) correspondence' (Vološinov 1994: 57). The questions also indicate a chasm in understanding between the speaker and the implied listener.

The title of 'Liverpool Echo' (*SFN* 44) is taken from the city's local paper and signals how the city resonates only faintly with its former glory while asserting the continuity of that past. For the Merseyside natives, The Beatles are not mere idols but neighbours and boyfriends to whom Liverpool 'cannot say goodbye'. The line picks up on their hit 'You say hello' ['and I say goodbye'] to indicate how the city will not forget the band it spawned and claims as its own. The 'you' in 'as if nostalgia means you did not die' is John Lennon who was murdered in 1981 and the switch between past and present tenses deepens the elegiac mood. The commemorative references to Pat Hodges, Matthew Street, and The Cavern, give solidarity to local readers while the 'loveless ladies' who cry incorporate the prostitutes and any Beatles fan who responds sentimentally to such lyrics as 'Aint She Sweet'. Duffy revisits Liverpool in a mournful sonnet 'North-West' (*FG* 64) and in 'Liverpool' (*RL* 18) discussed in Chap. 5. In 'Dreaming of Somewhere Else', Duffy uses non-rhyming sestets and patterns her loose colloquialisms with poetic alliterations, assonance, and dissonance while in 'Liverpool Echo' she blends titles to popular lyrics with a literary form of four quatrains, two tercets, and regular rhyme. This dialogue with literary tradition is what Carol Rumens notes in Elizabeth Bartlett (1924–2008), whose formative years, like Duffy's, were working class:

> The poems often enact interesting negotiations between the formal "big stanza" with its regular metre and rhyme, and vernacular looseness. Her line-formation never breaks faith with the rhythms of modern English speech. Yet the metrical "ghost" is a vital presence and reference. It not only satisfies the reader's often-neglected need for melody, but also allows the work to subvert, play with and ironically comment on English traditions and at the same time draw strength from them. Generations of love poems and elegies underwrite some of her grittiest settings. (1995: 15)

Postmodern Love

The backcloth to Duffy's love lyrics is usually abstract but the gritty urban settings to the dramatic poems perform how 'postmodern love mirrors economic exchange by emphasizing short-term amorous contracts between strangers, and the intensity of the affair (as in "Adultery"). Consumer culture as a whole proves hostile to amorous commitment' (Rowland 2003: 61). As Rowland indicates, 'Adultery' (*MT* 38–9) shifts the intense lyric voice into the dramatic monologue. The gender-neutral pronouns indicate that the adulterer is as likely to be female as male, for, according to the Office of National Statistics, in 1990, divorce was at a peak with a huge majority of women taking the initiative and the difference between women and men citing adultery as the cause being at its most narrow.[6] Typically, however, Duffy expresses and explores the complex psychology of the adulterer in such a way that the reader can position him or herself as speaker, the betrayed, sympathetic confidant/e, or detached observer. She dramatizes the guilt, the secrecy, the broken marriage, and the ensuing grief as the speaker reflects on whether the consequences outweigh the fleeting pleasures: 'and all for the same thing twice. And all / for the same thing twice'. The repetition and the hovering position of 'all' at the end of the line increases the volume of the lover's self-questioning. The vocabulary of profit and loss probingly captures a culture's consumerist mentality and 'You did it' is ambiguously the speaker's self-blame, self-congratulation, or another voice's condemnation. If 'adultery comes out of the flawed scripts of romance and nuptial bliss' (Rowland 2003: 69), the lovers in 'Terza Rima SW 19' (*SFN* 20) seem to lack a script at all. Narrated in the third person, the action is set on Wimbledon common in South-West London, and the reader is placed as onlooker to 'Two lovers walking by the pond'. The man is more expressive and tells the woman he wants her but she secretly vacillates between 'he loves me, he loves me not' and thinks the relationship might last a year or two. The ambivalent last line, 'and later she might write or he may phone', clashes with the tight terza rima form and suggests a lack of rules for courtship. Also, since the terza rima originated in Dante's Alighieri's *Divine Comedy* (c 1300), a kestrel in the background diving to kill a mouse or vole can seem like a 'deus ex machina' that mocks their foolish attempts to get together. 'Postcards' (*SM* 48), also narrated in the third person, recounts the light-hearted cards and messages between two people based in London and Lancashire in a long-distance correspondence. Presumably indifferent to political allegiances, the man puts the words 'I love you' in thought bubbles of famous people that include Chairman Mao, Reagan, or Thatcher.

[6] 'Divorce rates data, 1858 to now: how has it changed?' http://www.theguardian.com/news/datablog/2010/jan/28/divorce-rates-marriage-ons

Finally, the mood darkens when a card with the cliché, 'wishing you were here', arrives from the man without a stamp. It leaves the reader mirroring the recipient in wondering whether the sender has died and whether the fantasy relationship was beautiful, unhealthy, or sad.

In these relationship dramas, the Duffyesque 'withholding' of the core context destabilizes any ground of certainty or fixed notion of Truth. The 'we' in 'Where We Came In' (*SFN* 24) are a couple who have separated, each has a new lover, and all four have a meal in a restaurant. However, the original couple still shares a degree of understanding, exhibited in private references, jokes, and gestures. The poem is circular—the last word 'And' starts the sentence with which the poem opens, 'old loves die hard'—to illustrate the point. Duffy further punctures this scenario of mature modern arrangements with internal monologue in which the man and wife unconvincingly persuade themselves that they are currently better off: 'I think / of all the tediousness of loss but, yes, / I'm happy now. Yes. Happy. Now.' 'Correspondents' (*SM* 50) is in the voice of a Victorian Englishwoman who switches between a rather stiff mode of discourse in public and the language of passion she writes in letters to her 'lover'. Releasing desires that are sublimated by social repression, she finds the fabricated relationship more invigorating than her respectable marriage: 'I have called your name over and over in my head / at the point your fiction brings me to'. 'Telegrams' (*SM* 51), too, depicts a fantasy affair in which the woman finds herself deceived by the male lover when he divulges that he is married. The conventions of telegram writing—capital letters and no punctuation but a 'STOP' at the end of a phrase—mediate a certain comedy through exaggeration: 'THOUGHT IT ODD YOU WORE STRING VEST STOP / AS SOON AS I MET YOU I WENT OVER THE TOP STOP'. More tragically, 'Eley's Bullet' (*TOC* 30–1) has the plot and suspense of a novel potently condensed into a poem. The reader painfully looks on as a man who loves a married woman ends up killing himself after she calls off the affair and thereby blasts his dreams. Like so many characters, he cannot resolve the clash between 'the mind's mad films' and the place in which he spends his days. Thus, whether set in the past, present, or fiction, the poems dramatize and confront the paradox that 'We are the fools who dwell in time / outside of time'.

The Mad and Bad: 'our secret films'

There is a polemic to Duffy's indictments of economic injustice and greed but her constructions of lovers, the mad, and the bad are more morally ambiguous. Padel comments,

Duffy's eighties monologues, spoken by both abusers and abused (a murderous psychopath, a man beaten to make a false confession in a police cell), came over as witty, hard-hitting voicings of people who did not understand how mad, bad or badly off they were, in times we were living through, and became a poetic comment on that time. (2002: 21)

As already mentioned, the controversial policy to turn out patients from psychiatric hospitals into the community was accompanied by fears that the mentally ill would commit random acts of violence on the public. 'Liar' (*TOC* 28) portrays one woman who fabulates to the extent that she stole a child in the park, was arrested, sent to jail, and pronounced 'sadly confused' by a 'top psychiatrist'. By switching the pronouns, Duffy conjoins the condemned woman's make-believe, the judge's sexual fantasies of the 'Princess of Wales', and the reader's dreams: 'She lives like you do, a dozen slack rope-ends / in each dream hand, tugging uselessly on memory / or hope. Frayed.' The subject is only an exaggeration of the human tendency to fabricate a better life than the one in which we find ourselves: 'Hyperbole, falsehood, fiction, fib were pebbles tossed / at the evening's flat pool; her bright eyes / fixed on the ripples. No one believed her. / Our secret films are private affairs, watched / behind the eyes. She spoke in subtitles. Not on.' The poem is a means to put the subtitles on and make 'our secret films' available, at least to ourselves. As we view life through these outsiders' eyes we find new truths: '[Duffy] presents a gallery of psychopaths, mental curiosities, disturbed women and children, but like the American Indian each shows us a rinsed vision of the world' (Mackinnon 1988).

The disorientating monologues by social outsiders indicate how individuals' inner speech defies the terms of official and rational discourses. 'Psychic experience', as the 'semiotic expression of the contact between the organism and the outside environment' (Vološinov 1994: 56) is what Duffy touches in 'The Cliché Kid' (*MT* 18). In conversation with a doctor, the 'kid' can only supply images of normal things being the wrong way round—the dad in a ball gown and mother playing cards. The youth suffers a 'lonesome heart' and describes himself as 'bonkers'. Similarly, 'And How Are We Today?' (*SM* 27) presents the 'psychic experience' of a mentally unbalanced person negotiating the border between their inner and outer worlds. They suffer a sense of persecution, 'the little people in the radio are picking on me / again', and imagine copying a strange act they had read in the newspapers because it would get attention. However, the untethered consciousness—'I live inside someone else's head'—can belong equally to the patient or the doctor for whom 'it is no use / sneaking home at five o'clock to his nice house'. In 'Before You Jump' (*SFN* 38), dedicated 'for Mister Berryman', the poet who committed suicide in 1972, a compassionate voice pleads with the suicide to climb down and 'Forever come into the warm' but the subject needs 'one voice' as opposed to their conflicting inner voices, in order to be calm. Duffy creates an emotive pastiche of Berryman's confessional mode, weaving in biographical details such as his turbulent relationships and religious conversion. The speaker switches between first and second person pronouns in the manner of Berryman's *Dream Songs* and in the manner of someone battling strange voices when mentally off balance. As O'Brien approves, 'Duffy is unusual in being able to present both continuity and individual disjunction in time, so that the individual peculiarities of her speakers' predicaments, which are sometimes extreme, acquire a representative role by default of any larger sustaining structure of sense in society at large' (1998: 163). The lack of 'any sustaining structure' that makes sense is communicated by Mister Berryman's chaotic soundtracks: 'Fame and Money better never / Than too late' and 'They're killing me: the images, the sounds / of what is in this world'. One vital force peeps through: 'And who shall love properly? // You must / or we die.' Talking of *Selling Manhattan*, Duffy stated, 'It tries hard to name love, which is missing in Thatcher's Britain. Our language is the best we've got, but it's not fully adequate' (Buckley 1989).

Just as Duffy humanizes debates around 'care in the community' through portraying sympathetically the search for love or the 'psychic experience' of madness, she explores attitudes and legislation concerning sexual offences through the 'semiotic expression of the contact between the organism and the outside environment'. In the disturbing evocation of child abuse, 'Lizzie, Six' (*SFN* 13),[7] the innocent voice in italics seems disconcertingly unaware that the adult is menacing and predatory: 'What are you thinking? / *I'm thinking of love.* / I'll give you love / when I've climbed this stair'. Placed as a powerless observer, the reader recoils against the adult's domination of the vulnerable six-year-old-child, as magnified by their voice having three quarters of the lines. 'We Remember Your Childhood Well' (*TOC* 24) more directly registers a period in the early 1980s when ideas about children repressing

---

[7] See also Selima Hill, 'A Voice in the Garden', *Saying Hello at the Station* (London: Chatto & Windus, 1984: 29).

memories of incest and abuse led to a concerted search to recover their stories. The issue came to public attention in 1987 with the 'Cleveland Scandal' where 121 cases were diagnosed at a Middleborough hospital but ninety six were judged false.[8] Furthermore, *The Courage to Heal* report (1988) was accompanied by a reaction that described a condition of 'false memory syndrome'.[9] In Duffy's poem, a challenge to the idea of false memory is played out in the denial of the adult voices that respond to unspecified but readily imagined charges against them: 'Nobody hurt you. Nobody turned off the light', 'Nobody locked the door'. The chilling situations that emerge through the adults' defences are sufficiently precise to impress their cruelty while also sufficiently unspecific to relate to anyone. Each of the three-line stanzas begins with the dismissal of an implied accusation: 'What you recall are impressions. We have the facts.' By repeating the first person plural pronoun, the speakers harrowingly accentuate the child's helplessness as the 'we' conspiringly contradict his or her version of their tortured upbringing. 'The skid marks of sin' consolidate various allusions to emotional and physical torment: rows; being locked up; a 'bad man on the moors'; unanswered questions; being forced; and being sent away to 'firm' people. Duffy typically places evocative mid-sentence words at the end of a line in order to maximize their imaginative 'fury': 'argued / with somebody else, bigger / than you'. Shifting between end and internal rhymes—'off the light', 'night', 'didn't occur', 'blur', 'sent you away', 'extra holiday'—the sinister suggestiveness reaches the auditory imagination. Also characteristically, Duffy displaces familiar clichés ('it ended in tears', 'there was nothing to fear'), imbues them with a potency they have leaked through overuse and exposes how dead platitudes gloss the complexity of verbalizing trauma. The monosyllabic 'Boom. Boom. Boom.' is syntactically the speech of the 'carers' but correlates to the effect of their voices in the child's head and the fearful pounding of the child's heart. These sounds are all the more potent when his or her version of events is markedly absent. The callously rhetorical question that opens the final stanza, 'What does it matter now?', mimics the way such cases get forgotten by authorities and the media but never by the victims.

---

[8] In 2007, one of the key doctors who diagnosed the abuse and several people affected by the scandal spoke out on British daytime television of the traumatic aftermath.

[9] The British False Memory Society (BFMS) was formed in 1993 and the American False Memory Syndrome Foundation (FMSF) in 1992.

The dramatic monologue's conventional function of developing readers' moral sensibilities is straightforward when spoken by a deserving case but troubling in what Marsha Bryant calls the 'killer lyrics', grouping Duffy with the American poet Ai (1947–2010): 'Ai and Duffy create speakers who perform hardened versions of cool masculinity, fashioning their identities through movies, music, and other forms of media. Moreover, their violent utterances violate poetic language' (2011: 151). While some readers view the speaker in 'Education for Leisure' as an evolving psychopath, the title veers towards presenting the youth as a victim of educational and economic policies. On the other hand, in 'Too Bad' (*TOC* 13), a hit man, possibly enrolled by the IRA, coolly confides that he murdered a man walking out of a pub. The reader is taken into an underworld in which men find crime a panacea for the normality of a 'dull wife' and cosy home. His unnervingly blasé tone and the 'too bad' of the title indicate that he has passed the point of reform. Duffy more hauntingly exploits the relationship between the poet as dramatist and the reader in 'Human Interest' (*SFN* 36) in which a man confesses to killing his wife for cheating on him: 'She turned away. I stabbed. I felt this heat / burn through my skull until reason had died.' He is in prison and paying 'interest' on what took 'thirty seconds to complete'. Spoken in exaggerated slang, this dramatic monologue provokes strong feelings of empathy and antipathy in a reader, an antidote to the passive voyeurism of soap operas or the news. Bryant comments, 'The speaker recounts his feelings and actions in working-class vernacular, projecting a vulnerable toughness with the intensity of a lyric', thus combining 'journalistic and literary tropes' in his 'jailhouse confession' (2011: 152). Readers might wrangle over the extent of his culpability but the poem's title infers that viewers of such goings-on are part of the problem: 'Nestled between complicity and critique, it evokes media's constructions of murderers and other perpetrators of violence as "human interest" figures, acknowledging our daily appetite for their criminal confessions' (2011: 153–4).

Thus, the dramatic monologue's provocation of empathy and antipathy is an antidote to the passive voyeurism of soap operas or the news. It also expresses and explores the complexity of psychic experience that these mass media tend to reduce. In 'Psychopath' (*SM* 28), we are repelled by the blatant boasts of a man who has abducted a girl from a fairground, sexually violated her, and thrown her into the canal, as he has done many times before: 'You can woo them / with goldfish and coconuts, whispers in the Tunnel of Love. / When I zip up the leather, I'm in a new skin, I touch it / and love myself, sighing Some little lady's going to get lucky / tonight. My breath wipes me from the looking glass' (*SM* 28–9). With reference to 'the looking-glass' as a symbol of the 'frequently iterated one-dimensional images' of masculinity peddled through popular culture, Jane Thomas illuminates how he acts out 'the negative and violent modes of self-articulation offered to him'; chillingly, 'the psychopath's obsession with his masculine identity necessitates the domination, violation, and obliteration of its perceived and threatening feminine opposite' (2003: 132–3). More warmly, Vernon Scannell observes, 'through a quite brilliant and convincing use of a patois, deriving from American TV films and city street vernacular, [Duffy] gets right inside the skull and skin of her frightening and sad creature' (1987/8: 36). Although set in the 1950s to distance the event (McAllister 1988: 70), Roberts points out that the accumulation of references to the period is overdone if Duffy simply aims to historicize the plot; rather, she demonstrates how, 'the speaker is defined, or defines himself, from the outside by these [cultural references], and there is no sense of interiority' (1999: 190). Like the intimate address and present tense of the other 'killer monologues', the psychopath comes close, too close, and insinuates that he was 'more sinned against than sinning' (Shakespeare, *King Lear* Act 3: 2). Not only is he a puppet of media power, but he found his mother with the 'rent man' and 'Dirty Alice' humiliated his manhood. As Bryant slickly puts it, 'This psychic archive not only adds depth to the psychopath's character but also links him to his victim through the trope of betrayed innocence' (2011: 164). We can thus deduce, more than he does, why he is taking revenge on women through serial rape and murder. Nevertheless, the reader rails against being required to *sympathize* with the murderer. Of course, the dramatic monologue *performs* the speech, allows us to find it suspect, and to dismiss it as the kind of defence any violator makes when he asserts that a woman 'asked for it'. However, in the naturalistic detail of the victim and the perpetrator's personal history, Duffy presents us with the knotty dilemma of the court room as opposed to the knee-jerk verdicts of tabloid headlines that she parodies in 'Poet for our Times' and 'Phone-In': 'the front page of a tabloid / demanding the rope for a bastard who killed a kid' (*PMP* 16).

The reference to the 'bad man on the moors' in 'We Remember Your Childhood Well' ignites images of The Yorkshire Ripper, Peter Sutcliffe, whose activities continued into the 1980s. It also applies to Myra Hindley and Ian Brady, the couple responsible for the 'Moors murders' of five victims in the 1960s. In 1985, a new grave was discovered, Brady confessed to two further murders, and the case was reopened. 'Naming Parts' (*SFN* 21), which can be approached as the drama of any domestic violence (Gregson 1996: 104), may also refer specifically to Hindley and Brady chopping up their victims. The 'sideways look' and 'my hands reach sadly for the telephone' suggest the voice of the brother-in-law, married to Hindley's sister, who witnessed one murder and informed the police. We taste the uncertainty of who says what and who did what as unidentified pronouns shift around: 'we forgive them nothing', 'someone is cared for who is past caring'. Alan Robinson discusses how the poem's 'referential instability' is nonetheless powerfully referential. Hindley's 'disorientated partial perspective' especially compounds 'the experiential turmoil that compels the reader to undergo the stressful breakdown in communication that is this poem's subversive technique as well as its theme' (Robinson 1988: 201). Duffy also writes of Hindley and Brady in 'The Devil's Wife' (*WW* 42–6), a monologue in which Hindley's linguistic coherence supports her conscious culpability: 'The Devil was evil, mad, but I was the Devil's wife / which made me worse.' In the monologue's last section, 'Appeal', she lists the various forms of sentence for murder as if weighing the relative merits of execution and life imprisonment.

While the psychopath, Brady, and Hindley are extreme cases, the protagonists of 'Human Interest' or 'Education for Leisure' speak in ordinary vernacular and push at the boundary between a normative and exceptional psyche (Bryant 2011: 157–8). As Bryant contends, these monologues disrupt the Browningesque convention that was based on a moral consensus; instead, they ask questions about what moral sensibility might mean in an image-driven culture, about by what principles we label evil, deviant, or diseased behaviours, and about a tendency to convict the socially oppressed. When in 'Absolutely' (*SM* 26) Duffy mentions Magritte, famous for the phrase, 'une pipe n'est ce pas une pipe', she implies the simulacrum of political or polite rhetoric that glosses 'nasties in childhood or the woodshed'. At the time of writing this book, there is public uproar over the alleged cover up of the government's link with a paedophile ring going back to the 1980s when 114 files went missing and the enquiry continues to be a 'circuit without reference or circumference' to truth (Baudrillard 1988: 170). Thus, her poetic confessions of crime bear some resemblance to Alan Bennett's successful television monologues, *Talking*

Heads (BBC 1988 and 1998), most hauntingly, 'Playing Sandwiches' (1998), the portrayal of a reformed paedophile, in which Bennett exposes how readily we scapegoat the vulnerable. Like him, Duffy implies a more humane view of deviant behaviour.

NATIONALISMS: 'MY COUNTRY'

O'Brien comments that Duffy's own experience of deracination made her particularly alert to the dissolution of England's 'broad consensual under-standing of itself' (1998: 161). However, he warns against expecting the poet 'to work as a social historian' and commends how she can 'suggest all that is *not there* in the social fabric—the kinds of consciousness, for instance, which have yet to discover themselves' (1998: 165). The seem-ingly incidental fragments from T.S. Eliot's modernist poem *The Waste Land* (1922)—'Those early hyacinths' ('The Windows'), the 'wicked' cards ('Naming Parts'), and the 'dull canal' ('Psychopath')—resonate with his poetic evocation of a crumbling culture. Unlike Eliot, however, Duffy reinforces the relationship between poetry and subjective interiority, as O'Brien summarizes:

> The private life might remain nothing to the passage of history, but as it finds expression it has a strength which can only be understood in its own terms. Duffy, as we know, is a fine love poet. It is a tribute to her that the pursuit of the true voice of feeling, and her feeling for the individual life, are so thought-provoking'. (1998: 168)

Although Duffy's arrangement of voices sometimes decentres any moral or social authority, her treatment of the mediation and casualties of war is 'double-voiced', meaning that the author's polemic is implied rather than direct (Bakhtin 1981: 325). In 'Missile' (*SFN* 53), the child's innocent truths enforce the poem's argument that dropping bombs is inhumane: she says that birds fly, spiders spin, and fishes swim, all follow-ing their natures, 'Except you, Daddy'. The monosyllabic 'Bang' horribly parallels the swiftness of nuclear destruction with a shot from a toy gun. During the 1980s, cruise missiles were brought to Britain but preceded by protests on Greenham Common. Judith Radstone, to whom Duffy's 'Warming Her Pearls' is dedicated, was a protestor in the Campaign for Nuclear Disarmament (CND) and her spirit hovers over 'Missile' while 'The bomb' is one of the items banned in 'The Act of Imagination' (*TOC*

25). In 'Borrowed Memory' (*SFN* 55), a very English couple model themselves as schoolboy or schoolgirl fiction characters, such as those in the Billy Bunter stories initially published in the weekly comic *The Magnet* and which feature the hero Harry Wharton mentioned in the poem. In retrospect, 'Fair Play Bob' and 'Good Egg Sue' substitute their memories with the tales of 'larks', midnight feasts, and sporting achievements: 'these fictions are as much a part of them / as fact'. The commentator gives the reader a broader view than the characters in seeing how these adventure stories, endemic to their grammar school educations, trained them to unquestioningly do their national duty. Without a sense of self that is distinct from the roles prescribed by their books and betters, they supported the war effort uncomplainingly, taking to air raid shelters 'with tons of tuck to see them through'. In later life, they watch anti-war protests on the television but are unable to register a different reality to the stories in their heads. In a different manner, 'Poker in the Falklands with Henry and Jim' (*SFN* 54) is also counter-discursive to patriotic propaganda. The war started in April 1982 when the Argentine government claimed the islands and Britain declared war, resulting in big losses on both sides. 'Henry and Jim' could be any English boys sacrificed for the British government's controversial attack for the sake of a small piece of territory (4700 square miles) to which its claim was highly questionable. Duffy follows a line of war poetry, such as Alun Lewis's 'All Day it has Rained', in which soldiers fill up their hours with idle pastimes while naggingly aware of a danger conspicuously absent from conversation. The allusions, 'God this is an awful game' and 'Poker', synthesize playing cards with the government's gamble in sending its men against the mighty Argentine force who were close to home. There is a 'bearded poet' in the room so the card game might include Argentinians and both sides know that 'one of us is just about to win'. As it happened, 649 Argentine and 255 British military personnel plus three Falkland Islanders died during the hostilities. As discussed in Chap. 1, the British tabloid paper's headline, 'Gotcha', became a symbol of nationalistic fervour that bled from and to its readers. Duffy characteristically deconstructs such oppositional notions of identification for all sides are grotesque in war: '*In my country / we do this*. But my country sends giant / underwater tanks to massacre'.

Through 'War Photographer' (*SFN* 51), Duffy again accords with Simic's call to poets: 'In place of historian's "distance" I want to experience the vulnerability of those participating in tragic events. … My own physical and spiritual discomfort is nothing in comparison to that of those being imprisoned and tortured tonight all over the world' (1985: 126). Her photographer acts as history's 'conscious part' and may well be based on Don McCullin who worked for the *Sunday Times* and who talks of the darkness in the dark room: "'Sometimes it felt like I was carrying pieces of human flesh back home with me, not negatives. It's as if you are carrying the suffering of the people you have photographed'" (O'Hagan 2010).[10] Similarly, the language of developing films—'spools of suffering', 'solutions sop in trays'—indicates how the photographer has been indelibly marked by the horrors. Duffy's speaker reflects on how he peddles pain by selling pictures to editors of Sunday newspapers whose readers will be momentarily moved but not enough to interfere with the pleasures of their morning bath or pre-lunch beers. However, he reins in the poem's reader by personalizing the agonies—'the cries / of this man's wife', 'the feet of running children in a nightmare heat'—to offset desensitizing journalism. Duffy likens the photographer to a priest solemnly preparing Mass, as if the Last Rites, and names the war-torn places like a requiem: 'Belfast. Beirut, Phnom Penh'. The list is both poetically alliterative and politically particular: Belfast was the seat of the Irish 'Troubles'; Beirut refers to the Lebanese Civil War that lasted from 1975 to 1990, seeing a mass exodus and fatalities; and Phnom Penh was the site of the Cambodian genocide carried out by the communist Khmer Rouge regime between 1975 and 1979, killing around three million. The end rhymes of the concluding two lines to each sestet allow a finality that jars with the lack of closure for the photographer and the victims that he filmed: 'From the aeroplane he stares impassively at where / he earns his living and they do not care.' The 'they' can be greedy newspaper magnates, their callous readers, and the traumatized.

'What Price?' (*SFN* 52) and 'Shooting Stars' (*SFN* 56) rekindle sensitivities about remembering the six million killed out of a Jewish population of nine million living in Europe, during a time when conspiracy theories questioned the validity of witness accounts. In 1978, Willis Carto founded the Institute for Historical Review (IHR) as an organization dedicated to publicly challenging the commonly accepted history of the Holocaust. The voices in 'Shooting Stars' are both confiding and imperative: 'remember these appalling days which made the world / forever bad'. The stars are metonyms for the Jews who had to wear the badge for identification and for which they were shot during World War II. As the verbs shift between past, present, and future tenses, we are shown the

---

[10] McCullin was a friend of Duffy during the 1980s.

contrast between the fate of a casualty, who describes his death by firing squad, and the apathy of future generations. While there is some recognition that the soldiers who killed them were 'young men' and 'boys' there is no compassion for the superiors who take 'tea on the lawn'. 'What Price' takes the discovery of what were purported to be Adolf Hitler's diaries in 1983 (but later proved to be forgeries). Through monologue, Duffy creates a character with an air of social superiority—'Wagner on the gramophone'—and Nazi sympathies: 'I know the Sons of David died, some say atrociously, / but that's all past. The roses are in bloom.' He takes pleasure in wine, a long life, children, and grandchildren. The irony of 'it makes one glad to be alive' is not lost on the reader in the context of the numberless dead and their unborn descendants. The assonance of 'wife', 'find', and 'wine' accentuates the speaker's blissful indifference to the treatment of Jews as disposable commodities. In the last two lines, the 'they' are the diaries that might fetch two million pounds while millions of human lives were deemed price-less. The speaker supports Thatcher—'she has the right idea'—in claiming back the Falkland Islands, making a subtle link between Thatcherism and Hitler's brand of nationalism. Again, Duffy sharply manipulates how the dramatic monologue can infer a lot more than the speaker intends, 'encourag[ing] ironic reflection in the reader as we feel invited at some point to adopt a judgment larger than the speaker's' (Sinfield 1977: 32). Her indictment of the preying interest in the diaries by the newspapers demonstrates how the poet writes another kind of history to accentuate a common humanity.

'Now I am Alien'

The British Nationality Act of 1981 removed the automatic right of citizenship to all those born on British soil and policies continued to limit and curtail rights to immigration. The Scarman Report that followed the racially motivated Brixton Riots (1981) found that 'racial disadvantage is a fact of current British life'. Discussing Duffy's poems of the 1980s, Linda Kinnahan comments, '[her] poetry explores the discursive constructions surrounding the issues of immigration, ethnicity and nationalism' (2000: 209). Furthermore, Duffy leads the reader to enter the conditions themselves. 'Foreign' (*SM* 47), the internal monologue of an immigrant, sympathetically presents the alienation of dwelling in a 'strange, dark city for twenty years', marked as different by 'your foreign accent': 'You think / in a language of your own and talk in theirs.' The speaker confides how they do honest work yet have to confront racist graffiti: 'you saw a name for yourself sprayed in red / against a brick wall. A hate name. Red like blood.' The heavy monosyllables accentuate how verbal threats will lead to physical violence and the author blends her voice with the speaker to directly address the reader: 'imagine that'. 'Imagining that' is precisely what poetry makes possible, but only up to a point. In 'Deportation' (*SM* 59), the sad, bemused, but gracious voice of a deportee on their way to the airport—'Now I am *Alien*'—counters the formal wording of the host country's inhospitable bureaucracy: 'Form F. Room 12. Box 6.' The reader sympathetically co-experiences how the speaker came to work, raise a child, and fulfil their human desires: 'Love is a look / in the eyes in any language, but not here.' The deportee's liminal perspective, 'Where I come from there are few jobs / the young are sullen and do not dream,' comments on the human sameness between people in his native land and the one that he is leaving. However, his social status has changed: 'The only connection between the two is provided by "supplication" and "gratitude" which define the existence and the self of the foreigner in a hierarchical dependence on the natives, thus denying the foreigner a position of subjectivity' (Michelis and Rowland 2003: 86).

Poems that arose from Duffy's post as writer-in-residence in East London schools between 1982 and 1984 record the growth of multicultural education. 'Girl Talking' (*SFN* 7) is narrated by a young Pakistani Muslim who relates how her cousin Tasleen suffered an unexplained illness and died. The reader inevitably infers so much more than the speaker reveals in her simple uncomprehending statements to an unidentified addressee: 'Something happened. We think it was pain. She gave wheat to the miller and the miller / gave her flour. / Afterwards it did not hurt.' However, the reader is forced to realize their ignorance about the community she describes and thus has to suspend judgment. In 'Head of English' (*SFN* 12), the teacher homogenizes 'those with English as a second language' who receive extra tuition and the context suggests an orderly girls' grammar school in the 1970s. The polyphonic 'Comprehensive' (*SFN* 8–9) interrogates the ideal of social cohesion through a system of comprehensive state schools that from 1965 were introduced in Britain and attended by 90 per cent of the population. Each of the seven stanzas is spoken by a different character to present in parallel the perspectives of African, Muslim, Indian, and working-class white British children. The schoolchildren are products of other people's sayings, and, lacking the means to articulate an independent consciousness, simply reproduce what they hear. The first speaker is

African and relates, 'My mother says You will like it when we get our own house'; Majid voices the dashed dreams of his family who migrated from an Indian village to London, 'People wrote to us / That everything was easy here', but his feelings lurk in what he does not say; Ejaz makes friends with another Muslim who informs him that sausages contain pigs' meat; a Northern Indian child is descended from the Moghul emperors but rendered powerless through not speaking English and misses the free milk as a result. (Duffy slips in a reference to the provision of free milk that was stopped for the over sevens by Thatcher, nicknamed 'milk-snatcher', in 1971 when she was Education Secretary.) Wayne is a disaffected working-class boy who supports his football team, the National Front, and blames 'all of them / coming over here to work' for not getting a job. His 'Paki-bashing', like 'pulling girls' knickers down', is to exert power over anyone different. Ian Sansom comments, 'when [Duffy] attempts to plumb the depths of Wayne's inarticulacy, risking stylistic disaster in an attempt to provide him with a voice, she ends up caricaturing and stereotyping his language-use so that he becomes nothing more than a cipher, a representative of all that is bad in British society—racist, ignorant, lazy' (1995: 20). Actually, Wayne's racist attitudes consist of words from his parents and popular media that have infiltrated his consciousness: his family revel in the 1978 film *I Spit on Your Grave*, in which a woman is systematically gang raped and left for dead, and Wayne regurgitates their pleasure as 'Brilliant'. Similarly, a white boy who wants to join the army fights his instinct to 'be mates' with the 'others', because they are different so he joins in with 'taking the piss'. His sister 'went out with one' and the floating cliché, 'There was murder', can refer to either or both racial groups. Michelle's family struggle due to her mother's poor nerves; she modestly aims for a job in a supermarket chain, adulates her pop group Madness, which peaked in the early to mid 1980s, and finds life boring. She has not lost her virginity 'yet' because she wants 'respect'. Like Wayne, her subjectivity consists in the languages of contemporary culture and although attracted to a 'Marlon Frederick', she judges him 'a bit dark'. As Roberts comments, 'it is the white children who speak disconnectedly, as if answering questions, and who consequently seem strange'. Thus, while not underestimating the displacement of migration, Duffy connects all the children as products of 'the deformities of Thatcherite Britain' (Roberts 1999: 187, 188). Kinnahan instructively dissects the ways in which the voices 'reveal the tension between assimilation and cultural plurality underlying debates over Britain's changing demographics' and goes further to identify how the 'ethnically marked positions' are also defined by a market relationship to each other: 'For Duffy, the discursive space of a British identity constructed partially in reaction to growing diversity and nurtured by Thatcherism's linking of race, family, free market, and nationalism in both policy and public utterance, slices up the "comprehensive" possibilities of a plural nation, threatening to insert spaces of silence between the voices making up this poem and, by extension, remaking Britain' (2000: 221).

In 'Translating the English, 1989' (*TOC* 11), the person claims England as 'my country' and lists its features using idioms typical of speaking a foreign language, such as sticking to the present tense and superfluous definite articles: 'The Fergie, the Princess Di'. England is characterized by pride in its famous writers, Shakespeare, Wordsworth, Dickens, that the speaker puts on a par with fish and chips, history, Empire, soap operas, the Royal Family, and the 'Channel Tunnel'—the undersea link between England and France begun in 1988 and completed in 1994. The speaker also catalogues Britain's less glorious underside: the right-wing media, drugs, alcohol, rape, polluted water, unsafe eggs, talk about the weather, and a north/south divide. John Redmond resists the implications of these realities, 'While the poem is meant to point up the lazy racism of the British by means of a witty "translation", it relies on caricature so much as to seem questionable' (2007: 254), but Peter Forbes observes: '"Translating the English, 1989" is a monologue which holds up a hideous distorted mirror to English Society. The voice is that of an atrocious interpreter-cum-tout and what it is saying is too concentrated an essence of sleaze to be true. You want to think. But it is' (1994: 111). The voice's discordant mix of high and low cultural references and registers both sports and queries postmodern culture's 'aesthetic populism' as described by Fredric Jameson: 'The effacement of the older (essentially high-modernist) frontier between high culture and so-called mass or commercial culture ... materials they no longer simply "quote", as a Joyce or Mahler would have done, but incorporate into their very substance' (1991: 2–3). Most pertinent is the commercialization of culture—'For two hundred quid we are talking Les Miserables', 'All this can be arranged for cash no questions'—corresponding to Jameson's view that postmodernity threatened to herald the victory of commodification over all spheres of life (1991). In an incisive reading of the poem, Kinnahan zooms in on the paratactic arrangement of phrases that counters more official marketing of the nation's characteristics: 'The act of representation—of translation—always involves selection and arrangement that is, the poem suggests, ideologically interested.

The idea of popular or high art as separate from this ideologically messy world is satirized in the final lines' (Kinnahan 1996: 253–5). These final lines begin with 'Plenty culture you will be agreeing'.

As discussed throughout this chapter, Duffy dramatizes how the twin forces of capitalism and consumerism cause psychic alienation across a spectrum of identities shaped by class, race, education, and gender. 'Mrs Skinner, North Street' (*TOC* 12) is a recognizable figure out of a soap opera. Like the optical illusion of the pretty-cum-ugly woman, she can appear as a vulnerable sad individual who has lost the community she once knew; on the other hand, she can emerge as a bigot who 'twitches the curtain' and mulls over the word 'xenophobic' attributed to her by her social worker. As Michelis summarizes: 'The poem draws a map of a post-industrial England which is divided into "us" and "them", where national identity is defined purely by economic success based on "Fear, morbid dislike, of strangers", and thus on a process of "othering" inherent to the colonial and imperialist tradition underlying the feeling of national pride' (2003: 94). While the city is Duffy's more common context, 'Model Village' (*SM* 21) takes a picture-book depiction of a rural English community and, as it were, draws back the net curtains to reveal a sick state of affairs. Gregson sees the characters caricature themselves: 'Behind the cosy clichés of childhood are the *louche* clichés of soap opera or pulp fiction' (1996: 105). Smith comments that the child's initiation into conventional linguistic signs—'Cows say *Moo*' and so on—'creates 'a "model" reality in the head which then shapes all the self's negotiations with the "real"' (2003: 160). This 'model reality' would explain the dissonance between the social roles each character plays and their suppressed desires to be someone else. The virgin spinster has missed her chance to marry a man she loves through being trapped as carer to her bitter mother whom she murders in the style of 'a paperback'. When alone, the vicar fantasizes about smoking, dressing as a choirboy, and having sadomasochistic sex with the choir mistress. The librarian 'peddle[s] fiction' to the villagers: 'Believe / you me, the books in everyone's head are stranger …'. However, the farmer digging away for something is an allegory for the elusive 'something else' that permeates Duffy's lyrics: 'When I shovel / deep down, I'm searching for something. Digging desperately.'

The voice in 'Talent Contest' (*TOC* 19) ostensibly comments on a show at the end of a pier, but, like the farmer, comes to question the futility of it all. Initially, he applies the low vernacular of 'piss' and ''em' to the other poor quality acts in order to feel superior then realizes that he, too, is conning the audience about the 'talent' on display: 'A doubt like faraway thunder / threatens to ruin the day, that it's squandered on this.' Here, both participants and spectators would stave off the knowledge that they have wasted their time and money trying to have a good time. Such cheap thrills are poor substitutes for the 'something else' they seek. The poems on drinking also belie a nagging doubt about the authenticity of drunken pleasure. The humour of 'Drunk' (*MT* 24)—'Suddenly the rain is hilarious', 'what a laugh'—and the sequence, 'Make that a Large One', 'Still Life with hangover', and 'Rounds' (*William* n.p.) have a Duffyesque undertone that marks the loneliness and lack of fulfilment for which alcohol abuse is both a cause and symptom: 'I could've been anyone // Me // Wishful drinking'. However, the pertinently playful lines in these poems also accord with Bakhtin's observation of carnival, where 'Verbal etiquette and discipline are relaxed and indecent words and expressions may be used. ... The familiar language of the market place became a reservoir in which various speech patterns excluded from official intercourse could freely accumulate' (Bakhtin 1965: 203–4).

Dorothy McMillan summarizes: 'Duffy's use of dramatized voices is the strategy of a kind of passionate non-alignment on the part of the modern poet. The manipulation of other voices is perhaps a characteristic of writing in a plural society or one which is changing too rapidly for most of its members to comprehend it. Thus, Duffy as "state of the nation" poet makes the effort to comprehend the incomprehensible' (Gifford and McMillan 1997: 553). With Duffy, however, the realism invites us to interpret the poems as documentary but, echoing 'The Dummy', the speaker in 'Talent Contest' (*TOC* 19) states, 'Beware the ventriloquist, / The dark horse, whose thrown voice juggles the truth.' The lines can, of course, be wittily self-referential but 'Descendants' (*TOC* 22–3) reinstates the poet's role as recorder and prophet. Set in the future, it is narrated by an ignorant man who hates 'the bastard past' so he throws into the sea his girlfriend's book of poetry, that, by implication preserves and reanimates the past. Accordingly, this chapter has illustrated how poetry restores the 'conscious part' to history through the 'fury' of the imagination (Simic 1985: 126).

REFERENCES

1986. *Thrown voices* (London: Turret Books).

Bakhtin, M.M. 1965. *Rabelais and His World*, Trans. H. Iswolksy, in Morris (1994), 195–206.

Bakhtin, M.M. 1981. In *The dialogic imagination: Four essays*, ed. Michael Holquist. Austin: University of Texas Press.

Barry, Peter. 2000. *Contemporary British poetry and the city*. Manchester: Manchester University Press.

Baudrillard, Jean. 1988. In *Selected writings*, ed. M. Poster. Cambridge: Polity Press.

Bryant, Marsha. 2011. *Women's poetry and popular culture*. New York: Palgrave.

Buckley, Marian. 1989. Interview with Carol Ann Duffy. *City Life Magazine,* June 15.

Dunmore, Helen. 1999. Waiting for the world's wife. *Poetry Review* 89(2): 80–81.

Forbes, Peter. 1994. Talking about the new generation, Carol Ann Duffy. *Poetry Review* 84(1): 4–6, 111.

Forbes, Peter. 2002. Winning lines. *Guardian*, August 31.

Gifford, Douglas, and Dorothy McMillan. 1997. *A history of Scottish women's writing*. Edinburgh: Edinburgh University Press.

Greenlaw, Lavinia. 2009. The public poet. *Granta*, May 5.

Gregson, Ian. 1996. *Contemporary poetry and postmodernism: Dialogue and estrangement*. Basingstoke: Macmillan.

Jameson, Fredric. 1991. *Postmodernism, or, the cultural logic of late capitalism*. London: Verso.

Kinnahan, Linda. 1996. "Look for the doing words": Carol Ann Duffy and questions of convention, 245–268. Acheson and Huk.

Kinnahan, Linda A. 2000. Now I am Alien: Immigration and the discourse of nation in the poetry of Carol Ann Duffy, 208–225. Mark and Rees-Jones.

Mackinnon, Lachlan. 1988. Review of *Selling Manhattan*, *Times Literary Supplement*, March 18–24.

McAllister, Andrew. 1988. Carol Ann Duffy. *Bête Noir* 6, 69–77.

Michelis, Angelica, and Antony Rowland (eds.). 2003. *The poetry of Carol Ann Duffy: 'Choosing tough words'*. Manchester: Manchester University Press.

Michelis, Angelica. 2003. "Me not know what these people mean": Gender and national identity in Carol Ann Duffy's Poetry, 77–98. Michelis and Rowland.

Mousley, Andy. 2013. *Literature and the human*. Abingdon: Routledge.

O'Brien, Sean. 1998. *The deregulated muse: Essays on contemporary British and Irish poetry*. Newcastle on Tyne: Bloodaxe.

O'Hagan, Sean. 2010. Shaped by War: Photographs by Don McCullin. *Observer,* February 7.

O'Rourke, Daniel (ed.). 2002. *Dream state: The new Scottish poets* [1994]. Edinburgh: Polygon.

Ong, Walter. 2002. *Orality and literacy: The technologizing of the word*. London: Routledge.

Padel, Ruth. 2002. *52 ways of looking at a poem*. London: Chatto and Windus.

Redmond, John. 2007. Lyric adaptations: James Fenton, Craig Raine, Christopher Reid, Simon Armitage, Carol Ann Duffy. In *The Cambridge companion to twentieth-century English poetry*, ed. Neil Corcoran, 245–258. Cambridge: Cambridge University Press.

Rees Jones, Deryn. 1999. *Carol Ann Duffy*. Plymouth: Northcote House.

Reid, Mark. 1992/3. Near misses are best. *Orbis* 1992/1993: 34–38.

Roberts, Neil. 1999. Carol Ann Duffy: Outsidedness and Nostalgia. In *Narrative and voice in postwar poetry*, 184–194. Essex: Longman.

Roberts, Neil. 2003. Duffy, Eliot and impersonality, 33–46. Michelis and Rowland.

Robinson, Alan. 1988. *Instabilities in contemporary British poetry*. Basingstoke: Palgrave.

Rowland, Anthony. 2003. Love and masculinity in the poetry of Carol Ann Duffy, 56–76. Michelis and Rowland.

Rumens, Carol (ed.). 1995. *Two women dancing: New and selected poems by Elizabeth Bartlett*. Tarset: Bloodaxe.

Sansom, Ian. 1995. Wayne's world. Review of *Selected Poems*, *London Review of Books*, July 6, 20.

Simic, Charles. 1985. Notes on poetry and history [1984]. *The uncertain certainty*, 124–128. Ann Arbor: University of Michigan Press.

Sinfield, Alan. 1977. *Dramatic monologue*. London: Methuen.

Smith, Stan. 2003. "What like is it?": Duffy's *différance*, 143–168. Michelis and Rowland.

Stabler, Jane. 1991. Interview with Carol Ann Duffy. *Verse* 8(2): 124–128.

Thomas, Jane. 2003. "The chant of magic words repeatedly": Gender as linguistic act in the poetry of Carol Ann Duffy, 121–142. Michelis and Rowland.

Vološinov, V.N. 1994. *Marxism and the Philosophy of Language* [1929]. Trans. L. Matejka and I.R. Titunik, [1973], Morris, 50–61.

Wilkinson, Kate. 2014. Carol Ann Duffy: A great public poet who deserves her public honour. *Guardian*, December 31.

CHAPTER 4

Words Between Women

*Few of the poems fail to send tingling subtle nerve-ends to the present ...
New myths, with deeply buried personal roots, are being forged, strange
and raw and haunting. (Rumens 1999/2000)*

'THE DREAMS / OF WOMEN WHICH WILL HARM NO ONE'

Duffy's poems register sixty years of social change surrounding gender
roles and their intrinsic sexual politics. The poems' contexts stretch from
post-war ideologies of repressive domesticity to contemporary views on
the fluidity of sexual identities and arrangements. For example, the sexist
1950s is the setting for the grandmother's voice in 'A Clear Note' (*SFN*
31) that covers three generations, and 'The Female Husband' (*Bees* 20) is
spoken by an assertive post-gendered woman who reinvents herself at the
cusp of the new millennium: 'till I reached the tip / of the century and
the lip of the next—it was nix to me / to start again with a new name, a
stranger to fame.' This timespan saw the availability of the contraceptive
pill—1961 for married women and 1974 for single women, which enabled
women to take control of the connection between sex and childbirth—
and the decriminalization of homosexuality in 1967. These revolutions
were bound up with second-wave feminism associated with the 1960s and
1970s. During the 1980s and into the 1990s, a phase of 'power feminism'
was followed by discourses around a 'third wave', characterized by diver-
sifying the concept of 'woman'. 'Third-wave' slid into the terminology

© The Editor(s) (if applicable) and The Author(s) 2016
J. Dowson, *Carol Ann Duffy*,
DOI 10.1057/978-1-137-41563-9_4

of 'post-feminism' that continues into the twenty-first century. Feminist theories that run through these 'waves' converge around the descriptions of female development by Sigmund Freud and Jacques Lacan. These theories find too prescriptive, essentializing, and demeaning Freud's account of how a girl child discovers that she is the castrated Other to the male norm, and subsequently turns away from her mother. More sympathetic for feminists, is Lacan, who viewed femininity as a construction in language that could thus be changed through language.[1] With reference to Lacan's concept of the 'mirror stage', in which an infant identifies with its reflection before language names him (or her), Patricia Waugh observes how feminist novelists since the 1980s 'push their representations to the limits of the signifying order, attempting to reverse the development from the imaginary to the symbolic', and, to this end, employ 'the subversive potential of fantasy' (1989: 169). It is this 'subversive potential of fantasy' to delve and liberate women's unarticulated desires that we find dramatized in Duffy's female-centred monologues, narratives, and lyrics. They feed and interrogate the potency of women's imaginations as they negotiate their socially scripted identities.

It is through the surrealist suspension of rational thought that many poems reach beyond the language of phallocentric signification to actualize more authentic female subjectivity. 'Dear Norman' (*SFN* 41)[2] is framed as a letter divulging how such a woman's erotic fantasy happens in the everyday. The woman writes of how she turns the paperboy into a diver 'for pearls' and swims with dolphins. Through this trip of her imagination, she exercises some agency over her needs—'I can do this'—naming the boy 'Pablo'—'because I can'. Pablo can signify a Spanish Everyman but also the poet Pablo Neruda for she gives the boy a line from one of Neruda's love poems in the original Spanish that translates as 'Body of woman, white hills, white thighs'. Such projected desire for her undulating body satiates her longing. She finds 'this,' presumably sex with the paperboy, easy and difficult. The last full stanza begins, 'As I watch him push his bike

---

[1] Toril Moi, author of the influential essay 'Female, Feminine, Feminist', revisits feminist responses to Lacan and Freud in 'From Femininity to Finitude: Freud, Lacan, and Feminism' (2004).

[2] According to Duffy, the poem is addressed to the Liverpool poet, Henry Graham, whose first name was Norman. I had placed her as the mother in 'Dear Norman' by Robert Richard that was the *Independent* newspaper's Story of the Year in 1994 and used on school examination syllabuses. http://www.independent.co.uk/life-style/the-independent-story-of-the-year-dear-norman-1423179.html

off in the rain', repeating the last line of the previous stanza as if replaying the scene over and over. The rhyme—'rain', 'name', 'pane'—accentuates how the woman's daydream is merely but powerfully fabricated by language: 'I have re-arranged / the order of the words.' The imaginary letter ends with her self-reflexive anticipation of tomorrow's fantasy in which she will 'deal with the dustman'. This kind of departure from 'mimetic or expressive realist conceptions of the fictional text' (Waugh 1989: 169) correlates to the feminist novels described by Waugh: 'Many of these texts are aesthetically self-reflexive in an axiomatically "postmodern" way, but I would argue that all articulate the processes of fictionality as functions of human desire and imagination rather than as an impersonal, intertextual play of signification' (1989: 169). Female desires are what Duffy's poetic sculptures express, explore, and nurture: 'The dreams / of women which will harm no one' ('A Clear Note', *SFN* 31). In loosely chronological order of history and Duffy's poetry volumes, this chapter traces the interplay of female fantasy and contemporary culture.

'The Untold Want'

As Waugh observes, it is through 'the subversive potential of fantasy' that women writers disturb the language of sexual difference that they unconsciously internalize and perpetuate. It is through her fantasies that Norman's letter-writer shapes her desires and makes her own meaning out of them. Thus, in the fictionalized realism of the dramatic monologue, the poet can disrupt normative rational representations of female subjectivity. Several poems satirize or undermine the voices of education and the family, institutions that constrict the developing female. They sometimes dramatize how women, too, hand down the laws of patriarchy. The speaker of 'Litany' (*MT* 9) is a girl who has to wash out her mouth after saying the 'f' word in front of her mother's company whose sombre mood resembles a church service. She scathingly rejects 'the code I learnt at my mother's knee' that she sees repellently lived out by her mother's peers whose domestic showcases—'*candlewick bedspread three piece suite display cabinet*'—are dictated by women's magazines and belie their 'terrible marriages'. Duffy cleverly periodizes the repressive atmosphere in the allusions to 'stiff-haired wives', referring to the bouffant hairstyles of the 1960s, 'pyrex'—the kitchenware that proliferated in the 1940s, cellophane and polyester—new artificial materials, and 'American Tan' stockings, a popular neutral colour that just hinted at the flesh beneath.[3] These older women's undigested misery is contingent with their brusque insistence on formality, manifest in 'poised hands over biscuits' and likened to 'cellophane round polyester shirts'. Their programmed avoidance of uncomfortable realities, such as 'cancer, or sex, or debts', contrasts to the girl's natural urge for freedom, symbolized as a butterfly wordlessly 'stammering' in her 'curious hands'.

The synchronicity of free expression and self-realization is similarly illuminated in the darkly comic poem, 'Mouth, with Soap' (*SM* 44). The title links to the last line of 'Litany' where the girl's forced apology is 'the taste of soap'. Both narratives scrutinize the cliché, 'wash your mouth out with soap', a proverbial injunction against bad language. Like the women in 'Litany', the poem's subject minds her 'Ps and Qs'—the very English expression for polite speech and behaviour, does not swear, suffers her periods, euphemized as '*Women's Trouble*', in mute privacy, does the domestic chores, and provides sex for her husband on Saturday nights. She 'clacks her wooden tongue', indicating the wooden spoon of her dull domestic occupation and the vehemence of her scolding. Her tyrannical censorship of language is 'the tight vocabulary of living death' that masks 'a constant drizzle in her heart'. This constant drizzle of unfulfilment resembles 'The Problem that has No Name' described by Betty Friedan (1963: 11–27):

> The suburban doctors, gynecologists, obstetricians, child guidance, clinicians, pediatricians, marriage counsellors and ministers who treat women's problems have all seen it, without putting a name to it, or even reporting it as a phenomenon. What they have seen confirms that for woman, as for man, the need for self-fulfillment—autonomy, self-realization, independence, individuality, self-actualization—is as important as the sexual need with as serious consequences when it is thwarted. (1963: 314)

Friedan's survey of women in America over the years 1942–1959 unwrapped the deadly 'dailyness' of prescribed marriage and motherhood that had suffocated them. She found that they 'were taught to pity the neurotic unfeminine, unhappy women who wanted to be poets or physicists or presidents' (1963: 11). Women confessed to being lonely, feeling they had failed to live up to unattainable ideals, and seeking a panacea

---

[3] American Tan hosiery is associated with the dress code for the Royal family and the extent to which it is flattering or ageing is a topic of ongoing discussions. See, http://www.xojane.co.uk/clothes/american-tan-tights-are-they-ever-ok

in tranquillizers, alcohol, and psychiatrists. The housewife in Duffy's 'Recognition' (*SM* 24) is more aware than the women in 'Litany', 'Mouth with Soap', or Friedan's survey that she has neglected self-care through raising three children, loving her husband 'through habit', and doing the household chores. Too late, she realizes that a mirror reveals 'an anxious dowdy matron' in the place of the younger version of herself when she was swept off her feet by her man. In thus condensing the life of a frustrated woman, the poem links to such works as Fay Weldon's *Praxis* (1978) that interrogate the confusion each female undergoes as she is moulded into roles by the unhappy generation before her.

Duffy's 'Big Sue and *Now, Voyager*' (*SM* 45) is woven from the American film (1942) that pertinently took its name from a Walt Whitman poem titled 'The Untold Want': 'The untold want by life and land ne'er granted, / Now, voyager, sail thou forth, to seek and find'. Whitman's phrase, 'the untold want', corresponds to Friedan's 'The Problem that has No Name' and Duffy indicates Friedan's post-war era by references to the black and white television and sherry trifles. In *Now Voyager*, the film's heroine, played by Bette Davis, was initially large, ugly, and single but escapes the control of her mother, develops into an attractive woman who finds love, albeit with a married man and never formalized. In Duffy's poem, Big Sue lives alone in a Greater London flat, is called names relating to her size, comforts herself with food, devours *Now Voyager*'s story of a woman who sought and found herself, and loves the famous line, 'don't let's ask for the moon. We have the stars'. The poem's narrative stance invites pity for Sue the fat singleton, the recognition that 'her dreams are as valid and hopeless as anyone's' (Padel 1990), and also frustration that she does not take control of her life and 'sail forth'.

Whereas 'Big Sue' is situated in popular culture, the speaker in 'Havisham' (*MT* 40) originates in Charles Dickens's canonical bildungsroman *Great Expectations* (1860). Regardless of the gap between their historical and social contexts, both monologues invite compassion for a lonely woman with unfulfilled dreams. In Dickens's novel, Miss Havisham was jilted by her fiancé on their wedding day and never recovered from the betrayal. In order to avenge the male sex, she manipulates the young Pip into falling for her beautiful ward Estella whose frozen heart breaks the hero's. Seeing events through Pip's eyes, the reader views her intention to make him suffer as unmitigated cruelty. Anticipating the revisionist dramatic monologues of *The World's Wife*, Duffy conversely conflates Havisham's woe to any contemporary reader's, running no-holes-barred vernacular—'Beloved sweetheart bastard'—across the unrhymed quatrains. The isolated and bitter word 'spinster' enacts why she cannot bear to be known as 'Miss', just 'Havisham'. Duffy's Havisham is consumed by desire for her absent husband's body and the strength of her emotion is not only presented through the harsh consonants and vocabulary about 'love's hate' but also through violent symbols, such as stabbing the wedding cake, which visualize a pain she cannot verbalize. The inexpressibility of her passion is further projected through colour symbolism: green for jealousy; puce for anger; a red balloon for life 'bursting in my face'. Thus, the same question of whether women are inexorably consigned to untold wants and thwarted dreams parallel the tragic figure in the nineteenth-century novel to the female voyeur of *Now Voyager*, and possibly to the contemporary reader.

'IT DOES NOT LOOK LIKE ME'

By foregrounding 'the untold want', Duffy explicitly muddies the distorting mirrors of socialized femininity. She also draws attention to the male gaze: sometimes she blows it up to deflate it; sometimes she reverses it by women gazing on or fantasizing about men; and sometimes she presents female subjectivity outside the male gaze altogether. In her influential essay, 'Visual Pleasure and Narrative Cinema', Laura Mulvey appropriates psychoanalytic theory to scrutinize 'the way film reflects, reveals and even plays on the straight, socially established interpretation of sexual difference which controls images, erotic ways of looking and spectacle' (Mulvey 1975: 6). As Mulvey explores, phallocentrism depends on the construction of woman as castrated, a construction that Duffy frequently exposes, complicates, or reverses. She often weaves in the language of film—'The soundtrack then was a litany' ('Litany'), 'the fizzy movie tomorrows' ('Before you were Mine')—to appropriate how the contemporary psyche assimilates cinematic imagery: 'As an advanced representation system, the cinema poses questions of the ways the unconscious (formed by the dominant order) structures ways of seeing and pleasure in looking' (Mulvey 1975: 8–9). As in 'Big Sue and *Now, Voyager*', in 'A Provincial Party, 1956' (*SFN* 40), Duffy has the reader watching a woman watching a film. The voice is that of a young wife—married for just two years—who feels rather prudish in a gathering to watch a pornographic movie. The poem swiftly periodizes the 1950s *mise en scène* with a black plastic sofa, chrome ashtray, petticoats, nail varnish on the ladder in a stocking, the discomfort of tight suspenders, a Cyril Lord carpet, and the 'Magic Moments' music. What is actually going on in the film's sex scene is a little unclear but there are two men 'up to no good'. Other women in the room are uninhibited and make the viewer uneasy as they cackle loudly, smoke, and perform sexual acts in full view. The woman watching thinks how these antics would make her mother blush, contrasts the cautious sex she has with her husband, 'with the light off', and fears the film will give him ideas, for he 'smiles / at the young, male host with film-star eyes'. Is he envying the host's sexual adventures or releasing a latent homosexuality? Either way, his wife's commentary points out the gap between the film and his performance. Furthermore, 'Her disorientation is accentuated by the fact that the film allows her no satisfactory subject position' (Robinson 1988: 197).

Thus, through the speech of women, Duffy destabilizes the male gaze as it is described by Mulvey: 'Woman then, stands in patriarchal culture as signifier for the male other, bound by a symbolic order in which man can live out his phantasies and obsessions through linguistic command by imposing them on the silent image of woman still tied to her place as bearer of meaning, not maker of meaning' (Mulvey 1975: 7). The woman in 'Alliance' (*SFN* 26) is horribly 'tied to her place' as enabler of her man's self-regard. She is French with an English husband who bullies her, humiliates her nationality, gets drunk, and 'plonks his weight down on her life'. She stays put for the sake of their children but refuses to let him come near. The monosyllabic phrase, 'her heart slammed shut', mimics the finality of her emotional shut down. The imperceptible shifts between interior monologue and third-person narrative also mediate how the wife struggles to make her own meaning: 'What she has retained of herself is a hidden grip / working her face like a glove-puppet.' 'The Brink of Shrieks' (*SM* 23), an Everywoman's confiding monologue, can read as a co-text or sequel to 'Alliance'. As the title suggests, the speaker is a woman at her wit's end who wants to brain her husband who is depicted through shorthand allusions to stereotyped masculinity—he swaggers, swears, ends up in a ditch, presumably due to drink or violence, and then withdraws: 'See him, he's not uttered a peep in weeks. / And me? I'm on the brink of shrieks.' The popular cliché, 'Up to the back teeth', is animated by a context in which someone on the edge of madness is literally lost for words and resorts to well-worn phrases. The sonnet form rubs in how her relationship is antithetical to idealized love. ('The Brink of Shrieks' was omitted from *Selected Poems* (1994) but resurrected for the *New Selected Poems* (2004), indicating its continuing relevance.)

While most often it is the female speakers who expose man's orientation to control women, the men who speak some monologues unwittingly reveal their fantasies of power. 'You Jane' (*SFN* 34) evokes the famously mythologized line, 'Me Tarzan, You Jane', associated with various popular novels and films during the twentieth century. Duffy takes the seemingly innocuous and romantic boast to expose the brutal aspects of archetypal masculinity that such habitual iconography can mask. The phrase reinforces both Freudian and Lacanian accounts of sexual difference, whereby the woman is only relative to a man as his 'Other', as they are reflected in the poem's I/she pronouns. Duffy's modern Tarzan reveals his blatant narcissism as he delights in his muscle and the services of wife—'Look at that bicep. Dinner on the table / and a clean shirt'. She cooks, washes, irons, and gives him sex at the weekends, donning suspenders at which he gazes with pleasure, even though 'she has run a bit to fat'. The speaker's belief in his superman body is repulsive as he boasts of his laddish drinking, farting, and easy 'hard-on' that he pushes at his uncomplaining woman. Between his lines, we glimpse Jane's quiet desperation, yet she snuggles up to her husband and colludes with his vainglory: 'Man of the house. Master in my own home. Solid.' As Alan Robinson comments, 'He is a caricature of subhuman machismo, peremptorily staccato in utterance, actuated solely by animal appetite' (1988: 196). In 'Human Interest' (*SFN* 36), however, the division between oppressor and victim is more blurred. The man is imprisoned for stabbing his girlfriend when he found she had cheated on him. The confessional form of the dramatic monologue allows his defence—that he just acted out of love—to win the reader's sympathy. Alternatively, it can read like the self-deception of a 'Tarzan' whose dominated woman took comfort elsewhere. If we put 'Human Interest' in dialogue with 'You Jane', men's speech is proved to be the courier of phallocentric gender codes, albeit often unconsciously. In 'Statement' (*SM* 32), Duffy's camera again zooms in on masculine aggression, signified by a contorted face and clenched fists. However, the title frames the narrative as a witness statement by a son who abhors his father's violence to his mother. Now grown-up, the narrator concedes that the anger of his Irish 'Da' was attributable to the political situation but also relays its impact on the family. His drunken father would bruise his mother's breasts, yell through the night, and had not attended to his wife sexually since their other son was conceived twenty-one years earlier. The older sibling giving 'the statement', who cried '*Mammy, / Mammy*' at the time, is now an adult but forever scarred by the past.

'Standing Female Nude' (*SFN* 46), the dramatic monologue of a life model, explicitly reverses the male gaze. Duffy's nude exposes how patriarchal language fixes the female form for the purposes of pleasure. She clearly resists such fixity: for a start, she is speaking to him, and in repeating to herself and the reader, as silent eavesdropper, the artist's plea to 'be still', she evokes the imperative of feminine passivity that she is refusing. The model both endorses and mocks the Freudian idea of an Oedipus complex by stating that the artist links her to his mother, dipping his brush into the paint to 'possess' her. Like the writer's pen, the painter's brush signifies the male penis that exercises control over the woman. Empoweringly, she calls him 'little man' and positions him with her as a socialized Other, in that both 'make our living how we can'. Furthermore, she reduces his creativity to phallocentric scopophilia: 'he stiffens for my warmth'. Duffy sets the monologue in France—the man's name is Georges and he pays her in francs—and accentuates the painter's pretensions about the status of his art. While the public might rate him a 'genius', she experiences his cold room and his need to paint in order to eat. Furthermore, Duffy's nude envisages how her portrait will be hung in a gallery where the Queen of England will be 'gazing / on my shape', and will parrot 'magnificent' in unconscious mimicry of male voyeurism. The pretensions of art critics are also undercut in the phrase 'the bourgeoisie will coo' and in the prostitute's vulgar terminology for the parts they will admire, 'Belly nipple arse'. Here, the poem echoes Stevie Smith's 'Salon D'Autumne' (1937) that impersonates the erotic and sadistic scopophilia of critics who look at pictures of naked ladies: 'This is the Slap school of art, / It would be nice / To smack them / Slap, slap, slap, / That would be nice' (Smith 1981: 240–1). Duffy's final swipe is the nude's concluding: 'It does not look like me.' When reading the poem aloud, Duffy emphasizes the 'me', as if the nude is announcing her sense of self that eludes the artist's attempt at representation. The woman's ownership of her body—in the emphatic 'me' and 'my shape'—is crucial to her self-realization.

If 'Georges' refers to the French Cubist Georges Braque (1882–1963), 'it does not look like me' is as much a witty comment on abstract art as a feminist refusal of the artist's version of her. Both readings can be put in productive dialogue and push towards the dynamism of postmodern feminism that celebrates the artistic release from realism. Duffy's ekphrastic 'Three Paintings' (*SM* 41–3) also disturb male, supposedly naturalistic, 'ways of seeing and pleasure in looking' at a woman. 'The One–Eyed Flautist Plays for the Prince', based on the painting 'The One–Eyed Flautist' by an unknown artist associated with the French School in 1566, directly disables the male gaze in that the speaker only has one eye.

In Browningesque manner, Duffy has the flautist address an audience in the poem, a prince who finds it uncomfortable to look at the deviant form: 'Your gaze drops / to the floor, you fumble awkwardly.' More painfully, the flautist, seeing how the prince's mistress is uncomfortable and leaves the scene, longs to be whole in her eyes. Thus, Duffy cleverly privileges the gaze of the woman over the anxiously disfigured man and invites sympathy for how he feels inwardly subhuman. However, the flautist can transform his pain at being discarded into heavenly music, just as the poet can transport both writer and audience to a realm beyond the reductive typology of gender norms.

Duffy capitalizes on surrealism's defiance of narrative coherence to penetrate areas of the unconscious in which phallocentrism is embedded and where it can thus be uprooted. She reworks Max Ernst's disturbing painting, 'The Young Virgin Spanking the Infant Jesus in Front of Three Witnesses' (1926), in 'The Virgin Punishing the Infant', the second of the 'Three Paintings' sequence. Biographically, Ernst was angry at what he saw as brutality in the Catholic Church and Duffy confirms yet softens his intervention in religious sentimentality. Ernst's picture disrupts ideologies of feminine purity and passivity, particularly as perpetuated in Catholic iconographies of the Virgin Mary. Usually portrayed in blue to symbolize her purity, in Ernst's painting, Mary wears red, a universal symbol for sexuality and passion, and the baby's bottom is disturbingly crimson from the force of the mother's beating. Duffy's monologue is in the condemning yet sympathetic voice of the onlookers, taken from the figures peeping through the window in Ernst's picture. In contemporary idiomatic speech, they relay how Mary longed for a child that was ordinary, who said 'goo goo' not 'I am God', and how her husband Joseph's absorption in his work exacerbates her isolation. The evocation of looking at a painting in which the dominant social group watches in judgment on a woman beating her baby potently presents a kaleidoscope of perspectives. At the poem's core, however, Duffy takes Ernst's anarchic portrayal of maternal love to re-inscribe its authenticity and force. The third of 'Three Paintings', 'Jane Avril Dancing', is based on the famous Parisian cancan dancer who mesmerized Toulouse Lautrec (1864–1901) and featured in many of his works. Through the voice of the diminutive (4'6") artist who desires the dancer but is socially and sexually impotent, Duffy exposes and diminishes the male gaze: 'I thought her lovely still. I am a man susceptible / to beauty.' The 'still' means both passive, as in the 'be still' in 'Standing Female Nude', and 'always'. The logic shifts between the coherent female voice, '*What are you staring at? Buy me a bleeding drink! Jane Avril / yelled in rough red French*', and the inchoate longing of the man who watches her: '*la la la* Jane Avril dancing'. So, a dancer in Parisian low culture who is stared at on the posters associated with the Moulin Rouge hypnotizes Lautrec who finds himself speaking in the language of *her* unconscious that expresses itself in music and movement: '*la la la*'. Thus, in all three pictures Duffy destabilizes the male gaze and disrupts narrative logic to reconfigure representations of female normativity.

'The Way My Mother Speaks'

If, as Lacan asserts, 'the unconscious is structured like a language' and language is imposed on women by the patriarchal symbolic order, how can women represent a sensed female identity in the language that assigned them to 'lack', to otherness? As previously discussed, one method is to rupture or deconstruct the artistic and linguistic signs that fix her. Some of Duffy's poems expose the unconscious collusion of women in the socialization of girls; in other poems, it is the woman who derives scopophiliac pleasure; elsewhere, Duffy constructs female subjectivity apart from men altogether. 'Small Female Skull' (*MT* 25) epitomizes feminist deconstructions of the phallocentric concept of 'woman' in the self-reflexive monologue of the subject gazing at her own skull: 'For some time, I sit on the lavatory seat with my head / in my hands, appalled.' As Avril Horner comments, Duffy's figure echoes Shakespeare's Hamlet when he holds Yorrick's skull and also Auguste Rodin's sculpture, 'Le Penseur' ('The Thinker'), which, thus appropriated prove that women too can philosophize, and, what is more, can do so seated on the lavatory. Horner also sees in the reference to 'small' a retort to nineteenth-century medical-philosophy that elided the smaller size of women's brains with an inferior ability to think (Horner 2003: 100–2). Duffy's surrealist collage reveals the speaker accepting and loving the person beneath the skin, 'much lighter than I'd thought'. She holds the skull to the mirror as if to fuse a distinctly female self with its reflection. Thus, she completes healthily the mirror stage towards self-identification described by Lacan.

Therefore, along with female agency in language, positive female–female identification is a path to self-realization. 'A Clear Note' (*SFN* 27–31) consists of three parts, each one spoken by a woman representing her generation. Their internal monologues reveal a nexus of desires and restraints that repeats from mother to daughter and that also unravels as time moves on. The first part, 'Agatha', relates the life of a mother, presumably a Catholic since she was born in Ireland, who moved with her husband to Glasgow, and had eight children. The 'scunner' would come home from work and take her for sex before removing his boots, never kissing her goodnight nor noticing her dejection. The pejorative epithet 'scunner' expresses her aversion towards him that she kept to herself. She further fulfils the script for feminine self-abnegation by working as a nurse for the dying. Agatha has lost the will and words to express and thus to realize herself: 'I had a voice once, but it's broken / and cannot recall the unspoken words / I tried to whisper in his closed ear. / *Look at the moon. My darling. The moon.*' Like Friedan's housewives or the women objectified in Duffy's male monologues, Agatha can see no way out, 'till one of us is dead'. Agatha tells her daughter, Moll, how she [Agatha] was once good looking, confident, and had dreams. She charges Moll and Moll's daughter, Bernadette, to remember how she was before she aged and lost her looks, identity, and dignity. However, the bonds between grandmother, daughter, and granddaughter compensate for the misery brought on by her marriage: 'What laughs, Moll, for you and me / to swim in impossible seas. You've a daughter / yourself now to talk through the night. / I was famous for my hats. Remember.' Moll, now forty-nine years old, who speaks part two, echoes these lines; and they are echoed again by Bernadette whose monologue is part three. Whereas Moll suggests greater fulfilment and freedom than Agatha—her husband still loves her after twenty-five years of marriage; she smokes, drinks, and has some independence of mind—she is still tied to the kitchen and 'there would be fights' if she flew out to visit her daughter due to his suspicion that she would be unfaithful. Like her mother, Moll still feels the 'untold want': 'There's something out there / that's passing me by. Are you following me?' This rhetorical question to her daughter asks whether this longing is inexorable for women. Bernadette, however, *is* socially liberated—'For we swim with ease in all / possible seas'—and her grandmother's 'silence / and lovelessness' place her 'years away / from the things that seem natural to us'. Like the heroine of *Now Voyager*, Bernadette has heeded the 'clear note' of her 'thousand mothers': '*Away, while you can, and travel the world.*'

'A Clear Note' dramatizes the interactions between women's psyche and their conditioning as exemplified in the poems discussed earlier. It again presents how women are most trapped by a limiting inner vision but also how they can challenge and change the pattern of history. As Moll puts it, '*Never have kids. Give birth to yourself*', and the poem ends with the

WORDS BETWEEN WOMEN 135

shoots of spring flowers appearing from the grandmother's grave. Dreams give women a psychological exit from stifling circumstances and the strength to act. When Agatha's heart freezes, she asks, 'Is it mad to dream then?' … 'I had forgotten how to dream', and Moll dreams of walking 'out the door' … 'But then / there's the dinner to cook'. Nevertheless, she can roam 'inside myself, have / such visions you'd not credit. The best times / are daydreams with a cigarette.' Finally, Bernadette imagines her mother thinking of her and affirms, 'The dreams / of women which will harm no one.' The ability to dream is one answer to Freud's 'great question … "What does a woman want?"' (Jones 1955: 421).

Like the bonding across the generations in 'A Clear Note', in 'The Way My Mother Speaks' (*TOC* 54), Duffy's mother's phrases reverberate in her daughter's consciousness and renders her 'free, in love / with the way my mother speaks'. In similar vein, 'Before You Were Mine' (*MT* 13), depicts how the girl, also autobiographically Duffy, delights in imagining the life of her mother before she married and had a child. It is based on a photograph, in which her mother is laughing with her female friends, and on her mother's stories of how she would dance, date, and stay out late, and how she would consider her mother's scolding a small price to pay for the fun. In 'Cord' (*FG* 61–2), dedicated to Ella, it is Duffy who is the mother unbreakably bonded to her daughter. Drawing on images from fairy tales, she appropriates the archetypal quest narrative to a girl seeking her umbilical cord and finding the magnetism between mother and baby in the magic all around her. This life-giving nature of a harmonious mother–daughter dyad is reinforced by Naomi Wolf: 'The links between generations of women need mending if we are to save one another from the beauty myth, and save women's progress from its past historical fate— the periodic reinvention of the wheel' (1991: 283). Susie Orbach also sees a healthy relationship to the body as resting on 'an account of the feminine psychological development that occurs in the female to female ambience of the mother-daughter relationship' (2005: xxvii). These contemporary sociologists resonate with Virginia Woolf's cry for a female literary lineage: 'for we think back through our mothers if we are women' (1977: 83).

Feminist Talking Heads: *The World's Wife* (1999)

The so-called Girl Power of the 1990s can be seen as a retort to Freud's question, 'What does a woman want?' The Spice Girls' debut hit 'Wannabe' (1996) explicitly recites, 'I'll tell you what I want, what I really really want'.

The brazen female 'I', that presumes to speak for young women collectively, unashamedly wields control: she insists that a lover appreciates her, does more giving than taking, and satisfies her in bed. 'Wannabe's lyrics also assert the supreme value of female friendships: 'If you wanna be my lover, you gotta get with my friends (gotta get with my friends), / Make it last forever friendship never ends'. Duffy's witty sequence of dramatic monologues that she performed through the second half of the 1990s, before they were published as *The World's Wife* (1999), resound with similar self-possession: the women declare what they do and do not want in a man and several prefer the company of women. As indicated in the volume's title, Duffy takes the popular saying, 'the world and his wife', to overturn the atavistic concept of woman as man's accessory. Her thirty heroines, taken from history, myth, and popular film or music, are transposed into contemporary Everywoman types. The book connects with the period's many revisionist works that redeem Woman from the polarities of purity or evil, such as Liz Lochhead's 'The Complete Alternative History of the World, Part One' (1991:12): 'I'm not your Little Woman / I'm not your Better Half / I'm not your nudge, your snigger / or your belly laugh. / I'm not Jezebel // I'm not Jezebel // and I'm not Delilah / I'm not Mary Magdalen / Or the Virgin Mary either'. As Toril Moi avers, 'since patriarchy has always tried to silence and repress women and women's experience, rendering them visible is clearly an important anti-patriarchal strategy' (1997: 107). Furthermore, she famously argues, 'Feminists ... must therefore always insist that though women undoubtedly are *female* that in no way guarantees that they will be feminine. This is equally true whether one defines femininity in the old patriarchal ways or in a new feminist way' (Moi 1997: 108). The diversity of Duffy's wives (and sisters) blasts any female essentialism, feminine homogeneity, and any 'binary system related to "the" couple, man/woman' (Cixous 1997: 91). They can be irreverent—'By Christ, he could bore for Purgatory' ('Mrs Aesop' 19), vulgar—'We were a hard school, tough as fuck, / all of us beautiful and rich' ('Mrs Beast' 73), pleasure-seeking—'Remember the skills of the tongue, / to lick, to lap, to loosen, lubricate, to lie / in the soft pouch of the face' ('Circe' 47), violent—'*Kill each mother's son*' ('Queen Herod' 9), beautiful ('Salome' 56–7), ugly ('Mrs Quasimodo' 34–9), tender—'I nibbled the purse of his ear' ('Delilah' 28–9), and vulnerable—'I ... was soft, was pliable'—albeit as an act ('Pygmalion's Bride' 51–2). They want sex, sometimes with men, sometimes with women, and sometimes both from ('from Mrs Tiresias' 14–17). Apart from 'Anne Hathaway' (30), marriage—

unsurprisingly, given the book's title—comes across no more positively than in Duffy's other volumes. Most reviving is maternal love: 'I saw her at last, walking, / my daughter, my girl, across the fields' ('Demeter' 76).

Duffy milks the dramatic monologue's appeal to the reader to identify, sympathize with, and judge the speaker, often all at once. Sometimes, the wife directly addresses the 'girls', as in 'Eurydice' (58–62) and 'Mrs Beast' (73). All speakers assume women's empathy and a consensus that all men are fools—'that's him, pushing the stone up the hill, the jerk' (Mrs Sisyphus' 21), or cheats—'Here you come / with a shield for a heart / and a sword for a tongue / and your girls, your girls' ('Medusa' 41). Most unequivocal is the four-lined 'Mrs Icarus' (54) who watches her husband fly too close to the sun due to his undoubtedly male hubris. She announces, as if on behalf of all womankind, 'he's a total, utter, absolute, Grade A pillock'. Similarly, Mrs Darwin (20) mocks her husband's grand theories of evolution when she quips that the chimpanzee reminds her of him. Regarding men's sexual performance, 'Frau Freud' (55), the wife of the Austrian psychologist renowned for his theory of 'penis envy', mocks his obsession with the male organ and comes out with a string of popular euphemisms for it. In this fourteen-line anti-sonnet, Freud's wife feels pity, not envy, for her husband's phallus that is 'not pretty'.

At their crudest, then, the wives simply supplant male with female power and nurture female community, enhanced by knowing looks and laughter at live readings. However, although the monologues can seem ingenuous because of their entertainment value, they also confront the formulaic influences of myth by rewriting them with a complex psychology not found in the originating stories. Eurydice is explicit: 'Girls, forget what you've read. / It happened like this –' (61). Her side of the story about Orpheus sending her back to the underworld by looking round on their way out is that it was she who wanted him to return her there because she felt more at peace with the dead than in the daylight world of 'our life': marriage to Orpheus was a living death. She mocks her poet-husband's arrogance and refers to him as the 'Big O' mimicking a big empty mouth to suggest that his poetry was vacuous and that he bragged of great orgasms. Thus, Eurydice sounds like a woman of any place or time having a gossip but who is inwardly drowning. Similarly, the enjoyment of 'Mrs Aesop' is in her impertinent mockery of her husband's tedious talk, their dull marriage, and his failings to fulfil her sexually, due to his 'little cock that didn't crow'. Yet, like Eurydice, beneath the female bravado is an undertow of sadness and frustration. 'Mrs Rip Van Winkle' (53), takes the proverbial story literally by relating how the man who slept for a hundred years uses Viagra and arouses his aged wife from her slumber for some pleasure. Again, Duffy validates women's sexual needs and also charts history, for it was in 1998 that Viagra became available as a treatment for men's erectile dysfunction.

Duffy asserts, "'My aim is to find hidden truths or fresh ways of looking at familiar things. In some ways, several poems in *The World's Wife* are love poems about men; they're poems of regret that perhaps the initial relationship has ended through selfishness. But I see this as a loving book'" (Wood 2005). As she suggests, some monologues thrive on their strong narrative thrust whereby the audience revels in her fanciful appropriation of familiar stories. 'Mrs Midas' (11–13), for example, draws in her audience by their knowledge of the myth but adds a scene of their marriage before Midas is granted his wish to turn everything he touches to gold. His wife elaborates on what that means when, at a mundane level, food, the toilet, and wildlife become cold objects. As always, Duffy plays with idioms, clichés, and proverbs: 'Look, we all have wishes; granted. / But who has wishes granted?' More seriously, the wife depicts how their happiness was ruined by her husband's lust for wealth and mourns: 'I miss most / even now, his hands, his warm hands on my skin, his touch'. 'Mrs Faust' (23–7) is married to a man whose acquisitiveness takes over until he has no soul. Other wives do love their husbands, at least at first. Mrs Quasimodo, like her husband, has a physical defect yet she relates how they lived happily until he went off with the beautiful gipsy girl, Esmerelda in Victor Hugo's *The Hunchback of Notre Dame* (1831) from where Duffy's Quasimodo is taken. His rejection means she hates herself for being ugly and, unable to conform to expectations of feminine beauty, she goes into self-exile. Feeling an outcast, she avenges her husband by cutting down all the bells and thereby also deprives the human race of the means to celebrate communal occasions. 'Mrs Lazarus' (49–50) is Duffy's invention around the Biblical account of the man who died but was raised to life again by Christ (*The Bible*, John 10). Duffy wittily shifts the usual emphasis on the sisters' joy at being reunited with their brother to the implications for his widow. Taking poetic licence with the original timespan of three days, Duffy persuasively presents the scenario of a woman who has endured her husband's extended illness, the trauma of his death, elaborate public mourning, and her own private agony, through a highly charged exploration of grieving: '[I] howled, shrieked, clawed / at the burial stones till my hands bled, retched'. The emotional intensity is heightened by the consonance, dissonance, and assonance with which the poet is so adept. Through Mrs Lazarus, she also relates the 'hidden truths' in what follows loss: packing up the clothes, unexpectedly coming across one of Lazarus's hairs in a book; missing him physically; but eventually she moves on and finds comfort with another man, the schoolteacher. This twist in the narrative raises questions about fidelity to the deceased that confront every bereaved partner.

In her characters from classical myths, Duffy follows the playful treatment of Ovid in *The Metamorphoses*. Their unifying themes of 'mutability, love, violence, artistry, and power' (Wheeler 1999: 40) are made relevant through the contemporary idioms. As already discussed in 'Eurydice', the monologues humanize the women, exposing their betrayal or neglect by men. However, they also retain Ovid's highly fantastical depiction of the characters' shape shifting. 'Penelope' (70–1), the archetypal wife-in-waiting, is in a line of modern rewrites, from James Joyce's Molly Bloom in *Ulysses* (1922) to Margaret Atwood's *The Penelopiad* (2005). Duffy's version of the longsuffering woman gives her an autonomy lacking in Homer's epic of Odysseus who came back after a long journey only to leave again. The situation would connect with the wives of contemporary serviceman who wait fearfully for news. However, Duffy's patient Penelope refuses sentimentality, gets used to her husband's absence, and becomes, 'self-contained, absorbed, content'. Through her embroidery, she creates alternative worlds 'of love, lust, loss, lessons learnt' in which she revels. Again, it is the power of daydream that transforms her and renders the more vivid experience. 'Thetis' (5–6), the sea goddess, takes various forms to accommodate a stream of men: 'So I shopped for a suitable shape. / Size 8. Big mistake. / Coiled in my charmer's lap, / I felt the grasp of his strangler's clasp / At my nape.' It is difficult not to find a feminist lens on her story of how she would dance to the tune of a man but then 'learn' that it brings abuse, domination, disappointment, and rejection. Moreover, it is in having the prophesied child and becoming a mother that Thetis is fulfilled. 'Medusa' (40–1), the gorgon whose gaze could turn men to stone so her head was cut off, tells a tale of 'love gone bad'. In Duffy's version, she loves her husband but he is unfaithful—'I know you'll go, betray me, stray from home'—and it is gnawing jealousy that manifests as snakes in her hair. Instead of the malicious figure depicted in myth, she is a lonely woman who laments the loss of her looks and her man's attentions: 'Wasn't I beautiful? / Wasn't I fragrant and young? // Look at me now'. 'Circe' (47–8), who in myth turns Ulysses's men into pigs, is, according to Ovid, a woman in love and slighted. In Duffy's monologue, the enchantress devours the bodies of the pigs with a mix of revenge and sexual enjoyment as 'the sweetmeats slipped / from the slit, bulging, vulnerable bag of the balls'. The constant rhyming mimics Circe's magic spells and, like a radical feminist, she speaks of men *as* pigs. However, she also challenges such generalized aversion by establishing their individuality: 'each pig's face / was uniquely itself, as many handsome as plain, / the cowardly face, the brave, the comical, noble, / sly or wise, the cruel, the kind'.

Thus, *The World's Wife* may not be anti-men but it is rated 'the most radical book of poetry to be published for years in that it systematically undermines the myths by which masculinity has been sustained for millennia' (Smith 2000). In Ovid's *Metamorphoses*, Pygmalion falls in love with the sculpture he made, a near parallel to Narcissus who falls in love with his own image. Satirizing men's inability to love anything other than themselves, 'Pygmalion's Bride' (51–2) is in the voice of the sculpture he loves but only when she is his inanimate object. Initially, she stayed still as a statue –'Shtum'—but is as good as dead, so she warms herself up to get close to him but he runs off. 'Mrs Sisyphus' (21–2) is married to a man who neglects her due to being tied up in his dead-end job. In mythology, Sisyphus is a king punished for being deceitful and condemned to interminably push a huge stone up a hill only to watch it roll down again. The pleasure here is clearly that of the storyteller whose exaggerated rhyme— 'jerk', 'kirk', 'irk', berk', 'dirk'—parodies and rejects the symbolic order of language.

While the sex war is maintained and enjoyed in the humour and female empowerment, elsewhere, Duffy muddles oppositional formulations of sexual difference without rendering the categories 'man' and 'woman' superfluous. In 'Delilah' (28–9), she arguably emasculates but also humanizes the archetypal strong man Samson for he wants 'to learn how to care'. He renounces his machismo for the qualities of a New Man, arguably a utopian ideal in women's imaginations. The first recorded use of the phrase is 1982 in a review of the film 'Tootsie' and during the 1990s it was in widespread circulation, but as Tom de Castella reflects, 'The New Man was once a radical way to describe a male who wholeheartedly accepted equality in domestic life. … Today the New Man is like a relic of gender history' (2014).[4] At his bequest, Delilah cuts off every lock of

---

[4] '"Tootsie" has enough rowdy, inconsequential fun in it to take the curse off Hoffman's sentimentalized notion of The New Man, but it's also in the nature of a lucky tightwire act

her husband's hair in order to weaken him—a new spin on the Bible story in which she is the sneaky femme fatale (*The Bible*, Judges 16). 'Pilate's Wife' (18), however, describes her husband's feminine hands and cowardly nature in a disparaging way. In the Biblical account, she warns him in a dream to let the Christ go but Pontius Pilate weakly capitulates to the crowd.

In 'from Mrs Tiresias' (14–17), also plucked from Ovid's tales, Duffy uses the figure of the mythological prophet with female breasts to imagine being the wife of a man who cross-dresses or who has a sex change. Tiresias is depicted as the 'old man with wrinkled dugs' in T.S. Eliot's *The Waste Land* and Duffy reinforces the allusion by giving the wife's new lover 'violet eyes' that reproduce 'the violet hour' in which Eliot's Tiresias speaks. Typically, Duffy plays the story for laughs but subtly asks if we view sexual orientation as dictated by nurture or nature. When her Tiresias takes a male lover when he becomes a woman, his wife takes a female one. Discussing the poem, Jeffrey Wainwright (2003) refers to the part in Ovid's tale where Juno and Jupiter have a quarrel over whether men or women derive more pleasure from sex and Tiresias, in his unique position of having been both, is able to answer but annoys Juno by letting out the secret that women have the better time. Accordingly, Duffy's poem signifies how female sex is best. Like the 'de // da de da de da' in 'Girlfriends' (*TOC* 43), the 'wet red cry in the night', uttered by Tiresias's wife with her female lover, corresponds to Lacan's term *jouissance* for specifically female orgasmic pleasure that exceeds intelligible language.[5] As the authors concur in *Backwards in High Heels: The Difficult Art of Being Female*, '[Sex] is also the one most uncomplicated area where women really do beat the men hands down' (Kindersley and Vine 2000: 314).

Thus, in postmodern flirtation with the grand narratives of history, Duffy takes stories from different periods to undercut the binary formulations of sex and gender that they perpetuate. The recurring clashes and exchanges between men and women, sexual orientations, or high and low cultures, are evocatively portrayed through new contexts. On the level of substituting famous men with women, we have 'Queen Kong' (31–3), who is larger than

that comes close to tripping him up,' *Washington Post* (17 December 1982). The *Oxford English Dictionary* defines the New Man as someone 'who rejects sexist attitudes and the traditional male role, esp. in the context of domestic responsibilities and childcare, and who is (or is held to be) caring, sensitive, and non-aggressive' (OED.com 3b).

[5] For some discussion about Lacan's theories of *jouissance* see Jacqueline Rose (1982) and Toril Moi (2004).

the huge gorilla originally created in the 1933 film *King Kong*, and 'Elvis's Twin Sister' (66–7), which is prefaced by Madonna's famous line, 'Elvis is alive and she's female'. His sister lives like a nun in the rock star's estate, Graceland, and her speech is littered with the titles of his songs. It is a tribute to his music but her humble simplicity is also an antidote to her brother's egotism. 'The Kray Sisters' (63–6) is a comical narrative of what the language of hardened criminals sounds like in the mouth of women. Just as the brothers had a role model for boxing in their maternal grandfather, Duffy's Kray sisters lost their mother at birth and learned their 'vocation' from their grandmother, a 'tough suffragette'; she is a version of Emily Wilding Davison (1872–1913), famous for losing her life from injuries incurred when trying to attach a Votes for Women sash to the king's horse on Derby Day. The sisters inhabit a more modern world and 'wanted respect' for their ability to drive, go into a bar, and have sex: 'We admit, bang to rights, that the fruits / of feminism—fact—made us rich, feared, famous, / friends of the stars'. Like the bisexual Ronald Kray, the sisters allude to their female pin ups, 'Vita and Violet'. Vita Sackville West was the upper-class bisexual friend and lover of Virginia Woolf while Violet Trefusis was another of Vita's lovers.[6] Thus, Duffy typically meshes icons of high literature and popular culture. The monologue ends with the sisters feeling vitalized by the popular hit from Nancy Sinatra, 'These Boots are Made for Walking', released in 1966. We can refer back to the bully husbands in 'Statement' and 'A Clear Note' whose boots kept their women subservient, and to the women who wanted to walk out of the door in parts two and three of 'A Clear Note'. If there is any coherent perspective in the tale, the Kray Sisters lament the loss of feminism's potency and they value female sisterhood over heterosexual partnerships, berating girls who got 'Engaged' or became 'some plonker's wife'. In their manifesto, the slogan, 'A boyfriend's for Christmas, not just for life', parodies the popular campaign for dogs that started in 1978.

The violence in women like the Kray Sisters can be unsettling, just like the revisionist fairy stories in *The Bloody Chamber* (1979) in which Angela Carter nails the idea that women are made of 'sugar and spice and all that's nice'.[7] 'The Devil's Wife' (42–6) does not mention Myra Hindley, wife

---

[6] Sackville West is the subject of Woolf's novel *Orlando* (1928) that includes an indirect allusion to the affair between Vita and Violet; pertinently, Orlando transforms from a man to a woman half way through Woolf's novel. It was adapted to stage in 1989 and to film in 1992.

[7] This is taken from the nursery rhyme, 'What are Little Boys made of?', from The *Baby's Opera* by Walter Crane (circa 1877). Interestingly, in verse 4, 'what are young women made of?', the answer is 'ribbons and laces, and sweet pretty faces'.

of her co-murderer Ian Brady, but such details as her 'peroxide hair' and the Yorkshire dialect—'nowt'—make her recognizable. Duffy does not ask the reader to sympathize with the speaker but to examine the psychology at work when a man and woman bring out the menace in one another. 'Queen Herod' (7–10), wife of the king who had all the boys under two put to death to make sure that the prophesied Messiah, the Christ child born in Bethlehem, could not survive, is the one responsible for the ghastly act. In the Bible's version, all the women are wailing but in Duffy's tale, the Queen is visited by three queens, not the wise men from the East, and has all the boys killed in order to protect her daughter. Interviewed about *The World's Wife*, Duffy believes a woman would do anything to protect her child: "'I was also thinking of the Fairies in the story of Sleeping Beauty ... who come bearing gifts—not of gold, frankincense and myrrh, but grace, strength and happiness. And I imagined this as a sort of filmic poem, with the camels, etc."' (Wood 2005). On the level of its narrative, 'Mrs Herod' is indeed highly imaginative and asserts the supremacy of women over all types of men: 'Who? *Him. The Husband. Hero. Hunk. / The Boy Next Door. The Paramour. The* Je t'adore. / *The Marrying Kind. Adulterer. Bigamist. / The Wolf. The Rip. The Rake. The Rat. / The Heartbreaker. The Ladykiller. Mr Right.*' The Queen enjoys sex with the three visiting queens who warn against the birth of all *man*kind and lead her to destroy it: 'No *man*, I swore, / *will make her shed one tear.*' Using collective pronouns, she declares that women will walk through blood for their children for behind their mild lullabies lies the strength of an army.

In *The World's Wife*, Duffy creates an array of women who collectively demonstrate many models of their sex, thus defying Freudian essential-ism or cultural typology. Whereas Chaucer's wife of Bath, whose tale, in its turn, was influenced by Ovid, answers Freud's ultimate question by revealing that women want 'sovereignty', Duffy, expresses, explores, and validates the multiplicity of women's desires. At one end, we have Anne Hathaway, about whom little is known except that Shakespeare famously left to her the 'second best bed' in his will. Duffy overturns the assump-tion that she was relegated to second best by suggesting that this was the spare-room bed used for their mutual lovemaking. At the other end of the female spectrum, what the women really really want is to have it all: sex, freedom, loyal fulfilling husbands, and the choice to reject the need for men altogether. Duffy is adamant that the poems are about love and there are celebrations of man–woman love in the laments for its departure and disappointments. 'from Mrs Tiresias' or 'The Kray Sisters' embody sexu-ality as a continuum across demarcations of gender. Nevertheless, most powerful and generative is maternal love, as depicted in 'Thetis' (5–6), for whom giving birth turned her 'inside out', or 'Queen Herod' who would stop at nothing to safeguard her child. The book's last monologue, 'Demeter' (76) models the serene relationship between the goddess of harvest and her daughter, Persephone. It resounds with the love flagged in the volume's dedication to 'May and Jackie and Ella with love', Duffy's mother, her then partner, and her daughter.

FEMININE GOSPELS: 'AND HER PLEASURES WERE STORIES, TRUE OR FALSE'

Following on from *The World's Wife*, in *Feminine Gospels* (2002), Duffy also deconstructs the 'gospel' truth about femininity as it pervades myth in seemingly ineradicable forms. The world's wives speak back against the silencing and fixing of women as man's appendage then prove their anti-feminine sexual desires, humour, greed, jealousy, violent impulses, and autonomy. However, the poems in *Feminine Gospels* reflect Julia Kristeva's argument in her influential essay, 'Women's Time': 'the struggle is no longer concerned with the quest for equality but, rather, with difference and specificity' (Kristeva 1997: 200). Instead of tackling Freud's essentializing account of feminine development, Kristeva observes women's attempts in the contemporary arts 'to break the code, to shatter language, and find a specific discourse closer to the body and emotions, to the unnamable repressed by the social contract' (1989: 204). Duffy's poetic shatterings of narrative coherence correlate to contemporary fictions that evade the either/or of realist counter-discourse and postmodern self-reflexivity. We have seen the many angles from which Duffy's fictional women individually express an unconscious 'want' or their conscious fantasies. As Waugh states: 'Given the acute contradictoriness of women's lives and sense of subjectivity, it is not surprising that many contemporary women writers have sought to "displace" their desires, seeking articulation not through the rational and metonymic structures of realism but through the associative and metaphorical modes of fantasy' (Waugh 1989: 171).

In *Feminine Gospels*, disjunctive surrealist images dig out the essentializing myths about women buried deep into the collective and individual unconscious. 'The Long Queen' (1–2) is a personification of all the stereotypes in ancient, fairy, folk, and modern tales that are signified by castles, towers, woods, rags, and swooning. The length of the lines and the whole poem mediate the longevity of these stories:

What was she queen of? Women, girls,

spinsters and hags, matrons, wet nurses,

witches, widows, wives, mothers of all these.

Her word of law was in their bones, in the graft

of their hands, in the wild kicks of their dancing.

No girl born who wasn't the Long Queen's always child.

The narrator replicates how femininity is conceived in the polarized extremes of the pretty princess or the ugly hag. The italicized key words—*childhood, blood, tears, childbirth*—the four laws for women, mark how the biologically determining factors of being female are elided with self-fulfilling assumptions of femininity: 'when a girl / first bled to be insignificant, no cause for complaint'. Duffy ends by asserting how women unwittingly acquiesce in the conspiracies to hide their pain by handing down stories, 'true or false', that, for example, teach a woman that the pain of childbirth 'was worth it'. These stories are 'the light music of girls' but 'the drums of women'; the nimble rhythm imitates the young women's optimism while the heavier tread fits the vigour of their elders. The personified queen 'of all the dead / when they lived if they did so female', is a restive play on words: it means that the archetype of feminine suffering rules the entire female population and it also celebrates the strength of mind and heart that women wield. 'The Map-Woman' (3–7) also uses 'the associative and metaphorical modes of fantasy', in its defamiliarizing tale of someone whose skin bears the marks of her experience, 'her own small ghost', and who finally removes it to reinvent herself: 'There it all was, back // To front in the glass.' The mirror here indicates how the skin she constructed was but a simulacrum because the familiar landmarks of her life were 'only façade'. We might view the description of the woman removing her skin as debunking fears around ageing, but it correlates more to what Waugh notes in postmodern fictions: 'The alienation and estrangement from their bodies experienced by the female protagonists as a consequence of their gender positioning releases a desire for transformation not simply of the body as an individual corporeal unit, but of the whole social structure' (Waugh 1989: 170). 'Sub' (29–31) is a light-hearted and surreal account of a woman who rewrites history by inserting herself into famous male feats: she can be famous in sport, land on the moon, or be one of the Beatles pop group. However, the catch is that she has to alter her biological make-up and flatten her breasts, overcome her periods, and avoid pregnancy. In other words, her female body means that such equality is impossible and she is forever assigned to the realm of the 'also-ran'. In 'Work' (20–1), however, women take on both female and traditionally male roles: they farm, fish, work in factories and take part in the construction, computer, and marketing industries. The lists of jobs cover different historical periods, rural and urban environments, proving the superhuman feats that women have always done. Elaine Feinstein comments, '"Work" takes a single mum, working her fingers to the bone to fill her larder, and develops her problem through a rhetoric of absurdity that leaves her at the heart of the capitalist internet trying to feed a planet. Sometimes the gritty details make a familiar point surprising' (2002).

'Beautiful' (8–14) provocatively links the life and death of Princess Diana of Wales (1961–97) with the beauties of classical myth, literature, and popular culture: Helen of Troy, Cleopatra, and Marilyn Monroe (1926–62). Duffy condenses the stories of each heroine, but as they are not named they operate as archetypes. She weaves in signifiers to make them recognizable while the contemporary idioms conflate ancient with modern times. Helen, supposedly 'a daughter of the gods', Zeus and Leda, is 'drop-dead / gorgeous', the cliché becoming chillingly literal when the full story is unravelled. As 'the face that launched a thousand ships', she is said to have started the Trojan War when she was seduced and abducted by Paris. Always admired and flocked by suitors, her 'beauty is fame', but she pays for it, treated variously as a goddess or witch. In legend, she was either taken up to Olympus or hung from a tree. Duffy inserts an image of the superior and liberating love between women in the 'little bird inside a cage' of her maid who loved Helen more than all the suitors. Cleopatra is 'tough beauty': she models how to defy prescriptions of feminine passivity and refuse the gaze of men. She uses her looks for power, wielding it first over Caesar and then Mark Antony. Monroe, however, is 'dumb beauty': she increasingly constructs herself through the gaze of the camera, her marriages becoming shows for her expanding audience—'the US whooped', 'the whole world swooned', 'the audience drooled'. Monroe's identity is sketched by allusions to her relationships with Frank Sinatra and President John Kennedy, by her addictions, and then by her probable suicide, when, according to Duffy, she finally resembled herself, perhaps by exercising some choice or perhaps because she was always inwardly dead. Diana, whose 'beauty is fate', is presented through snapshots that include her appearances on the [Buckingham Palace] balcony, the legendary photograph of her alone on a bench outside the Taj Mahal, the gaze of the press, the contingent gaze of women who wanted to look like her, and the flags at half-mast after her death on 31 August 1997, with 'History's stinking breath in her face'.

These poems can be placed in dialogue with the work of Wolf and Orbach on 'body instability' (Orbach 2010) that especially afflicts women. As Wolf states in *The Beauty Myth: How Images of Beauty are Used against Women*: 'Culture stereotypes women to fit the myth by flattening the feminine into beauty-without-intelligence or intelligence-without-beauty; women are allowed a mind or a body but not both' (1991: 59). Duffy strips away any glamour from beauty and any sense that these women were blessed by their looks to reveal how they were objectified, imprisoned, and killed by voyeurism. The phrase, 'beauty is fate', directly echoes Wolf's observation that a woman's 'face is her fortune' (20). As Wolf elaborates: 'The fixation on "beauty" of the 1980s was a direct consequence of, and a one-to-one check and balance upon, the entry of women into powerful positions. The triumph of "beauty" ideologies in the eighties came about as a result of real fear, on the part of the central institutions of our society, about what might happen if free women made free progress in free bodies through a system that called itself a meritocracy' (1991: 28–9). Duffy's connections between Princess Diana and the other heroines illuminate how deeply the beauty myth is entrenched in the population's psyche, and how these famous beauties magnify the tragedy that nearly all women are well schooled in the beauty myth: 'Many of us are not yet sure enough ourselves that women are interesting without beauty' (Wolf 1991: 84).

In the Introduction to the 1997 edition of *Fat is a Feminist Issue*, Orbach notices little change in the twenty years since the book's first publication in 1978: 'But how we eat, what we eat, how much we eat, even whether it is okay to eat and the relentless struggle to get our bodies to be the way we want them to be are still major preoccupations for women of all ages today. Food and its place in women's lives continues to be painful and troublesome' (2006: 367, 2010: vii). As she analyses in her later study *Bodies* (2010), the issues continue into the twenty-first century. Duffy's 'The Diet' (*FG* 15–16) chillingly confronts the compulsion to conform to social requirements for thinness: 'She starved on, stayed in, stared in / the mirror, svelter, slimmer', until she became 'anorexia's true daughter'. Appropriating elements of Lewis Carroll's 'Alice in Wonderland', the narrative defies rational logic as the tiny woman wanders round in all sorts of places until she resides in the gut of a Fat Woman and is subject to an 'avalanche munch of food': 'She knew where she was all right, clambered / onto the greasy breast of a goose, opened wide, then / chomped and chewed and gorged; inside the Fat Woman now, / trying to get out.' The tone and sense are hard to gauge but the images magnify the contradictions about femininity when it comes to the body: 'Just as the "slim" woman seems to conform to and accept the cultural expectations discussed above, the self-inflictedly *emaciated* woman is a horrible parody. She is both an exaggeration and an *implicit* denial of these cultural norms, just as the fat women *explicitly* denies them' (Waugh 1989: 177).

'The Woman who Shopped' (*FG* 17–19) takes what came to be known as 'retail therapy' to absurd lengths until the woman loses her senses. The first recorded use of the phrase was in *The Chicago Tribune*, 'We've become a nation measuring out our lives in shopping bags and nursing our psychic ills through retail therapy.'[8] The recourse to a cure for 'psychic ills' echoes Friedan's survey of women thirty years previously. The stages of the woman's life correspond to the script of making herself pretty, then desirable, entering a marriage contract, setting up house, and consuming from all levels of the department store until she actually becomes the store: 'Her skirts / were glass doors opening and closing, her stockings were / moving stairs, her shoes were lifts, going up, going down'. Kit Fryatt observes here the trope of allegorical literature—'the microcosm-macrocosm analogy': 'because the self is inside the world, the world must be inside the self' (2002/3: 83). Although evading a moral or realist perspective, it is difficult to fix a viewpoint when the woman is an object of both ridicule and sympathy. Duffy's imagery of glass exaggerates 'the deep cultural ambivalence towards femininity … Moreover, within the context of a late capitalist consumer society, these contradictions are rendered even more acute through the alienating effects of commodification' (Waugh 1989: 177). Women are unwitting yet complicit targets of fashion and marketing industries: 'It cannot be about women, for the "ideal" is not about women but about money' (Wolf 1991: 232). When Duffy's shopper decides to 'have a sale', 'crowds would queue overnight / at her cunt, desperate for bargains'. This odd image is a grotesque parody of prostitution and the commodification of women's bodies. The gothic imagery in the last line, 'Birds shrieked and voided themselves in her stone hair', is a horrific implication that her acquisitions and the sale of her body leave her as good as dead.

These comi-tragic depictions of female objectification not only link to cultural commentators, such as Orbach and Wolf, but also to such novels as Atwood's *The Edible Woman* (1969) and Fay Weldon's *The Fat*

[8] Mary T. Schmich, 'A Stopwatch On Shopping', *Chicago Tribune*, 24 December 1986.

Woman's Joke (1967). Reviewing such works, Waugh writes: 'As a consequence of their social alienation, women experience their bodies as parts,
"objects", rather than integrated wholes. However, their dissatisfaction
with and desire for a "better" body can form the basis of a genuinely subversive fantasy of social change. ... The experience of fragmentation and
disintegration can become the starting point for a reconstruction for the
bodily ego' (1989: 178). Waugh argues that whereas Freud put fantasy
down to wish fulfilment that stems from dissatisfaction, feminist writers
prove 'a more positive articulation of the possibility of connecting our
desires to a potential world outside them' (168). This is what the girls
and teachers do in Duffy's extraordinary twenty-page 'The Laughter at
Stafford Girls' High' (*FG* 35–54). They first reject the rules, then vent
their unexpressed desires, and finally fulfil them, whether composing
poems, treading the boards, climbing mountains, or loving women. Set
in the 1960s, the surreal narrative is of a giggling epidemic that ultimately
closes the school. It denounces, documents, and treasures old-school culture: 'the chalky words rubbed away to dance as dust /on the air, the
dates, the battles, the kings and queens, / the rivers and tributaries, poets,
painters, playwrights'. The poem's length, the far-reaching lines, and
the light-footed assonance imitate the girls' uncontrollable laughter that
overturns the rigid and endless routine of the women teachers and students who are equally trapped in a repressive system. The details of the
environment, curriculum, and ethos are threaded through the comic tale.
Same-sex love is increasingly licensed: 'Miss Batt and Miss Fife' are initially 'good friends'—'each woman's silently virtuous love'—but they end
up free of restraint to express their mutual passion. The girls blossom and
flourish through their communal power and freedom while the teachers
leave the school to find a life for themselves. Only 'Mrs Mackay', married for twenty-five years, walks into the sea, and the well-qualified Head,
Doctor Bream, ends up incapacitated in an asylum. The fast pace and
strong rhythm mediate the exhilaration of living life to the full through
breaking conventional codes. The poem corresponds to Lacan's notion
of the unconscious as a continuum of shifting signifiers, and Duffy makes
the substance of the desires as solid, valid, and in excess of what phallocentric language can signify: 'her lips split from the closed bud of a kiss /
to the daisy chain of a grin and how then she yodelled / a laugh with
the full, open, blooming rose of her throat, // a flower of merriment'
(37). This is the *jouissance* described by Lacan and taken up by Kristeva,
a term significantly untranslatable into English and so pertinently marked

by the women's infectious laughing. This *jouissance* approximates to the pleasures of exercising their rights, discovering their unique natures, and of releasing their sexual drives.

'WHAT CAN A WOMAN DO?'

We have seen how Duffy's poems document and examine continuities and shifts in ideologies of sex and gender from the 1950s to the early twenty-first century. Her dramatic monologues potently disempower the male gaze as analysed by John Berger: 'This pattern, which leaves out women as individuals, extends from high culture to popular mythology: "Men look at women. Women watch themselves being looked at. This determines not only the relations of men to women, but the relation of women to themselves"' (Berger 2008: 47). Duffy proves how poetry particularly can rework the unconscious languages that perpetuate such myths. As Ian Gregson notes in representations of the male image in post-war poetry: 'What is fascinating about the poets I discuss in this book is the extent to which their work registers the changes in understanding of gender which have taken place over the past fifty years. Poetry is especially effective in this context because its techniques effect a radical de-familiarizing of its material. Because gender norms had established themselves so rigidly during the nineteenth century their subversion requires especially subtle and complex aesthetic means, so that the grip of their familiarity can be broken' (1999: 3). Although some women in Duffy's poems suffer an 'untold want', other monologues suggest that they are able to find, express, and release their desires. We can further read particular poems in relation to significant cultural commentaries, such as Mulvey on narrative cinema, Waugh on postmodern feminist fictions, Wolf on the beauty myth, and Orbach on women's unstable relationship to their bodies, manifest in eating disorders or other problematic conditions.

   In speaking of the indelible pangs of losing her mother and of being a mother, forty-nine-year-old Moll asks, 'What can a woman do?' ('A Clear Note', *SFN* 28). While admitting, '"Which of us doesn't have a criticism of her mother"' (O'Connell 2012), in various ways, Duffy's 'subtle and complex aesthetic' (Gregson 1999: 3) scotches the Freudian script for 'normal' male and abnormal female development. In 'Boy' (*TOC* 29), for example, the grown man is stuck in the Oedipal complex and still wants his mother: 'I think of myself as a boy. Safe slippers.' He confides that he contacted an older woman, some kind of nurse who bathed him and whom he calls 'Mummy', and now he advertises in a paper's Lonely Hearts column, hoping to find another kindly maternal figure. Instead of turning away from their mothers, as Freud prescribed, Duffy emphasizes regenerative relationships between women. *Feminine Gospels* ends with celebrations of a mother's joy in her daughter, 'The Light Gatherer' (59–60) and 'The Cord' (61–2). Such lyrics correspond to Wolf's conclusion that the links between generations of women need enforcing to rescue them from the self-perpetuating beauty myth. She asserts: 'Gill Hudson, editor of *Company* women's magazine, reveals the extent to which the beauty backlash has propagandized the young: '"Young women", she says, "absolutely don't want to be known as 'feminists' because "feminism is not considered sexy." It would be stupid and sad if the women of the near future had to fight the same old battles all over again from the beginning just because of young women's isolation from older women' (Wolf 1991: 283).

REFERENCES

1994 *Selected poems* (Harmondsworth: Penguin).

1999 *The world's wife* (London: Anvil).

2002 *Feminine gospels* (London: Picador).

2004 *New selected poems 1984–2004* (London: Picador).

Berger, John. 2008. *Ways of Seeing*. London: Penguin Books.

Cixous, Hélène. 1997. *Sorties: Out and out: Attacks/ways out/forays*, 91–103. Belsey and Moore.

Feinstein, Elaine. 2002. A casual kind of confidence. *Guardian,* September 14.

Friedan, Betty. 1963. *The feminine mystique*. New York: Dell Publishing.

Fryatt, Kit. 2002/2003. Seeking and finding a difficulty. Review of *Feminine Gospels, Metre* 13: 83–84.

Gregson, Ian. 1999. *The male image: Representations of masculinity in postwar poetry*. Basingstoke: Macmillan.

Horner, Avril. 2003. "Small female skull": Patriarchy and philosophy in the poetry of Carol Ann Duffy, 99–120. Michelis and Rowland.

Jones, Ernest. 1955. *Sigmund Freud: Life and work*, vol. 2. London: Hogarth Press.

Lochhead, Liz. 1991. *Bagpipe Muzak*. Harmondsworth: Penguin.

Moi, Toril. 1997. Feminist, female, feminine, 104–116. Belsey and Moore.

Moi, Toril. 2004. From femininity to finitude: Freud, Lacan, and feminism. *Signs: Journal of Women in Culture and Society* 29(3): 841–878.

Mulvey, Laura. 1975. Visual pleasure and narrative cinema. *Screen* 16(3): 6–18.

O'Connell, Alex. 2012. The poet who refuses to rest on her laureate. *Times,* November 3.

Orbach, Susie. 2005. *Hunger strike: The anorexic's struggle as a metaphor for our age* [1986]. London: Karnac Books.

Orbach, Susie. 2006. *Fat is a feminist issue.* London: Arrow Books.

Orbach, Susie. 2010. *Bodies.* London: Profile Books.

Padel, Ruth. 1990. In otherness together. Review of *The Other Country, Times Literary Supplement,* May 11–17.

Robinson, Alan. 1988. *Instabilities in contemporary British poetry.* Basingstoke: Palgrave.

Rose, Jacqueline. 1982. Introduction to Lacan, "God and the *Jouissance* of The Woman". In *Feminine sexuality: Jacques Lacan and the ecole freudienne,* ed. Juliet Mitchell and Jacqueline Rose, 137–138. London: Macmillan.

Rumens, Carole. 1999/2000. Trouble and strife. Review of *The World's Wife, Poetry Review* 89(4): 33–34.

Smith, Stevie. 1981. In *Me again: The uncollected writings of Stevie Smith,* ed. Jack Barbera and William McBrien. London: Virago.

Smith, Laurie. 2000. With one bound she was free. Review of *The World's Wife, Magma* 16: 16–21.

Wainwright, Jeffrey. 2003. Female metamorphoses: Carol Ann Duffy's Ovid, 47–55. Michelis and Rowland.

Waugh, Patricia. 1989. *Feminine fictions: Revisiting the postmodern.* London: Routledge.

Wheeler, Stephen M. 1999. *A discourse of wonders: Audience and performance in Ovid's metamorphoses.* Philadelphia: University of Pennsylvania Press.

Wolf, Naomi. 1991. *The beauty myth: How images of beauty are used against women.* London: Vintage.

Wood, Barry. 2005. Carol Ann Duffy: *The World's Wife.* Conversation with Carol AnnDuffy.http://www.sheerpoetry.co.uk/advanced/interviews/carol-ann-duffy-the-world-s-wife

Woolf, Virginia. 1977. *A room of one's own.* London: Grafton.

CHAPTER 5

Poetry and the Public Sphere

In 21st-century British society it is no longer possible, or even desirable, to write relevantly or meaningfully in response to, say, a royal anniversary or a national event. And anyway, can any single writer—poet, play-wright or novelist—fully apprehend the British mood and give it lyrical expression? (McCrum 2008)

POETRY MAKES SOMETHING HAPPEN

While the poetry discussed in other chapters nurtures personal interiority as a private, discrete, and generative space, 'public' is conceived as the realm of communal experience. Although Charles Simic lamented in 1985, 'One can read literally hundreds of pages of contemporary poetry without encountering any significant aspect of our common twentieth-century existence' (127), the growth of mass media and information technology might rapidly render a 'public' poem superfluous. Additionally, as McCrum intimates twenty years after Simic, in the contemporary climate of cultural diversity, some homogenous national 'mood' might be hard to pitch. McCrum also hints that Duffy might echo the sentiments of fellow working-class poet Tony Harrison in his poem 'Laureate's Block': 'There should be no successor to Ted Hughes. / "The saponaceous qualities of sack" / are purest poison if paid poets lose / their freedom as PM's or Monarch's hack' (Harrison 2000: 15). Indeed, on her royal appointment, a handful of watchful critics did perceive that Duffy's work had become

© The Editor(s) (if applicable) and The Author(s) 2016
J. Dowson, *Carol Ann Duffy*,
DOI 10.1057/978-1-137-41563-9_5

'serviceable' (Puss in Boots 2012). However, as outlined in Chap. 3, she has always animated the poet's role as a cultural commentator, stating in 1988: "'the poet is merely bearing witness. … What I am doing is living in the twentieth century in Britain and listening to the radio news every day. … Poets don't have solutions; poets are recording human experience. If I'm moved by something or intrigued, or interested, that's what I am going to write about"' (McAllister 1988: 72). In 2014, she more assertively claims the poet is a vital interpreter of the times: "'Poetry provides an important alternative voice to journalists or pundits or academics as a way of dealing with things that matter to us all"' (Duffy, Wroe 2014). Duffy manages to accommodate individual diversity by her belief in poetry's unique capacity to reach and express shared emotional truths: 'We find in poetry the echoes of our deepest feelings and most serious moments' (*Stylist* 2011). Thus, even when speaking of public affairs, she explores and expresses how they 'matter' at the level of human interiority.

Several poems penned during Duffy's Laureate years (2009) are commissioned invitations to mark an occasion, but she insists: 'There always had been a public element to my work, particularly during the Thatcher years, and I think all poets, to a greater or lesser degree, need to have a finger on the national pulse' (Wroe 2014). She takes the national pulse regarding events that engage the entire population—a General Election, a Royal Wedding, the Scottish Referendum—and also privileges groups whose heartbeat is overlooked, notably the grieving relatives of racial murders or of the Hillsborough disaster, and voters disillusioned by bankers' bonuses or MPs' fraudulent expenses. 'Translating The British' (*Mirror* 2012), a poem on the London Olympics 2012, written specially for *The Mirror*, is in the voice of 'the people' wanting a piece in the pie of opportunity. While rehearsing the names of the beloved British heroes of the Games, it demands money back from the Bankers, funding for cycle lanes, and 'school playing-fields returned'.[1] She captures the new momentum for sport, for celebrating a diverse new Britishness, and for inspiring anyone to become a hero: 'We saw what we did. We are Nicola Adams and Jade Jones, / bring on the fighting kids. / We sense new weather. / We are on our marks. We are all in this together.' The plural first person pronouns

---

[1] 'One school playing field sold off every three weeks since Coalition was formed', *Daily Telegraph*, 13 December 2013. http://www.telegraph.co.uk/education/keep-the-flame-alive/10516870/One-school-playing-field-sold-off-every-three-weeks-since-Coalition-was-formed.html

build up solidarity in a slice of the public who feel deprived of chances, alienated from politics, and distanced from media hype around celebrity culture. It proves how 'poetry is about the personal mattering, in public. On its own frail but stubborn level, it challenges controlling public perceptions merely by existing and being shared'. Padel also advocates the relationship between poetry, free expression, and democracy: 'Where freedom of expression is forbidden, and the private becomes political, poetry is seen for what it is: a form of expression crucial to everyone' (Padel 2002: 25).

Thus, Duffy enacts her principle that, '"Original laureates were spin doctors for the monarchy—now it is the music of being human, to call into question what needs to be called into question and to praise what needs to be praised"' (Duffy, Lawson 2011). In 'The Twelve Days of Christmas', written for the *Radio Times* (2009), she establishes a public voice that does not sacrifice her integrity and poetic independence: '"Twelve Days" proved that poetry is still capable of creating a political storm' (Wilkinson 2014). The sequence condenses what needs to be questioned and praised along with what Duffy prizes: social inclusivity, football, human rights, and, most of all, art and poetry. The twelve verses touch on soldiers far from home, global warming, the cults of celebrity and beauty, natural disasters, honour killing, mistreating refugees, and neglecting the vulnerable. With outspoken astringency, she exposes the popular carol's rarefied sphere in which lords and ladies enjoy gold rings with an entourage of dancers and drummers. On *her* 'tenth day', 'Lords don't leap / They sleep', a witty slight on a complacent aristocracy and the unelected peers in Parliament's House of Lords. The poem was reprinted in the *Mirror* with the sub-line 'grim version for our times' (Shaw 2009). Typical of her later work, Duffy also offers uplift through hymning the 'magic' of Barack Obama, Fabio Capello, Joanna Lumley, Anish Kapoor, and Alan Bennett, and through 'swan songs' for the late poets U.A. Fanthorpe and Adrian Mitchell. One *Daily Telegraph* blogger approves 'Her anti-establishment— if predictable—politics' but finds this 'seasonal ramble' 'embarrassingly bad' (Marre 2009). In the same paper, however, Lorna Bradbury admires Duffy's 'campaigning zeal for the possibilities of poetry' (2009). In the Glasgow broadsheet, *The Herald*, Mark Smith cites the editor of the *Radio Times*, '"we've now got a confident poet laureate with a strong distinctive voice who is prepared to grapple with the big issues"', and Alan Riach, Professor of Scottish Literature: '"This is poetry as journalism … This is not the ivory tower. It's something that is concerned with the real world"' (2009). Referring to W.H. Auden's famous dictum, 'poetry makes nothing happen', Duffy proposes, '"I wonder if the opposite could be true. It could make something happen"' (Bradbury 2009).

In his study of eighteenth-century book-reading 'critically debating' public forums, Jurgen Habermas observes that in the twentieth century, 'the world fashioned by the mass media is a public sphere in appearance only' (1994: 171). Douglas Kellner elaborates: 'the media rarely encourage participation in public action. In these ways, they foster social passivity and the fragmentation of the public sphere into privatized consumers' (2000: 269). However, Duffy's overt alliance with the left-leaning *Guardian* broadsheet and *The Mirror* tabloid indicate how she adds the voice of poetry to these potent mediators of intellectual and mass cultures. Furthermore, by printing her poems in both papers, she effects an exchange between the book-reading public associated with *The Guardian* and the readership of the *Mirror* in which a proportion of pages are at basic reading ability. In 2012, however, *The Mirror* launched a 'We Love Reading' campaign and claimed Duffy as one of its supporters (Parry 2012). Fittingly, then, her 'public' poems exchange views and unsettle a clear divide between the 'general public', meaning those whose interests are largely consumerist and patriotic, supporting the Royal Family and war heroes, and a 'critically debating public' who welcome new ideas and agitate for social change. In tune with Habermas, Lavinia Greenlaw exhorted the new Laureate, 'I hope Duffy will be encouraged to be a public poet in the best sense: that is someone actively engaged with society at all levels and willing to offer a trenchant response' (2009). As if in reply, reviewing *The Bees*, Dominic Hale spots 'its (typically Duffyesque) bravery, the way it does not shirk from confrontation' (2012). Invited to write a poem for *The Guardian* to mark the 2010 General Election, Duffy shuns the big story for the side-lined travesty of empowerment when voters were turned away because officers closed polling station doors at 10.00 pm. The title and tone of 'Democracy' (7 May 2010) are bitingly ironic— 'here's a drawbridge, here's a moat … / What's your hurry? Here's your coat'—and the end-rhymes portray officials' platitudinous attempts to placate the crowd. The symbol of drawing up the bridge so that common people cannot enter the castle conjures a bygone feudal age that continues in the form of a 'cut throat' contemporary bureaucracy.

While explicitly anti-Thatcherite during the 1980s, Duffy continues to oppose any abuse of power but ploughs a non-partisan furrow. In 'Politics' (*Bees* 12), the potent satire is tinged by her characteristic sympathy for men and women who find themselves embroiled in corrupt systems: 'How it makes your face a stone / that aches to weep, your heart a fist, / clenched or thumping, your tongue / an iron latch with no door.' The inclusive pronoun 'you' merges the poet or reader with the politician and both Left and Right political wings are implicated in denying their humanity: 'your right hand / a gauntlet, a glove puppet the left'. The 'iron latch' signifies Conservative Prime Minister, Margaret Thatcher, nicknamed the 'Iron Lady' for her tough policies, and 'education education education' mimics Labour Prime Minister, Tony Blair, in his famous speech, 2001.[2] The capitalization and repetition of 'POLITICS' in the final line represent the raised voices, bullying tone, and hollow rhetoric of political speech. Mark Brown comments, 'It is a powerful, passionate commentary on the corrosiveness of politics on politicians and the ruinous effect on idealism', and cites Judith Palmer, Director of The Poetry Society: '"I think that what [Duffy] has managed to do is capture in poetry the sense of disbelief, the strangled despair, which leaves most of us just shaking our heads, open-mouthed and inarticulate. ... that "bloody hell" feeling most people felt every time they listened to the latest detail of the expenses scandal"' (2009). In 2013, Duffy picks up the animal allegory of 'Weasel Words' (*TOC* 14) in a witty and acerbic jibe at a Government Minister's complaint that 'badgers had moved the goalposts'. He was speaking about a pilot scheme to cull badgers in West Somerset that would be extended by up to three weeks because it had not reached its target. The absurd scapegoating of badgers typifies a government's slippery rhetoric that Duffy mocks: 'Because the Badgers are moving the goalposts / The Ferrets are bending the rules. / The Weasels are taking the hindmost. / The Otters are downing tools.' The poem's title, '22 Reasons for the Bedroom Tax' (Kennedy 2013), satirizes the hollow justifications for reducing benefit to tenants in social housing if they have a spare room, legislation introduced in April 2013 under the Welfare Reform Act, 2012. Robert DiNapoli notes how the broadcast speech of politicians 'bulldozes the play of living language to a shopping-mall car-park desolation of flat, dead surface with no depth or resonance. At the other end of the spectrum, all literature worth the name says more than it says' (2014: 37).

The tough task with a 'public' poem, then, is to speak for and to a public, conceived variously as the entire population or as a specific group, while also saying 'more than it says' through the aesthetic pleasure of

---

[2] Tony Blair, launching Labour's education manifesto, University of Southampton, 23 May 2001.

ingenious language that has 'depth' and 'resonance'. In largely eschewing the traditional forms of public poems, the ode, the epic, or formal elegy, Duffy has to find ways of being both direct and imaginative. This she does through the 'music' of poems, retaining their affective power through evocative sounds and symbols. As one reviewer of *The Bees* put it: 'Has there even been a Poet Laureate with such accessibility or one with such an eagerness to engage with social or political issues without compromising the poetic sensibility?' (Colton 2012: 46). Duffy proves how poetry awakens the reader's sensibilities to tragedy and celebration or to the unwarranted aggrandizement of a hero, idol, politician, or monarch by reducing them to life-size. In order to echo 'our deepest feelings and most serious moments', she sometimes speaks in the voice of 'Poetry'—'If poetry could tell it backwards then it would' ('Last Post', RL 13), or blends the emotional intensity of lyric expression with a collective pronoun—'the hive, alive, us' ('Hive', Bees 31). Mostly, she views public matters through a personal lens—of someone participating, or otherwise affected, or her own (Lawson 2011). In 'Pathway' (*RL* 32), an elegy to her father, a beautiful vision ends with him stripped and shivering in a cold bed, an oblique reference to the neglect by the subsequently discredited Liverpool Care Pathway on which he had been placed before he died in 2011 (Donnelly 2013). Duffy comments, 'It is a controversial area, but again this was a moment where something very private and personal happened that also had one foot in a public debate and that is the sort of thing that I have always written about ... It was one of many such set ups to be condemned'" (Wroe 2014). Writing in *The Times*, Eric Wagner corroborates Duffy's method: 'I would like to think of Carol Ann Duffy and her electric eclectic verse as a lightning rod for the poetic impulse of Britons', adding that true poets do best when they 'make the personal universal', surely the 'true job of the laureate' (2009).

POETRY AND THE NEWS

Simic narrates his discomfort with the mass mediation of atrocities and commends poets to respond 'in times of madness': 'I am really describing the pressure of reality on the contemporary poet, the way in which the world's daily tragedies are brought to us every morning and evening. It's really the raw data of history given to us so soon after the event and in such detail that makes each one of us a voyeur, a Peeping Tom of the death chamber' (1985: 126–7). In a piece for *The Times* about a charity poetry reading in aid of the Haiti Earthquake appeal, Duffy, like Simic, draws attention to the inhumane voyeurism of watching the news, 'The bloodstained rubble of Port-au-Prince remains heaped in the TV corner of each of our living rooms', and urges 'politicians, bankers, builders and businessmen to deliver a better world, especially to the poor' (*Times* 2010). She also admits that images of horror challenge the scope of words: 'It was not difficult to feel that there was nothing that poetry could do to help the amputees, the orphaned, the homeless, the traumatized, the hungry, thirsty and sick'. However, she found a source in a woman dug out after six days who was singing with gratitude, 'the life bursting out of her', and equated the woman's joy to how poetry 'enters us' and 'reflects our brightest mornings or deepens in our darkest nights' (Duffy 2010). Poetry reporter and journalist, Jeffrey Brown, in Carrefour a year after the earthquake, similarly testifies:

> On this day there is much reciting, singing, shouting lines, sometimes back and forth, in Creole and French. I can make out references to the quake, cholera, hunger, death, but also to pleasure, fellowship, drinking, and love, love, love. ... In one tiny corner of Haiti, men and women gathered together to tell their histories, their lives, their hopes and joys, anger and sorrows. Poetry happened.
>
> I report on poetry. In an age of chattering 24-hour news, of the latest celebrity this or that, it is barely conceivable. But it also makes a kind of sense. Literature has long provided me with a connection, a way in. I have seen the world, traveled the world through poetry and learned much from it of the power and process of giving an account. (2014: 567–8)

Duffy, too, often centres 'love, love, love' as in human compassion and kindness: 'All day we leave and arrive at the hive, / concelebrants. The hive is love' ('Hive', *Bees* 31). Her Third Day of Christmas parodies the carol's 'Three French hens' with 'Three Welsh lambs' that do not know they baa in Welsh, and commends, 'Newborn babies—one, two, three— only know / you human be.' ('The Twelve Days of Christmas' 2009)

Since political polemic is anathema to poetic aestheticism, public poetry's 'music' can thus be in firing the imagination and reviving our sense of a common humanity, endorsed by collective pronouns. It can 'make something happen' by 'giving an account' in language that reaches parts of the unconscious and emotions that other discourses do not. In 'Far Be

It' (*NSP* 139), Duffy foregrounds the obscenity of 'sieve[ing] the news /
for poetry' to profit from others' tragedy. Nevertheless, she replicates the
horrific television image of a boy 'who bled / from the stumps of arms /
and wasn't dead' but adds her quasi prayerful response in which she likens
the victim to the crucified Christ: 'Brought to my knees, I genuflect, /
shaking with rage and shame / at the TV set.' In this way, the poem
both values and discredits how we become 'Peeping Toms of the death
chamber' as war is brought to our screens. Importantly, it also revives the
human feelings against which television can inoculate. 'Loud' (*FG* 25–6)
is prefaced by an extract from a report, cited as 'Afghanistan, 28 October
2001', on how parents with mutilated children were told to have them
smuggled across the border to find help in Pakistan. This information
drives Duffy's subject to shout and scream and howl at the daily news
coverage of inhuman acts. She is beyond words at the radio's coverage
of how an innocent church congregation were sprayed with bullets: 'gib-
berish, crap, / in the cave of her mouth'.[3] Duffy's assonance, dissonance,
and onomatopoeia vibrantly replicate the woman's wish to wake up the
world to the unutterable nature of human violence. The woman confesses
to her former voyeuristic pleasures in mass media—relishing the salacious
exposures of MPs' homosexuality or the 'royal kiss on the balcony'—but
she can no longer look on passively: 'She bawled at the moon and it span
away / Into space. She hollered into the dark where fighter planes buzzed
at her face. / She howled every noise in the world / Sang in the spit on
the tip of her tongue: the shriek of a bomb / the bang of a gun'. The ono-
matopoeic verbs depict both the sounds of the horrors and her inarticulate
responses to them. In 'Tall' (*FG* 22–4), surreal images stand for the collective speechless shock following the attack on New York's twin towers,
11 September 2001. A woman grows ever higher until she is above the
planets from where she sees earth's natural and human disasters that she is
powerless to avert. Just like the woman in 'Loud', 'she howled' at all the
dead, then stooped to catch 'their souls in her hands as they fell / from the
burning towers'. This gesture evokes an intense compassion for humanity, for both perpetrators and victims, which transcends sectarian dogmas.

---

[3] http://www.telegraph.co.uk/news/worldnews/asia/pakistan/1360879/Christians-
massacred-at-prayer.html These lines are also relevant to the racist murder of nine people at
prayer in Charleston, South Carolina, 18 June 2015. http://www.usatoday.com/story/
news/nation/2015/06/17/charleston-south-carolina-shooting/28902017/

War

War is one area of public life in which poetry is always embraced since the extremity of its suffering defies words. As Laureate, Duffy has to negotiate differing expectations—for poetry that validates sentimental patriotism, or that pays due respect to the nation's servicemen, or that colludes with prevailing anti-war attitudes. She does this by 'bearing witness' and by pinpointing shared human feelings. Verse 1 of 'The Twelve Days of Christmas' depicts a soldier who has 'no partridge, pear tree', is comforted by a 'card from home', but knows an imminent bullet would rob a family of 'father, husband, / brother, son' (2009). In *The Guardian*, mindful of the escalating conflict in Afghanistan and the pending Iraq inquiry, Duffy commissioned 'war poetry for today'. Her Introduction dwells on the continuities and shifts in the poet's role:

> Poets, from ancient times, have written about war. It is the poet's obligation, wrote Plato, to bear witness. … British poets in our early 21st century do not go to war, as Keith Douglas did and Edward Thomas before him. They might be poet-journalists like James Fenton, the last foreign correspondent to leave Saigon after it fell to the Viet Cong in 1975, or electrifying anti-war performance poets, like the late Adrian Mitchell, or brilliant retellers of Homer's Trojan wars, like Christopher Logue. War, it seems, makes poets of soldiers and not the other way round. Today, as most of us do, poets largely experience war—wherever it rages—through emails or texts from friends or colleagues in war zones, through radio or newsprint or television, through blogs or tweets or interviews. With the official inquiry into Iraq imminent and the war in Afghanistan returning dead teenagers to the streets of Wootton Bassett, I invited a range of my fellow poets to bear witness, each in their own way, to these matters of war. (Exit Wounds 2009)

As indicated here, bearing witness involves scrutinizing the ways in which war is mediated. In Duffy's own poem, the end rhymes ('track' 'black', 'rack, 'sack', pack' and so on) clue her reference to Iraq and she confronts the fruitless search for Weapons of Mass Destruction (WMD) from 2001 to 2009. The colloquial title, 'Big Ask' (*Bees* 9–10), marks the magnitude of the principles at stake and ironically confronts the Labour Party's reluctance to progress the Iraq Inquiry, announced in July 2009 but still not published five years later[4]: 'Sexing the dossier' alludes to the infamously

---

[4] Justin Parkinson (2014) 'Set up Afghanistan war inquiry, MPs urge government', BBC News website, 13 May. http://www.bbc.co.uk/news/uk-politics-27377977 See also, Peter

dodgy file that fudged the facts over the WMD, the torture of suspected terrorists, and the manic witch-hunt for ringleader Saddam Hussein. The voice apes the evasive answers of the leaders responsible for innumerable deaths: 'Your estimate of the cost of the War? / *I had no brief to keep track*', 'Guantanamo Bay—how many detained? / *How many grains in a sack?*' The challenging tone of Duffy's questioner connects to Adrian Mitchell's rebuttal of government cover-ups, 'Tell Me Lies About Vietnam', famously read at London's Royal Albert Hall, 11 June 1965.

The inside cover blurb to *The Bees* states, '[Duffy's] celebrated "Last Post" … showed that powerful public poetry still has a central place in our culture.' In 'Last Post' (*RL* 13), commissioned by the BBC to mark the deaths of the last two survivors, Henry Allingham and Harry Patch, from the trenches of World War I, she respects the millions dead while opposing war for robbing life from those who served and those who loved them. The title refers to the bugle call played to remember the fallen while the two opening lines from the anti-heroic 'Dulce et Decorum Est' by Wilfred Owen (1975: 79) emit an anti-war undertone. The filmic flash-back to the lives that might have been, 'crammed with love, work, children, talent, English beer, good food', is both a tribute to the men and an indictment of war. Similarly, some elegiac consolation in how tragedy illuminates the value of each human life permeates 'The Falling Soldier' (*Bees* 13–14) where Duffy flashes back to the time before battle and poetically films how the man's life might have turned out, had he survived. Based on Robert Capa's iconic photograph of a Republican in the Spanish Civil War, she imagines what the soldier's posture might suggest if not in the context of violent combat: he might be flopping back for a 'kip in the sun', enacting a breakdance with his friends, or boyishly sliding down a hill with joy. Each snapshot is accompanied by a voice-over about the 'much worse' reality of his vain fight for the sake of democracy. In 'Premonitions' (*Bees* 81–2), she uses the same device of rewinding, this time from the point of her mother's death, and offers an imaginative resurrection. Duffy believes the grief at losing her mother fed into her treatment of the public commemorations and states, '"Poetry can't be documentary. I'm not sure that any of the arts should be—but poetry, above all, is a series of intense moments"' (Winterson 2005). Accordingly, Duffy attends to how war intensifies human experience. The title of 'Passing Bells' (*Bees* 80), first

Taylor (2013) 'The Iraq war: the greatest intelligence failure in living memory', *Daily Telegraph*, 18 March.

printed in the *New Statesman*, October 2010, is taken from Owen's bitterly ironic, 'Anthem for Doomed Youth', that starts: 'What passing-bells for these who die as cattle? /—Only the monstrous anger of the guns' (1975: 76). In dialogue with Owen's bleak depiction of the inglorious and invisible deaths of a generation of young men, Duffy's elegy for all soldiers assures their loved ones that each is not forgotten by depicting every ring of a familiar bell, whether on a church, shop door, or bicycle, as a reminder of his soul passing on.

For the centenary of World War I, Duffy edited an anthology, *1914: Poetry Remembers*, writing in the Introduction: 'we hear the proper note of outrage which all remembrance of the carnage of this War should contain, which the brave dead of all nations deserve, and which we hear clearly, still, in Siegfried Sassoon's declaration against "the sufferings"' (2013). Whereas Sassoon was gagged for his declaration, Duffy galvanized her contemporaries to compose their own poem to place alongside a piece of World War I writing for the anthology. Her piece, 'An Unseen' (*RL* 35), echoes Owen's 'The Send-Off' (1975: 97–8), evoking the agony of love and fear in the soldier who leaves and the one who watches him go 'to the edge of absence'. The most haunting and gut-wrenching lines capture the utter bleakness of a lost script for life: 'all future / past, an unseen. Has forever been then? Yes, / forever has been'. A *Guardian* reader chose *1914: Poetry Remembers* as one of her 'books for 2013', commenting on 'the beauty of language to express physical and emotional pain: the waste of young lives and the futility of war' (Walmsley-Collins 2013). Just as Duffy mentions the sorrow of the 'dead soldier's lady' in 'The Twelve Days of Christmas', the lens of 'Repatriation Day' (Near 2012: 9) is the intense pain of personal loss: 'the bride's a widow and the child is fatherless'. The elegiac sonnet is set around the custom of saluting the coffins of men and women who died in action as they were carried through the quiet town of Royal Wootton Bassett. As one mourner said, referring to the proposed change in route: 'It's really been the major cause of the public awareness and the public ability to appreciate those who've fallen on their behalf.'[5] Television made the ceremony available to the wider public but Duffy's unflinching emphasis on the human drama sustains the affective power of the event. Most affectively, 'The Christmas Truce', printed in *The Mirror* (23 December 2011), dramatizes the legendary ceasefire between English, German, and French soldiers in the trenches in 1914. Duffy's poem accords with witness accounts of this miraculous eruption of the human spirit

[5] Julie Etchingham, n.d., http://fallenheroes.org.uk/farewell-wootton-bassett/

when the men shook hands and exchanged gifts. She emphasizes how the music of carols and songs were shared language that enabled the men to put aside the business of war. Her moving finale of 'the high, bright bullets / which each man later only aimed at the sky' rhetorically asks how on earth could they then resume their duties and kill the Fritz or Franz whom they had just met as a human brother? The Duchess of Cornwall said of the poem: 'Poetry is like time travel, and poems take us to the heart of the matter. This poem made me cry. It is such a touching and perceptive evocation—through its deceptively simple language and powerful imagery—of the truth of life in the trenches, and of that moment of hope when the sounds of wars were silenced.'[6] Writing from his position as a Public Broadcasting Service news correspondent, Jeffery Brown cites a cadet at The West Point US Military Academy, soon to be deployed to Iraq: 'Poetry is directly related to our func-tion as a military officer because, at the bottom level, we're all here training to take lives. And that's a concept that you really can't approach without art, without some sort of deeper understanding of the human condition, which is exactly what poetry is' (2014: 570).

POETRY AND PLACE

As in 'Pathway', Duffy's other Liverpool-based poems have one foot in her personal allegiances and one foot in public debate. Although Laureate, she says, 'A poem like "Liverpool", which was published at the time of the Hillsborough report, was something I would have written anyway' (Wroe 2014). Since her period as a student in Liverpool, she continues to be a fervent Reds supporter and offered 'Liverpool' (*RL* 18) to the *Liverpool Echo* that was 'proud to publish it' (14 September 2012). The poem tack-les the initial reports that blamed football fans for the deadly human crush at the match between Liverpool and Nottingham Forest in Sheffield, 15 April 1989. On the twentieth anniversary of the disaster, the Hillsborough Independent Panel was formed. It looked at previously withheld docu-ments, cleared Liverpool fans of blame, and held other public bodies responsible for multiple failures that led to the death toll.[7] Duffy's sonnet has the gravitas of a public elegy and the opening line, 'The Cathedral bell, tolled, could never tell', relates how the Anglican Cathedral, one

---

[6] 'First World War centenary: the war poem that moves the Duchess of Cornwall to tears', *Daily Telegraph*, 28 June 2014.

[7] In March 2015, there was further clarity over what went wrong. http://www.telegraph.co.uk/sport/football/teams/liverpool/11464983/Liverpool-news-Hillsborough-police-chief-admits-terrible-lie.html

of the City's grand landmarks, rang ninety six times to mark the number of local people who had died. 'Could never tell' also resonates with the secrecy around what happened, the mourners' unspeakable grief, and 'the slandered dead' who could not defend themselves. The poem expands the specific event to the larger principle of justice—'not a matter of football, but of life'—and ends with a Duffyesque uplift by invoking the beauty of truth, symbolized as 'the sweet silver song of the lark'.

With reference to the cathedral and the Liver Birds' statue, 'Liverpool' is what Peter Barry calls 'urban specific', but it is also 'urban generic' in foregrounding human moods (2000: 48–52). He lists 'literary co-texts' as one feature of the 'urban-generic' and Duffy's opening is redolent of Thomas Gray's pastoral 'Elegy Written in a Country Churchyard' (1751) while her lark of truth belongs to Keats's 'Ode on a Grecian Urn' (1820) that imagines untold stories around the figures depicted on the clay pot. 'North-West' (*FG* 64) itemizes the ferry, the Pier Head, the 'silvery bird', and the 'yeah yeah yeah' of The Beatles' lyrics, to specify Liverpool's famous associations, but the sonnet meditates on memory in more universal terms: 'Frets of light on the river. Tearful air.' Nevertheless, these poems connect with Barry's wish to re-register Liverpool's 'poetic claims': 'In the 1990s, as the city emerged from its traumatizing 1980s decade, it has produced a much more troubled and troubling kind of writing' (2000: 137–64). Barry also revives the 'poetic claims' of Hull, London, and Birmingham and refers to their 'hard lyric' treatment by contemporary poets. Duffy's 'Birmingham' (*RL* 19), written in August 2011, is one such stern reflection on the riots in Winson Green when the looters, aiming for the mosque, drove their car into three men who came out to defend local businesses. Duffy dedicates the poem to Tariq Jahan, father of one of the victims, who pleaded for calm and was subsequently praised for his heroic public service. The gritty 'hard lyric' voice speaks personally to the murdered men and also appeals for public penance and respect: 'I think we all should kneel // on that English street.' 'Stephen Lawrence' (*Near* 10) similarly mixes lyric intensity with public address—'Cold pavement indeed / the night you died, / abused and stabbed'—and zooms in on the bereaved parent. In *The Mirror*, the poem accompanied the report of Stephen's mother laying flowers on the paving stone that marks his death, following the conviction of two men nearly twenty years after the attack in 1993.[8] Duffy confronts the cruel facts of his murder while

[8] Tom Pettifor (2012) 'Stephen Lawrence: Mum Doreen lays flowers at the spot where her son died', *Mirror*, 7 January.

consoling his mother that her seeds of love have doubled his short lifespan, referring to Doreen Lawrence's campaign that harvested a public inquiry into institutionalized racism.

In these poems, Duffy blends a geographically and historically specific event with more widespread principles of justice and equality. She does not romanticize the cityscape, but she does insist on its place in contemporary poetry. 'The English Elms' memorializes the grand trees, the original Seven Sisters in London's Tottenham, which now only survive through art. The rather discordant pun, 'overwhelmed', is perhaps a self-conscious avoidance of pastoral sentimentality. The poem illustrates a diachronic poetic trope, 'perceiving through the city several layers of time, several epochs, simultaneously' (Barry 2000: 48). Similarly, 'The White Horses' (*Bees* 44–5) is 'chronotopically anchored' (Barry 2000: 83), meaning that a reflective 'out-take' occurs in a specific time and place. Based on the seventeen geoglyphs in England, many of which are in Wiltshire, the county named in the poem, the hill figures are hard to preserve. However, Duffy likens the white horse printed on the turf to a poem on the page and thereby asserts the human music of these primitive art forms. A poem on the floods in Cumbria, November 2009, 'Cockermouth and Workington' (*Bees* 55), is self-evidently chronotopically specific. The 'f' letter that snakes through the poem—'No folk fled the flood'—is on the cusp of a distracting tongue twister, but it mediates the deafening sound and rapid flow of the flooding waters. It also reverberates with medieval alliterative verse to diachronically evoke the place's historic landscape along with a bright future as the new bridge is built, foals are in the fields, and farmers are back at work.

The Things-of-Nature

Duffy is neither a 'city' nor a 'post-industrial' poet for her engagement with urban life is not at odds with her self-fashioned task of championing aspects of culture threatened by human insouciance and these include nature. However, as Nerys Williams explains, '"nature" now has a "suspiciously retro, neo-Victorian ring, even when the argument is recast to emphasize not just love of nature but proto-ecological knowledge and environmentalist commitment"' (2011: 158). For Duffy, characteristically, this knowledge and commitment mesh the need for progress alongside the need to preserve: 'Yes, I think a poem is a spell of kind / that keeps things living in a written line' ('Spell', *Bees* 56). Her entertaining 'The Counties' (*Bees* 42–3) was provoked by the Royal Mail's plan to delete every county from its database and contingently from postal addresses by 2016. Her additive method—the repetition of 'But I want to'—corresponds to the devices of oral poetry in which mnemonic needs determine speech patterns and syntax. A poem she often selects at readings, it revives the poet's role as community spokesperson. She characteristically draws on various cultural treasures and landmarks, from The Dorset Giant—a chalk hill figure in Cerne Abbas, or the Inland Revenue based in York, to the disappearance of Rutland, England's smallest county. Intertextual fragments display how Britain's counties are woven into literature that spans popular folk-songs ('The Lincolnshire Poacher'), children's stories (*Alice in Wonderland*), and above all, poetry, specifically A.E. Housman's *A Shropshire Lad* (1896) and John Betjeman's ironic 'In Praise of Slough' (1928, 1937). The last line, '*all the birds of Oxfordshire and Gloucestershire ...*', borrows from Edward Thomas's 'Addlestrop' that Barry dubs the 'rural-iconic poem' and 'the very heart of twentieth-century meadow-cred poetry' (2000: 6). However, as Barry also points out, the songbirds that Thomas heard from his train are not what they were (2000: 41). The decline in songbirds over the past twenty-five years is attributable to changes in farming techniques, the use of insecticides, the disappearance of hedgerows, and too many predators.

In 'The Counties', then, Duffy is not primarily concerned with environmental issues and yet the poem stands up to 'Ecocriticism', which, as Terry Gifford defines, 'may be the frame of our age, informed with a new kind of concern for "environment" rather than "countryside" or "landscape" or the "bucolic"' (1999: 147). Bate also addresses the challenge for contemporary poets to write about nature:

> The "crisis of representation" or "hermeneutics of suspicion" is at the core of all versions of postmodern literary theory. Ecopoetics, with its affirmation of not only the existence, but also the sacredness, of the-things-of-nature-in-themselves seems naïve in comparison. It needs to find a path through skepticism, to reach a clearing beyond the dense undergrowth of the proposition that language is a self-enclosed system. (Bate 2000: 251)

As noted above, Duffy's use of performable oral devices—lists, repetition, alliteration, rhythm and rhyme—assumes a public context in which to ventilate common concerns. 'John Barleycorn' (*Bees* 29–30) not only resuscitates the English folk song but also the way of life and places that it registers. Since Barleycorn is an allegory of the barley crop from which beer and whisky are made, the poem's narrative stresses the importance of good crops and the communities that evolve around them in agriculture and public houses. Barleycorn was renowned for his drinking and Duffy lists English pub names that record birds, flora, and fauna and those that signify quintessential aspects of British history and culture, from 'The Poacher' and 'Red Dragon' to 'Nelson' and 'Robin Hood'. The sprawling patchwork of references ends with the tragic vision of Barleycorn's world on the brink between survival and recession: 'And where he supped, / the past lived still; and where he sipped, the glass brimmed full.' This poem complicates the 'double vision-ing' discussed by Barry that 'arises from the tendency of cities to foreground time and change whereas the countryside … primarily connotes (when used as a cultural signifier) timelessness and continuity' (2000: 45). Instead, Duffy dramatizes how the countryside is subject to time and change and how rural and urban matters are connected. A poem like 'John Barleycorn' might be labelled 'post-pastoral', a term Terry Gifford proposes to 'enable "a mature environmental aesthetics" to sift the "sentimental pastoral" from the "complex pastoral" in a way which takes account of the urgent need for responsibility and, indeed, advocacy for the welfare of Arden' (1999: 149).

Duffy's 'Arden' is sometimes specifically Britain, but more often planet Earth and it always converses with other poetic depictions. 'Silver Lining' (*RL* 36), that invokes the popular proverb, 'every cloud has a silver lin-ing', records the grounding of flights caused by ash from the Icelandic volcano Eyjafjallajökull in April 2010, from the perspective of listening to the news. While documenting the harsh upheavals for people stranded abroad, Duffy moves to the upside of having a noiseless sky. She tunes in to the amplified song of British birds, 'the music silence summons', heard by the poets, George Herbert, Robbie Burns, Edward Thomas, and 'briefly us'. In *To the Moon*'s Introduction, she writes: 'In 1969, the USA first landed and walked on the moon and threatened to smudge a sacred poetic symbol. Since then, poets are already seeking new ways, through dialogue with scientists, to respond to the awesome ecological challenges of this century' (2009: xviii). In *The Bees*, bees and other endangered species, that include poetry, thread through the poems and in turn, rever-ence for 'the-things-of-nature-in-themselves' sustains the indispensability of Duffy's art. Inevitably mindful of Ariel's song, 'where the bee sucks', from Shakespeare's *The Tempest* (Act 5: 1), in 'Ariel' (*Bees* 11), Duffy affirms the sacredness of nature with characteristic self-reflexivity. Ariel's 'merrily / merrily' taken out of its pastoral dreamscape to twenty-first century farming methods satirizes the casually widespread use of toxic substances, 'neonicotinoid insecticides'—associated with honey-bee colony collapse disorder—that 'sour' the soil and threaten the whole ecosystem. The impact of colony collapse disorder is also registered in 'The Human Bee' (*Bees* 76–7), referring to the hire of people to do the work of bees in China where the disorder was acute. In 'Virgil's *Bees*' (*Bees* 23) the poet assumes the mantle of a priest or prophet and warns: 'where bees pray on their knees, sing, praise / in pear trees, plum trees, bees / are the batteries of orchards, gardens, guard them'. The poem's title alludes to Book IV of Virgil's *Georgics* that chronicles the life and habits of bees and Duffy's 'Hive' (*Bees* 31) also pays homage to the industry of bees as celebrated since ancient times. 'Drone' (*Bees* 78) honours the male that dies after mating with the queen bee, the four lines demarcating the brevity of his life.

Prior to the climate change summit in Copenhagen (December 2009), *The Guardian* asked artists and writers to produce new work in response to environmental concerns and 'Virgil's Bees' was Duffy's contribution.[9] Additionally, in the last verse of 'The Twelve Days of Christmas 2009', she crafts her poetic polemic: 'Did they hear the drums in Copenhagen, / banging their warning?' She names some of the world's leaders and asks whether these 'politicos' are twiddling their thumbs and striking bargains instead of striking a match to action. In the form of a letter, 'The Woman in the Moon' (*Bees* 49) is subtler in its lament for the fragile planet on which humanity depends: '*Darlings / what have you done to the world?*' Duffy's collage of the varying shapes and hues of the moon invites the reader's return of love for this ethereal symbol of nature's combination of constancy and cyclical change that is also an iconic symbol of poetic inspiration. The poem models what Bate describes, citing Heidegger: 'there is a special kind of writing, called poetry, which has the peculiar power to speak "earth". Poetry is the song of the earth' (2000: 251). Duffy's 'Atlas' (*Bees* 27–8), published on National Poetry Day 2009, also 'sings the earth' by naming several natural wonders of the world. In Greek mythology, Atlas was a titan who held up the celestial spheres but Duffy has him as a hero who supports Earth's seas, creatures, and mountains that are vital to its human population of billions. 'Parliament' (*Bees* 50–2) takes the songs of birds to grieve, mock, and heckle against extinctions resulting from human exploitation. Coral is erased by the

[9] '*Postcards to the Planet*, a climate change special, *Guardian Review*, 26 Sept 2009.

ferocious oil industry—'Oil like a gag / on the Gulf of Mexico'; rainforests are burned for 'cocaine, cash, looters'; and land disappears due to emissions of methane. As Hale comments, '"Parliament" is a stunning poem, with all the birds of the so-called "writer's wood" chorusing their two cents' worth in protest at humanity's disregard for the planet; here, again, Duffy speaks to the ancient traditions of literature in English, specifically to Chaucer's "Parlement of Foules", written in the 1380s' (2012).

Thus, when Duffy sings the earth, she takes account of the 'complex web of nature and environment' (Bate 2000: 23). The sonnet 'Oxfam' (*Bees* 19), written for the organization's literary festival, condenses into the frame of a charity shop the values of a contemporary public. 'Fieldnotes from a Catastrophe: Report on Climate Change' by American journalist Elizabeth Kolbert is priced at 40p; published in 2006, the report's low value indicates the fatal procrastination by governments and the public's indifference to such findings. 'Luke Howard, Namer of Clouds' (*Bees* 46) remembers 'the father of meteorology' (1772–1864) and the bee connection is indirectly made since his early work was a 'Microscopical Investigation of several Species of Pollen'. Duffy's poem revives his name and his passion for observing the weather system. She typically addresses global matters through a close-up of its personal implications. Here, 'love goes naming' refers to an intimate space in which a curl of hair resembles the shape of a cloud that Howard named. 'Nile' (*Bees* 32), in the voice of the great river, similarly proves how global shifts are experienced in the mundane for if the rivers dry up all is 'nil, null, void'. Printed next to the elegiac 'Water' (*Bees* 33), the poem links emotively to the last thirsty cry for water from the poet's dying mother. These poems prove Bate's belief when he asks 'What are poets for?' He dismisses philosophizing and moralizing—'though they often try to explain the world and human kind's place within it'—in favour of, 'they are often exceptionally lucid or provocative in their articulation of the relationship between internal and external worlds, between being and dwelling' (2000: 251–2).

NATIONHOOD

Based on his first-hand experience of the Balkan wars that resulted in 'a hatred so huge, so vicious and mindless', Simic warns: 'The marching music of the next century will undoubtedly be religion and nationalism' (1997: 25). Like Simic, Duffy is alert to inflammatory religious dogma that engulfs its followers (discussed in Chap. 2) and the fifth ring in 'Twelve

Days of Christmas' (2009) is 'religion's halo, slipped—a blind for eyes or gag for lips'. She also exposes the inhumanity of and devastating fall-outs from nationalistic conflicts, notably the Holocaust or The Falklands war (discussed in Chap. 3), and more recently, as mentioned above, in Afghanistan or Iraq. The role of 'National Poet' is a particular challenge when she professes no sense of national identity: "'When I go to Scotland I feel Scottish and when I go to Ireland I feel Irish," she says. "I suppose the one thing I don't feel is English"' (Ross 2012). Since she had satirized and indicted nationalist hegemonies during the Thatcherite years, how was Duffy to write about Dover's white cliffs, particularly with their inevitable and uncomfortable equation between chalky whiteness and Englishness? Commissioned by the National Trust to mark a successful public appeal to buy one of the last stretches of the famous landmark in private owner-ship, Duffy could justifiably collude with the principles of guarding wild-life and keeping the spot accessible to the public. Thus, in 'White Cliffs' (*RL* 22), she sidesteps patriotism and foregrounds how the place features 'in painting, poem, play, in song', a noble tradition to which she is merely adding. One reviewer of *The Bees* detected a 'self-imposed pressure to celebrate "heritage"' and 'an anxious English identity politics'; however, she also associates Duffy's 'spoken melody' with the 'Celtic influences, from her Scots-Irish ancestry', citing a line from 'Premonitions' addressed to her mother: "'the joy of your accent, unenglish, dancey, humorous"' (Rumens 2012). Duffy certainly draws on and contributes to the cultural resources of Britain rather than England and is increasingly a mediator between groups rather than an agitator for difference. *Academi*, the Welsh National Literature Promotion Agency and Society of Writers, published a leaflet in which Gillian Clarke notes that Duffy had been a long time visitor to Wales, regularly read in several venues throughout the country, and, with Clarke, tutored at Ty Newydd Writing Centre in Llanystumdwy where 'poems by the poet laureate are now engraved in local Welsh slate and hidden in the gardens' (Darlington 2015). Duffy prefaces *The Bees* with a dedication in Welsh to Clarke, as National Poet, godmother to Ella, and friend to the poet. 'My Favourite Drink' (*Pamphlet* 18–19) is set in 'The Red Dragon / in Penderyn / near Hirwaun / in mid-Glamorgan', but, typically, the remembered place sets off thoughts about love.

Duffy is decidedly, if erratically, claimed for Scottish literature, a claim with which she acquiesces, up to a point. She first read 'Drams' (*Bees* 34–8), a sequence about whisky, at the Scottish literary festival *Aye Write!* in March 2010. It has a light touch but covers several Duffyesque interests, from her family history—'my grandmother / Irish to his Scotch', and erotic love—tasting Talisker 'on your lips', to human 'joys, grief', and more privately, 'The unfinished dram / on the hospice side-table'. Most of all, the dram is a symbol for a short poem. As Hale, comments, '"Drams" is a wonderful sequence of haikus, at once personal and transcendent, amongst the standout poems in this collection [*The Bees*]. National identity is wrestled with in this poem, as it has been throughout Duffy's work (in such poems as "Originally"); the "sad flit" from "whisky to beer" brilliantly encapsulates transition and homesickness' (2012). Hale, a Scottish poet himself, concludes that her litany of Scottish poets—'With Imlah, Lochhead, / Dunn, Jamie, Patterson, Kay, / Morgan, with MacCaig', and, of course, 'Dour Burns's water'—is where Duffy aligns herself. 'Standing Stone' (*Pamphlet* 9–17), commissioned for the opening of the National Museum of Scotland (30 November 1998) is largely in Scottish dialect and takes the archaeological phenomenon of ancient stones to commemorate the country's history, fish, rivers, birds, and cities, from the Bronze age, through English colonization, to the present. Welsh poet, Sheenagh Pugh, admires the poem's evocation of 'the feeling of kinship and love that tends to sweep over you when looking at odds and ends of the long departed' (1999). However, it does not sentimentalize places or people but includes references to economic struggles and barbarity towards women, redolent of Heaney's bog poem 'Punishment' (2001: 37–8).

Nevertheless, the Scottish papers celebrate Duffy's continuing affinity with the country of her birth and paternal grandfather. In 2002, Scotland's daily broadsheet printed 'McGonagall's Burd', with the headline, 'Leading Scottish writer Carol Ann Duffy pens a new year poem for the *Sunday Herald*'. The poem parodies the doggerel that won the nineteenth-century writer his notoriety as the worst poet in British history. Duffy amusingly parodies McGonagall's mixed metres, Scottish colloquialisms, inconsequential sentiments, and weak imagery—'the moon's a petticoat shortbread'—proving her knowledge of popular Scottish culture as she expresses good wishes to the readers. Elsewhere, she hybridizes English with Scottish words and allusions, particularly since her appointment as laureate: in 'Sung' (*Bees* 71), a meditation on a tombstone, she writes 'trysts', 'bonnie', and 'a rose, red, red', with deference to Burns's immortal metaphor for romantic love. For twenty years she has taught at Moniack Mhor, a residential writing centre in the Highlands (Ramaswamy 2009), and *The Big Issue* reports that Edinburgh is her favourite city (Meiklem 2009). A regular at '"its most magnificent, most important and most generous book festival in the world"' (Duffy, Linklater 2009), she readily coined a poem 'Inside the Yurt', in honour of Catherine Lockerbie when she stepped down as its director (2009). Duffy was a driving force behind the four-month exhibition on poets laureate, 'Poetry at the Palace' (2014), in Holyrood House, Edinburgh, next door to the stunning parliament complex that was completed in 2004 following devolution in 1998. The exhibition was announced proudly in the Scotsman, endorsing how the Laureateship is officially for the whole United Kingdom (Ferguson 2013). Reviewing *The Bees*, Julian Colton detects an 'understandable idealization of things Scottish' but also a human belief 'that we should hold on to things of value, cherish those things which really matter like the environment, close family, the people we love and the wider social nexus which we all rely and depend on' (2012: 46).

In 'September 2014', Duffy uses love to problematize the elemental binary divisions in the historic Scottish referendum on independence. Respecting but transcending the manifestoes of both 'Yes' and 'No' campaigns, the metaphor of a river flowing across the border as 'shared currency', depicts the difficulty of extricating Scotland from its English relation, economically as well as geographically and emotionally. At the same time, she eulogizes what is distinctly Scottish: its dialect and poets— epitomized in 'Rabbae Burns'—its history and its landscape, 'the brave, bold, brilliant, land' of the thistle. Acknowledging the indelible scars of English colonialism, she expresses the shame and love that sympathetic English onlookers to the referendum could barely put into words: 'the thistle jags our hearts, / take these roses / from our bloodied hands'. As one *Guardian* reader exclaimed, 'As a yes voter, my eyes filled with tears on reading Carol Ann Duffy's poignant poem, "September 2014", on Saturday's front page—as if I had grasped that thorny thistle. So much said in so few words!' (Geyer 2014). Thus, refuting McCrum's scepticism about public poetry, Duffy incisively apprehends the British mood in an intense yet pluralized lyric voice to express how the collective response is felt as deeply personal.

The 'R' Factor

Refusing to be short-listed for the Laureateship in 1999, Harrison's 'A Celebratory Ode on the Abdication of King Charles III' imagines a Britain freed from the trammels of colonialism and obsequy to the Crown: 'More democratic, more adult / with no mystique of monarch cult, / let's begin by hauling down / the R in names that mean the Crown' (2000: 2). Since Duffy shares Harrison's left-wing verve, critics wondered how she would manage the 'R', the Royal factor, in her appointment. To repeated questions on the issue, Duffy responds that since Wordsworth's time 'there hasn't been any expectation that poets would write on command', and she was 'persuaded by her need to prove that poetry can still be central to Britain's cultural life' (Thorpe 2009). The absence of Laureate poems on royal babies inevitably invites comment and even parody (Low 2015). However, as stressed all through this book, Duffy foregrounds and fosters a shared humanity that transcends divisive categories. 'A Commonwealth Blessing for Girls',[10] written for and read at 'An Observance for Commonwealth Day' in Westminster Abbey, 14 March 2011, held no compromising imperial vestige of Rule Britannia but a theme of 'Women as agents for change'. The programme lists a commitment to gender equality in the spirit of human rights. To this end, 'A Reflection' by Dr Dambisa Moyo numbered areas of progress and also areas where women, although more than half the populations, constitute a majority of the most poor; at the other end of the social spectrum, they are barely visible as Heads of State or in other positions of influence. Duffy puts the same realities poetically and envisages what the women might do, given the chance: 'equality, a girl half / of the whole of the harmed world, healer; the joy of choice'. Providing a sense of ownership through naming, a method she frequently favours, the poem itemizes many countries in the Commonwealth.

A pre-Laureate poem, 'To Boil Bacon' (*NSP* 137–8), is the internal monologue of a housewife following a recipe when she hears on the wireless, 'the sudden abdication of a king', a reference to Edward VIII's controversial decision to marry the divorcee Wallis Simpson. As head of the Church of England, he could neither divorce his wife nor marry a divorced person whose spouse was still alive. The king's agonizing choice between love and duty perhaps chimes with the housewife's situation. Her rigid adherence to the recipe can suggest the same competing impulses as she struggles to keep house and feed her family, for, if she is boiling the bacon it is probably an inexpensive cut. Her tears, jerked by the onion, suggest her unspoken torment symbolized by the 'hard gold glinting' of her wedding ring. As Helen Dunmore comments, 'Much of Duffy's work demonstrates that public poetry is most telling when most unexpected' (1999).

[10]http://www.westminsterabbey.org/__data/assets/pdf_file/0009/47088/Commonwealth-Day-Observance-Programme-2011.pdf

'Rings' (*Bees* 24–5) dealt with a royal wedding in a 'most unexpected' way: although composed for the marriage of Prince William and Catherine Middleton at Westminster Abbey, 29 April 2011, it does not mention the couple by name but opens up its romantic imagery to any lovers, regardless of their status or sexuality. The poem plays with the central conceit: rings found in nature; rings made by human hands; or sounds that ring out. The harmonious rhythm emulates the symbiosis of dance or love making that culminates in a crescendo: 'here, / where nothing and no one is wrong'. In Duffy's lexicon, the couple are complete and 'at home' through love, whereas love gone wrong engenders feelings of homelessness and dislocation: the 'wrong taste', 'and the wrong sounds, / the wrong smells, the wrong light, every breath—/ wrong' ('Nostalgia', *MT* 10). In *The Guardian*, Duffy placed 'Rings' with other poems for nuptials stating, 'Britain has many countries, and one of them is Poetry. We go to our national art when we seek Coleridge's "best words" for ceremony and celebration' (23 April 2011).

Duffy's concession, 'There is a lot of goodwill towards the Queen in the country and that was also an important thing to honour in a poem', signals a maturation since 'Poet for our Times' that denounced a populist tabloid's royalist bent with its 'punchy haikus featuring the Queen'. Aptly, she prioritizes her professional duty to put poetry in public spaces and that includes 'ceremony and celebration'. As recorded in Chap. 1, Duffy uses her connection with Buckingham Palace for the benefit of poetry and when asked by Westminster Abbey to mark the 60th anniversary of the Coronation, she accepted because of the Abbey's connection with literature through its Poets' Corner. In the vein of Shakespeare's history plays, Duffy's 'The Crown' (*RL* 39) dwells on the tough vulnerability of the human who wears it—'The crown translates a woman to a Queen'. Duffy neatly states that for Elizabeth II it is 'no hollow crown' referring to a bleak passage spoken by Shakespeare's Richard II who never wore it with ease:

> for within the hollow crown
> That rounds the mortal temples of a king
> Keeps Death his court and there the antic sits,
> Scoffing his state and grinning at his pomp,
> Allowing him a breath, a little scene,
> To monarchize, be fear'd and kill with looks,
> Infusing him with self and vain conceit,
> As if this flesh which walls about our life,

Were brass impregnable, and humour'd thus
Comes at the last and with a little pin
Bores through his castle wall, and farewell king! (*Richard II*, Act 3: 2)

This lengthy extract illuminates the complexity of what on the surface might seem a rather straightforward royal tribute, for Duffy's 'The Crown' has the same iambic pentameter, the same meditative tone, and the same themes of weighty responsibility and human mortality that Shakespeare richly dramatizes.[11] It also proves how the Duffyesque imagination is always firstly literary and never panders to 'state' or 'pomp'. In like manner, when asked to write a poem for the ceremony of Richard III's re-interment in Leicester Cathedral (26 March 2015), Duffy skilfully condensed into fourteen lines the story of his unmarked death with a Shakespearean meditation on human mortality in the voice that is both king and human: 'Describe my soul / as incense, votive, vanishing; your own / the same' ('Richard', *Guardian* 26 March 2015).

Duffy again draws on her poetic myth-kitty in 'The Thames, London 2012' (*Guardian* 27 April 2012), written for the Jubilee Pageant in which the Queen and the Duke of Edinburgh sailed on a royal barge along the river as part of a flotilla of over 1000 boats. Spoken by the River, the poem tells the history of London's upheavals—the Great Fire, the Big Freeze, Fog, Flood, The Blitz, beheadings, drowning, and pollution—through fragments from the poets Shakespeare, Spenser, and T.S. Eliot. Like her namesake, Elizabeth 1, the current Queen does finally sail into the sunlight with the river 'gargling the Crown'. The verb 'gargle' can describe the wake from the boats as Duffy herself observed, 'seeing seven miles of the Thames seem to give voice to itself in the most extraordinary, surreal and moving way' (Duffy, 29 September 2012), but it also allows anti-monarchists to hear it as their trouble in swallowing the royal celebrations. Additionally, true to herself, Duffy edited *Jubilee Lines* designed to add 'Poetry's voice' to the Diamond Jubilee, 2012. The project involved commissioning sixty poets from the UK and Commonwealth to write on a particular year of the queen's reign, and Duffy's 'Thames' is the last in the anthology. In her Preface, she introduces the variety of poems with a statement that describes her own practice: 'The poems offer a fascinating mix of the personal and the public, the political and the poetic … [they]

---

[11] In 2012, 'The Hollow Crown' was the title to a new series of the plays broadcast on BBC 2.

reflect on who we were, where we have been, and what we have done'. She
delights in the events that they record, the films and songs with which they
resonate, and the range of styles, 'a truly democratic mix'.

POETRY MATTERS: '"IT'S A PERFECTING OF A FEELING IN LANGUAGE"'

As outlined in Chap. 1, Duffy can take considerable credit for raising
public awareness about how poetry matters. Reviewing *The Bees*, the
Express declares, 'Duffy is spearheading the current surge in poetry's
population. Her book sales are going through the roof, her staged readings regularly sell out and her latest collection, *The Bees*, is shortlisted
for the Costa Book Awards.... [Carol Ann] strides off into the night.
Nobody bows or curtsies but I have a feeling that one day they might.'[12]
As constantly noted, one Duffy trademark is the hybrid allusions to
high and popular cultures. In 'Philharmonic' (*RL* 24), commissioned
by the Royal Philharmonic Society to commemorate its bicentenary,
the cognoscenti would get her reference to the Society's early commission of Beethoven's ninth symphony in the 'deaf joy' of the composer. The ode depicts the orchestra's many instruments, from brass
to strings, but cannot resist the common cliché, 'all strings attached
to silver sound'. It reverberates with the kinship between music and
poetry through alliterative onomatopoeia—'Wounds in wood, where
the wind'—yet also demarcates the distinctiveness of sheer sound as 'a
songbird's flight'. Duffy asserts, '"I love music"', and that inspiration
'"has to come from a genuine impulse or a real connection. There is
no point in faking up a poem"' (Wroe 2014). Similarly, she had no
conflict in writing for The World Shakespeare Festival in 2012: 'of
course, Shakespeare is very important—he almost *is* the language. I
also feel very close to Stratford because I've been going there since
I was a teenager' (Wroe 2014). Her free-verse sonnet, 'Shakespeare'
(*RL* 31), projects how her own sense of a poetic self is modelled on
his: 'word-blessed, language loved best; / the living human music of
our tongues'.[13] In 'Chaucer's Valentine' (*RL* 9), Duffy digs down to

[12] Cited as the *Sunday Express* in publicity material: http://www.panmacmillan.com/
book/carolannduffy/thebees

[13] To accompany 'Shakespeare', artist Stephen Raw translated the verse into seven paintings, which unveiled in November 2012 and were exhibited in the foyer of the Swan Theatre,

the literary tradition behind popular customs. Initially printed on the front page of *The Guardian* (14 February, 2013), the title regards the first reference to St Valentine's Day as a time to celebrate romantic love in Chaucer's 'A Parliament of Foules'. Duffy takes his opening—'The lyf so short, the craft so long to lerne'—which in turn appropriates a Latin phrase, *Ars longa, vita brevis*, that translates an ancient Greek aphorism. As ever, the chain of references frames the poem with a self-enclosed literary allusiveness while its argument urges the reader to go out and love because life is short, a fact confirmed by the brevity of each line and of the whole poem. Aside from its co-texts, the tone and dedication, 'for Nia', are intimate, rendering a stand-alone love poem that any reader might be happy to give or receive: 'but be my valentine / and I'll one candle burn'. Continuing the process of handing on literary forms and themes, Duffy's poem was widely circulated via Twitter and Tumbler.

In 2002, Padel reported a paradox: on the one hand, poetry is happening more than ever, through festivals, competitions, prizes, in institutions 'from the Royal Mail to London Zoo' and poems are commissioned every day by 'town councils, hospitals, theatres, radio … Poems are bricked into pavements and written in glass on the windows of delicatessens. Poetry it seems has never been so popular'; and yet, 'poetry has also never had such a low profile in the media and literary community, nor so few readers proportionate to the numbers who buy and read other serious books' (46). Seven years later, Duffy is more optimistic:

> Most contemporary poets feel themselves to be members of the honourable tribe of poets: one which presently stretches from elders such as Dannie Abse, Roy Fisher, Edwin Morgan, Fleur Adcock, Elaine Feinstein, to new, younger voices such as Daljit Nagra, Jane Weir, Clare Shaw, and with so many in between. // The poets I've known and worked with over 25 years or so—reading in primary and secondary schools, in libraries, in prisons; performing in pubs, on stage or at festivals; running workshops in universities or community centres; undertaking residencies in football clubs, in factories, in art galleries, in hospices; supporting little magazines or judging glittering prizes; travelling abroad or writing in solitude—all share the certainty that poetry, the music of being human, matters deeply to a huge and growing number of people in this country. This is a certainty, a belief, which has been learned, earned, over and over again, from fellow poets, readers

Stratford on Avon.

and audiences. I believe that the continuance of the laureateship acknowledges that poetry is vital to the imagining of what Britain has been, what it is and what it might yet become. ('Sisters in Poetry', Guardian 2009)

Duffy certainly practises what she preaches and is tireless in getting poetry into places through various media and means. She contributed her name and a poem, 'Gesture' (*Bees* 79), to a fund-raising anthology for Macmillan Cancer Care (Goodyear and Morgan 2011) and on 30 August 2010, she premièred her poem 'Vigil' for the Manchester Pride Candlelight Vigil in memory of LGBT people who had lost their lives to HIV/AIDS.

Part of Duffy's success lies in not being a one-woman show. As previously mentioned, she collates poems through anthologies and through curations for *The Guardian* that in addition to war, sport, and weddings, include women and ageing—'Our society, I believe, is turning gradually away from its obsession with "yoof" and "slebs"' ('Older and Wiser' 2010). She also generously brings poets together for public events, as poet Jo Bell blogs:

> She is a pragmatist laureate who never stops using that shiny golden title to good effect, creating events that showcase poetry from all backgrounds, from all ages, on all subjects. She brings on new poets at her own readings in Manchester, and judges prizes that bring up new talents. She has lent her name as patron to organizations including Chorlton Arts Festival, Camden and Lumen Poetry, the Wenlock Poetry Festival, Ledbury Poetry Festival and (erm....) the Natural Beekeeping Trust. Yes.
>
> Her predecessor, Andrew Motion gave us the great gift of the Poetry Archive, but Carol Ann grabs the poisoned chalice of the laureateship with both hands and makes it a collection plate for British poetry. ... The Queen's Diamond Jubilee saw no bunting go up in my household, but CAD used it to give sixty contemporary poets exposure in her anthology *Jubilee Lines*. She gathered poets for readings in London and Edinburgh to raise money for victims of the Haiti earthquake [2009]. This week she is sticking her neck out again, using her celebrity to agitate against the books ban in prisons.[14]

In addition to agitating against the book ban for prisoners, Duffy was one of several public figures who opposed cuts to public libraries in 2012. Her vitriolic response to axing funds for the Arts, 'A Cut Back', was published

[14] https://belljarblog.wordpress.com/2014/05/19/jo-bells-always-there-awards-5/

in *The Guardian* (9 April 2011) with her notes explaining the specific losses to festivals, small presses, and educational initiatives. The poem's sub-line, 'after Louis MacNeice', alerts readers to the spirit and pattern of 'Bagpipe Music' in which MacNeice satirizes the philistinism of his contemporary government and public: 'It's no go the Government grants, it's no go the elections, / Sit on your arse for fifty years and hang your hat on a pension' (MacNeice 1964: 48). Duffy follows suit: 'It's no go, dear PBS. It's no go, sweet poets. / Sat on your arses for fifty years and never turned a profit. / All we want are bureaucrats, the nods as good as winkers. / And if you're strapped for cash, go fish, then try the pigging bankers.' She also took part in the 400th anniversary remembrance for the twelve Lancashire people accused of witchcraft, ten of whom were hanged and eight of these were women. She comments, '"I was struck by the echoes of under-privilege and hostility to the poor, the outsider, the desperate, which are audible still"' (Wainwright 2012). Her poem for the events, 'The Pendle Witches' (*RL* 14–15), registers the 'superstition, ignorance' of the rural Lancashire community towards the victims, 'unloved, an underclass'. As if to inspire greater tolerance, her poem historicizes the crude beliefs: 'But that was then—when difference / made ghouls of neighbours'. The unchanging part is the scenery and grey skies of Lancashire and the poem's verses are placed outdoors in the view of walkers along ten mileposts that also feature the name of one of the so-called witches. In her 'Study of Poetry in Public Places', Julia Forster echoes Duffy's faith that poetry can make something happen: 'Publishing poetry in public places is vital if we are to keep it at the forefront of the human consciousness, where it can inspire, heal and transform' (Forster 2006).

In 'The Pendle Witches', the three lines of each verse resemble a witch's spells to evoke the atmosphere of magic surrounding the trials and hangings. This orality conforms to Walter Ong's study of how highly literate cultures pit themselves against preliterate ones, presuming an unwarranted superiority when they cannot attain the fuller human consciousness of oral communities:

> In the absence of elaborate analytical categories that depend on writing to structure knowledge at a distance from lived experience, oral cultures must conceptualize and verbalize all their knowledge with more or less close reference to the human life world, assimilating the alien, objective world to the more immediate, familiar interaction of human beings. (Ong 2002: 42)

Poems written for a broad public are necessarily direct and offer some res-olution, aesthetically at least, in times that are baffling or overwhelming. Rumens comments on this aesthetic as a deficiency: 'Like the performance poem at the technical level, the eco-poem and the national celebration offer ready-made intellectual positions and too-easy closure' (2012: 75). Such reviewing illustrates how performable features are judged negatively in relation to the conventions of writing: 'The rhetorical tricks recurrent in *The Bees* are the staple of British performance poetry—sing-song rhythms, emphatic rhymes, a sense of relentless crescendo, excited and often allit-erative lists. Oh the lists, the lists, the lists. Too often they substitute a forced carbonated energy for the complex, sinew-thrust of written syntax' (Rumens 2012: 75).

Duffy braves such criticism in daring to use epithets, clichés, and devices that are staple formulae in oral communities. As Ong observes, 'The spoken word forms human beings into close-knit groups. ... Writing and print isolate' (2002: 73). As Ong also states, the oral effects of nar-rative, rhythm, or repetition that are designed to aid recall, bring poems close to the 'life world' of their readers. 'Achilles' (*Bees* 17), that endears Duffy to football fans, ends with her magic threefold repetition: 'his heel, his heel, his heel'. The poem is about the Achilles tendon injury that left England footballer David Beckham out of the 2010 FIFA World Cup. Published in the *Mirror*, Duffy told the paper:

> The public aspect of some lives provides a narrative, a story, for the rest of us to follow. We speak of 'living the dream', a 'fairytale existence' of 'legends' and of 'heroes'. Like Greek myths, such public lives can contain triumph and tragedy, and in a way we all learn from them, as we do from Ovid, or the Brothers Grimm, or Shakespeare. The narrative of David Beckham's public life is, I'm sure, far from over ... but this poem is written in sympathy for this part of his story and to draw a parallel with Achilles, who gave his name to Beckham's injury. (*The Mirror,* 16 March 2010)

One reviewer, commenting on her blend of 'the modern and the mytho-logical', discerns in Duffy's treatment of Beckham's vulnerable tendon, 'his redefinition of the ideal male' (Relich 2011: 27). However, it is up to the reader whether they hear any irony in Duffy's depiction of the god-like status assumed by the game's top players. Beckham himself did not and requested a handwritten copy of 'Achilles' in exchange for a pair of his boots. In 'The

Shirt' (*Bees* 18), Duffy adds to the many literary appropriations of the poi-soned shirt of Nessus that killed Hercules as well as Achilles. She strips the glamour from fame in the dramatic dialogue with a devastated player who has lost his touch and is vilified by fans while the media denigrate his manhood and his WAG (wife and girlfriend). The poet-speaker cuts to the quick of his mortality with, 'at the end of the day you'll be stiff / in a shirt of solid gold, shining for City'.

Although poets and other artists were integral to the early Olympic Games in ancient Greece, as Duffy pointed out when introducing a group of sport-related poems in *The Guardian* ('Play up! Play up!' 2010), poetry and sport became an unusual combination. As *The Times* declared 'in the 400-year history of poets laureate there has never been a poem like [this] one ['Achilles'], for she suggests that a footballer's injury is 'a central ingredient in our national life'. It reported Duffy's comment on Radio 4's *The World at One*, that if the public make ordinary people into heroes, they will be seen 'at their most human' (Hoyle 2010). In a similar vein, 'Munich' (*NSP* 136) remembers the deaths of England's football team in the plane crash, 6 February 1958. The colloquial language accentuates the casual ordinariness of the players as they went about their business with 'a game of cards at the airport', oblivious to their impending tragedy. When the Olympic Games were hosted by London, a 'Poetry Parnassus' brought together poets from the 204 participating nations: 'a jewel in the crown of the London 2012 Cultural Olympiad, [it] is being hailed as the largest gathering of poets in history. It is part of a remarkable popular renais-sance' (De la Vega 2012). De la Vega saw the weeklong event as part of a worldwide revival:

> Poetry is everywhere. Its verses have emerged from minority venues to form part of mass culture, of people's day-to-day lives. Never before has a poetry festival of this magnitude been held in the United Kingdom and it is being billed as the first time in history that so many poets from around the globe have come together in one place.'[15]

Duffy's commitment to narrowing the gap between poets and the people extends to reaching the young. She presented *The Times* Young Poets Prize in 2012 and is a major contributor to the popular 'Poetry

---

[15] The poems are published in *The World Record* (2012) ed. Neil Astley and Anna Selby, Tarset: Bloodaxe Books.

Live' events that aim to engage 15 and 16 year-olds by meeting the poets. Duffy's elegy, 'Simon Powell' (*Bees* 57), on the untimely death of the man who conceived and executed 'Poetry Live', is, as Germaine Greer writes, 'more intricate than it seems. The pattern is founded on the trochaic cadence of the name, which has the same repeated double note as a mourning bell, submerged in liquid half-rhymes, like a vision through tears' (Greer 2010). Typically, Duffy's epithet, 'poetry's pal', and reference to his blessed marriages join his professional work to his personal life while the 'us' denotes the bereaved poetry community that he partly built. As Laureate, Duffy launched 'Anthologise', a competition for secondary schoolchildren designed to stimulate their personal ownership of poems by selecting some they like. She plans to extend poetry's scope in schools:

> "What I'd like to do is create anthologies for other school subjects—for history, for geography, for maths," she says. "I think poetry can help children deal with the other subjects on the curriculum by enabling them to see a subject in a new way. … Poetry is a different way of seeing something, and seeing a subject in a different way is often a very good tool to better learning". (Moorhead 2011)

With the expansion of new media, Duffy's poems are widely available through the unregulated World Wide Web. Following Ong's prediction that information technology heralds a newly oral culture, Kellner views the Internet as a realm for democratic participation and debate:

> first broadcast media like radio and television, and now computers, have produced new public spheres and spaces for information, debate, and participation that contain both the potential to invigorate democracy and to increase the dissemination of critical and progressive ideas—as well as new possibilities for manipulation, social control, the promotion of conservative positions, and intensifying of differences between haves and have nots. (Kellner 2000: 280)

However, the extracts from blogs previously cited demonstrate how the pages on which Duffy's work appears, foster critically debating discussion groups that strengthen a progressive democracy. A Google search for 'Carol Ann Duffy' finds 837,000 pages that largely consist of the national papers, the BBC, educational study guides—some of which are 'lessons' on YouTube, many of which are interactive—and independent intellectual forums, such as 'The Rumpus', with its broadly appealing manifesto:

> We know how easy it is to find pop culture on the Internet, so we're here to give you something more challenging, to show you how beautiful things are when you step off the beaten path. The Rumpus is a place where people come to be themselves through their writing, to tell their stories or speak their minds in the most artful and authentic way they know how, and to invite each of you, as readers, commenters or future contributors, to do the same.

Its pages include a lively, intellectual, and informative review of *Rapture* that would please the poet: 'Actually, I know her name and I am in love with her: Poetry' (Miller-Mack 2013). The way in which contemporary media can operate a critically debating public sphere is also evident through letters to the newspapers and comments on the online articles.[16] Duffy believes 'we should strive to introduce poetry to the texting generation' (29 September 2012) and the ultimate compliment must be spawning a Twitter mimic 'Carol Ann Muffy'. Duffy, however, never compromises on what poetry uniquely does: '"It's a perfecting of a feeling in language"' (Moorhead 2011). To balance contemporaneity with a sense of continuity, Duffy also offers antidotes to the sterile aesthetics of virtual realities through her live performances and the tactile physicality of her twenty-first century books. She sometimes enhances her readings by including Scottish musician John Sampson, to draw out or add a musical undertow to poems and to continue the collaboration of laureates before her, such as John Dryden with Henry Purcell. Just as she writes with a fountain pen (as seen in the manuscript poems at Holyrood Palace), the aesthetic features of her hardback volumes appeal to the reader's senses. The embossed covers ask to be handled and hint of old commonplace or children's books. The cloth ribbon bookmark, or 'stylus', invites the reader to progress though the poetry volume like a diary, novel, or music LP.

'Do you think it hears and heals our hearts?'

In 1993, poet and critic Sean O'Brien astutely observed, '[Duffy] has always written from the apparent certainty that poetry has a place in the

---

[16] See, for example, the letters under 'Taking a Line on poetical correctness' (2008) *Guardian* 5 July.

public realm, that it deals memorably with matters of importance and that it illuminates as well as records the facts and imaginings of life' (1993). Five years later, surveying the variousness of contemporary poetry, its attendant lack of central poetic authority, and the paucity of newspapers' editorial attention to poetry in comparison to fiction or biography, he concluded: 'it's clearly important for poetry to go on staking its claim in public, in a language both appropriate to its subject and available to the general reader, whoever he or she may be. What we also need is an expansion of space for more considered public discussion of poetry that the times seem to find convenient or necessary' (O'Brien 1998: 12). Nearly twenty years on, we can see such developments and they are frequently attributed to Duffy:

> Can poetry change the world? Is that its purpose—to call its readers to arms? Carol Ann Duffy, who became poet laureate last year and is proving an electrifying presence, seems to believe it can. Her response to her new public role has been very different from that of most of her predecessors, prompting poems not on happy royal occasions but on war, the expenses scandal, the banking crisis, climate change. She recently argued that poetry was 'in the ascendant' among young people, and that as they rejected materialism they would channel their thoughts and ideas, especially on green issues, into poetry. (Moss 2010)

As indicated throughout this chapter, and the book, Duffy expresses contemporary human concerns but always foregrounds how poetry not only verbalizes but also compensates for them through 'art made of language'. She thus stands up to O'Brien's evaluative criteria:

> Poetry in public is often invited, and sometimes willing, to turn into comedy, or performance, or political succor, or moral outcry, or emotional reassurance. It can, of course, be all these things, but it is also more, and it risks losing its essential nature if it does not maintain a vigilant regard for its own interests as an art made of language. (O'Brien 1998: 20)

The 'public' poems in *Ritual Lighting* and *The Bees* especially balance their message with 'art made of language', authenticated by an 'invisible personal connection' (Duffy, 29 September 2012). A bee can both sting and make honey, just like a poet, whose 'honey is art' ('Bees', *Bees* 3) and the art is 'music scored / on the air' ('Poetry', *Bees* 16). In 'Poetry', Duffy playfully depicts how this art can permeate every crevice, so that thing and poetic symbol become interchangeable; thus, if a pint of Guinness becomes a metaphor for a nun then on seeing a nun the narrator thinks of the pint. In 'Music' (*Bees* 67–8), the mix of lyric, narrative, and familiar cultural references—to the Pied Piper, buskers, children learning the piano, snake charmers, funerals, the cliché 'Play it Again Sam', and Shakespeare's 'If music be the food of love, play on'—answer the rhetorical question about the power of music, and implicitly poetry's 'music of being human': 'Do you think it hears and heals our hearts?' Christina Paterson, for one, would say 'Yes'. She notes Duffy's increasingly persistent note of poetry's power to alleviate our harms: 'We are lucky, lucky, lucky to have this passionate, thoughtful, brilliant poet flying the flag for poetry, flying the flag for the healing power of words' (2009).

REFERENCES

2012 *Near* (London: Faber and Faber).
2009 *To the moon: An anthology of lunar poetry* (London: Picador).
2013 *1914: Poetry remembers* (London: Faber and Faber).
'December' (2009) *Christmas Pamphlet* (Nottingham: Candlestick Press).
'Inside the Yurt (for Catherine Lockerbie)' (2009) *Times,* 18 August.
'The Twelve Days of Christmas' (2009) *Radio Times,* 8 December.
2009 'Sisters in Poetry', *Guardian,* 2 May.
2010 'Older and Wiser', *Guardian,* 13 March.
2010 'Play up! Play up!', *Guardian,* 10 July.
2010 'Poetry is the music of being human', *Times,* 30 January: *Saturday Review* 2.
Barry, Peter. 2000. *Contemporary British poetry and the city.* Manchester: Manchester University Press.
Bate, Jonathan. 2000. *The song of the earth.* London: Picador.
Bradbury, Lorna. 2009. Can poetry change the world? *Daily Telegraph,* October. *Review* 3.
Brown, Mark. 2009. Carol Ann Duffy leaps into expenses row with first official poem as laureate. *Guardian,* June 13.
Brown, Jeffrey. 2014. Reporting poetry. *Poetry* 203(6): 567–573.
Colton, Julian. 2012. Review of *The Bees, The Eildon Tree* 21, 46.
Darlington, Miriam. 2015. The virtuoso thrush plays his melodies of spring. *Times,* May 2.
De la Vega, Carla. 2012. Cultural Olympiad: Poetry in motion. *Vision,* June.
DiNapoli, Robert. 2014. The play's the thing: Word-play and poetry. *P.N. Review* 40(4): 34–38.

Dunmore, Helen. 1999. Waiting for the world's wife. *Poetry Review* 89(2): 80–81.

Ferguson, Brian. 2013. Scots-born poet laureate Duffy to be star of the show at palace exhibition. *Scotsman,* October 25.

Forster, Julia. 2006. Critical openness: A study of poetry in public places. *Agenda,* July 5. http://www.agendapoetry.co.uk/documents/JuliaForster-Essaypdf.pdf

Geyer, Margaret. 2014. Awesome response to Scottish referendum. *Guardian,* September 21.

Gifford, Terry. 1999. *Pastoral.* London: Routledge.

Goodyear, Ronnie, and Annie Morgan (eds.). 2011. *Soul feathers: An anthology to aid the work of Macmillan Cancer Support.* Stony Stanton: Indigo Dreams.

Greenlaw, Lavinia. 2009. The public poet. *Granta,* May 5.

Greer, Germaine. 2010. Farewell to poetry's pal from Carol Ann Duffy, the nation's students, and me. *Guardian,* November 28.

Habermas, Jürgen. 1994. *The Structural Transformation of the Public Sphere: An Inquiry into a Category of Bourgeois Society.* Trans. Thomas Burger with Fredrick Lawrence. Cambridge: Polity Press.

Hale, Dominic. 2012. Review of *The Bees, Cadaverine Magazine,* July 23.

Harrison, Tony. 2000. *Laureate's block.* Harmondsworth: Penguin.

Heaney, Seamus. 2001. *North* [1975]. London: Faber and Faber.

Hoyle, Ben. 2010. David Beckham injury immortalized by Poet Laureate. *Times,* March 17.

Kellner, Douglas. 2000. Habermas, the public sphere, and democracy: A critical intervention. In *Perspectives on Habermas,* ed. Lewis Hahn, 259–288. Chicago: Open Court Press.

Kennedy, Maev. 2013. Bedroom tax brings out the beast in poet laureate. *Guardian,* October 11.

Lawson, Mark. 2011. Poet laureate Carol Ann Duffy. Interview, *Front Row,* BBC Radio 4, September 30. http://www.bbc.co.uk/programmes/b0151xt6

Linklater, Magnus. 2009. Carol Ann Duffy's tribute to departing head of Edinburgh book festival. *Times,* August 18.

Low, Valentine. 2015. Royal birth leaves left-wing poet laureate with writer's block. *Times,* May 6.

MacNeice, Louis. 1964. *Selected poems.* London: Faber and Faber.

Marre, Oliver. 2009. Carol Ann Duffy turns into a pub bore. *Daily Telegraph Blogs,* December 6.

McAllister, Andrew. 1988. Carol Ann Duffy. *Bête Noir* 6, 69–77.

McCrum, Robert. 2008. The royal family doesn't need a poet. *Guardian,* December 1.

Meiklem, Peter John. 2009. Duffy: Poet in motion. *The Big Issue,* July 30–August 5, 7.

Miller-Mack, Ellen. 2013. Review of *Rapture, The Rumpus,* August 23. http://therumpus.net/2013/08/rapture-by-carol-ann-duffy/

Moorhead, Joanne. 2011. Carol Ann Duffy: "Poems are a form of texting". *Guardian*, September 5.

Moss, Stephen. 2010. What is the future of Poetry? *Guardian*, June 18.

O'Brien, Sean. 1998. *The deregulated muse: Essays on contemporary British and Irish poetry*. Newcastle on Tyne: Bloodaxe.

Ong, Walter. 2002. *Orality and literacy: The technologizing of the word*. London: Routledge.

Owen, Wilfred. 1975. In *War poems and others*, ed. Dominic Hibberd. London: Chatto and Windus.

Padel, Ruth. 2002. *52 ways of looking at a poem*. London: Chatto and Windus.

Parry, Tom. 2012. *Daily Mirror* launches "We Love Reading" campaign. *Mirror*, January 16.

'Poet Laureate Carol Ann Duffy writes for injured David Beckham', *The Mirror*, 16 March 2010.

Pugh, Sheenagh. 1999. Why? Review of *The Pamphlet*, *Thumbscrew* 13: 26–29.

Puss in Boots. 2012. Politics, politics. Review of *The Bees*, *Gutter* 6.

Ramaswamy, Chitra. 2009. Crowning glory of jaffa cake sunsets. *Scotland on Sunday*, July 26, 10–11.

Relich, Mario. 2011. Review of *The Bees*, *Scottish Review of Books*, 8(1): 27–28.

Ross, Peter. 2012. Interview with Carol Ann Duffy. *The Scotsman*, December 2.

Rumens, Carol. 2012. Review of *The Bees*, *The Yellow Nib* 7, 75.

Shaw, Adrian. 2009. "The 12 days of Christmas": Poet laureate Carol Ann Duffy's grim version for our times. *Mirror*, December 7.

Simic, Charles. 1985. Notes on poetry and history [1984]. *The uncertain certainty*, 124–128. Ann Arbor: University of Michigan Press.

Simic, Charles. 1997. *The Orphan factory: Essays and memoirs*. Ann Arbor: University of Michigan Press.

Thorpe, Vanessa. 2009. Laureate puts political spin on 12 days of Christmas. *Guardian*, December 6.

Wagner, Eric. 2009. Skill, talent and a great heart are more important than her gender. *Times*, May 2.

Wainwright, Martin. 2012. Poet laureate Carol Ann Duffy on the Pendle witches. *Guardian*, August 15.

Walmsley-Collins, Fiona. 2013. Readers' books of the year 2013: Part 3. *Guardian*, December 28.

Wilkinson, Kate. 2014. Carol Ann Duffy: A great public poet who deserves her public honour. *Guardian*, December 31.

Williams, Nerys. 2011. *Contemporary poetry*. Edinburgh: Edinburgh University Press.

Winterson, Jeanette. 2005. Interview with Carol Ann Duffy. *Times*, September 10. http://www.jeanettewinterson.com/journalism/carol-ann-duffy/

Wroe, Nicholas. 2014. Carol Ann Duffy on five years as poet laureate: "It has been a joy". *Guardian*, September 27.

CHAPTER 6

Poetry About and for Childhood

*Whether I am writing for children or for adults, I am writing from the
same impulse and for the same purpose. Poetry takes us back to the
human. (Duffy, Winterson 2009)*

'CHILDHOOD IS THE ONLY REALITY'

Since children's poetry has scant recognition as an academic art, it
is tempting to omit this portion of Duffy's work from a book of criticism. However, it forms a large part of her oeuvre and involves the same
Duffyesque aesthetics. Indeed, several poems converse with pieces in the
adult volumes. Since this book's framing concept is 'poet for our times',
I put Duffy's poetry *for* children alongside her poetry *about* childhood to
illustrate how both kinds protect childhood as a distinct space and phase.
They thus counter an alleged crisis of 'age compression', that means, 'the
phenomenon by which girls are expected to dress and behave older than
their years' (Orbach 2010: 114). This phenomenon pertains particularly
to the early sexualization of children in the US but Orbach describes a
more widespread condition, for boys as well as girls, in which the healthy
processes of 'psychosexual maturity', whereby each developmental stage
has a precursor so that 'we crawl before we walk, we pull ourselves up
before we stand, we vocalize before we talk, we suckle before we chew',
is condensed or denied (2010: 129). In Duffy's poems, childhood is a
'country' from which we necessarily, if reluctantly, emigrate yet one that

© The Editor(s) (if applicable) and The Author(s) 2016
J. Dowson, *Carol Ann Duffy*,
DOI 10.1057/978-1-137-41563-9_6

shadows relationship and subjectivity throughout our adult lives: '"André Breton said, I think, that childhood is the only reality. The older I get, the more I'm becoming interested in childhood. It has to be my own—by which I mean that I can surprise myself by recalling that period. … I think, perhaps, childhood events shape everything that follows. So, if you presume to write poetry, then that too"' (Duffy, Stabler 1991: 124).

Duffy often reflects that writing for children was a natural progression from her lyrics that vibrate with '"A strain of nostalgia for childhood and the mysteriousness of its contours"' (Forbes 2002: 20). Several lyrics counter 'age compression' by dramatizing the gulf between children and adults. In 'An Afternoon with Rhiannon' (*TOC* 34), the adult considers how Philip Larkin feared a particular building in Hull but the young girl exclaims, '"*I like / buildings!*"' in 'a voice so new it shines' and the speaker ponders, 'A small child's daylight / is a safer place than a poet's slow, appalling, ticking night'. In the context of the poem, the sad poet is Larkin but it might self-referentially also be the poet, nostalgic for the daylight of her own childhood. 'Crunch' (*Bees* 63) also contrasts the shiny newness of a child's delight with the tedious complexity of adult life. Her mother ruminates on a burglary at their home that the police put down to the 'credit crunch', a euphemism for widespread debt and poverty, while the 'brightly young' daughter asks 'what's for lunch?' Her sparkling relish in the crunch of snow or a tasty apple outshines adults' distress when needing, having, or losing money. As Duffy states, 'Our children, by giving us their innocence and joy and worries of their living childhoods, remind us of our own gone childhoods. We bridge the gap between their present and our past with stories and poems' (*Daily Telegraph* 2005).

In an interview, Duffy explains how her sense of childhood's nostalgia and mystery relate to her early reading: "My grandfather gave me Alice in Wonderland when I was seven and I loved it so much that, when I finished it, I started writing some more of the story for myself. That book tipped me into this world of making up stories." She also cites Richmal Crompton's William books—"I was William the anarchist and rebel"—and, most importantly, Grimms' fairy tales' (Wroe 2007). While she appropriates Crompton's anti-hero for her largely satirical pamphlet, *William and the Ex-Prime Minister*, it is the echoes of Lewis Carroll and Grimm that resonate most in her poems for children. Duffy published adaptations of Grimm (1996, 1997), of folk stories from around the world (*Beasts and Beauties* 2004; *Rats' Tales* 2012), and wrote the words for a dance version of Rapunzel (2015). She would choose a collection of

Grimms' as a Desert Island book: "'I love fairy tale, actually. To me, it's very close to poetry, because it uses archetypal symbols. It doesn't need plots or explanation. It can move through time..... Writing for children ... brings more of your poet self alive. I was just lucky that my daughter brought this magic with her'" (Paterson 2009). According to 'Demeter' (*WW* 76), Duffy's daughter, Ella, brought 'spring's flowers' to 'winter and hard earth' and her poetry for children largely pertains to the years following Ella's birth in 1995. The publications started with *Meeting Midnight* (1999) and culminated in *New & Collected Poems for Children* (2009) [from which the page numbers in this chapter are taken]. She has also written stories for children and edited two anthologies of children's poetry. She has been a Poetry Society poet in schools and ran a poetry club for eight-year-olds at Manchester High School, the explicit voices in 'I Adore Year Three' (112). She contributes poems for online workshops aimed at years four, five, and six under the 'Junior' section of the Sheer poetry website. In addition to being used educationally in England, her poetry is in a *New Scottish Poetry Anthology* (Liddell and Gifford 2001), a text designed for the Scottish English and Communication Higher Still Examination. Incidentally, Duffy sews Scottish accents and dialects into such poems as 'Spell' (107) and 'The Scottish Prince' (46). The latter has a musical lilt and dance-tune refrain, thus meeting John Rice's tenet that 'songs and tunes' should feature in any book of Scottish poems (Rice 2001). The Scottish Poetry Library is a partner in The Children's Poetry Bookshelf website, set up during The Arts Council England's Children's Literature initiative in 2004, and *Meeting Midnight* features on the list of books recommended by the site's educational advisors.

While children provide a market for poetry, their literature struggles 'to establish its credibility as an intellectual subject' (Thomas 2011: 93) and scholarship largely attends to its mediation of cultural codes. In *From the Garden to the Street* (1998), Morag Styles surveys the genre's development over three centuries from pastoral to urban verse, as the title indicates. In similar vein, in his Introduction to *The New Oxford Book of Children's Verse* (1996), Neil Philip describes how 'the line running from Stevenson and Rossetti, through De la Mare, Farjeon, and Reeves, to Charles Causley has been disrupted by a more boisterous, less reflective street-smart poetry ... the focus is on shared not unique experience, on the rhythms of speech not the patterns of prosody, on school not home' (1996: xxxii–xxxiii). Duffy's writing for children took off after these studies ended and her work is less easy to categorize in such realist terms. The surge of writing for children that followed her mother's death from cancer in 2005, when Duffy felt too 'deafened' to write otherwise, was, she says, '"more like paddling than swimming"' (Paterson 2009). Perhaps the shallow waters of children's verse make the Duffyesque features—the lists, assonance, alliteration, repetition, and above all, rhyme—all the more translucent. Even more so than her poems for adults, the poems for children foreground their own processes and encourage the young reader to play with language as freely as the poet does. The parodies of 'Not Not Nursery Rhymes' (175–6), such as 'All the King's horses / And all the King's men, / Had to have omelette for dinner again' ('Humpty Dumpty', 176)—distances the reader from the original rhymes in a way that would make a child feel more grown up. Thus, the verses entice the child to make a subtle shift from being a passive conduit of nursery rhymes to an active player with words.

Duffy, then, engages the child by not infantilizing them. She offers different levels of cognition for a broad span of 'junior' or 'young readers' aged seven to eleven, along with any adult co-readers. As Winterson comments, 'The poems can be wonderfully silly but they are never patronising. ... The language is always as tight and fired with thought as her adult work' (2009). Eva Muller-Zettlemann illuminates how Duffy's first two books for children resemble her adult poetry in standing up to the 'formal and intellectual challenges of the postmodern avant-garde' (2003: 187). 'The Word' (162), for example, takes a paradigm familiar to children—they hide a gift in a secret place where it grows—but makes language the protagonist. The personified Word grows to a phrase, a sentence, a paragraph, a page, and finally a book: 'This is it. Look', says the Word to the reader. Muller-Zettlemann comments on this meta-poetic method: 'the ever-growing word strangely oscillates between beast and man. ... More importantly, though, by featuring the word as a self-sufficient, autonomous and ultimately uncontrollable phenomenon which has a distinct life of its own, Duffy's text manages to address post-structuralism's central tenet in a highly amusing manner' (194). Similarly, 'A Rhyme' (166–7) appropriates the friendship plot to Rhyme itself but in grown-up terms, for Rhyme takes the speaker to his room, pours a drink of rum, and then pours out his sad life-story, of how he was once in demand but now something of a relic, 'out on a limb'.

As in her other volumes, however, Duffy balances the intellectualism of linguistic self-reflexivity with 'the music of being human'. 'The Words of Poems' (1–2), that opens *New and Collected Poems for Children*, itemizes what poetry can do while enhancing the experiences dear to a child: a poem is a place to relive the joy of flying a kite, to compassionately reflect 'the wept tears on your face', to discover excitement comparable to magic spells or sparklers, and to record 'who you were' as you migrate to new worlds. While some poems seem to guard the innocence of a child's perspective, yet others introduce dangers and death, but as they feature in myth, fairy, or folk stories. As David Whitley asks, 'How does a writer who associates childhood so powerfully with disturbing aspects of contemporary experience write convincingly for children?' (2007: 103). He concludes that Duffy's strategies of estrangement allow horror and indeterminacy to stimulate children's imagination in a space decidedly separate from their life worlds. John Rieder, speaking of 'nonsense verse', also asserts how the language does not 'fall out of referentiality altogether', but 'the truncated or suspended referentiality' makes [the verses] peculiarly appropriate for children' (1998: 49). Therefore, if we expect to sniff the socialist, feminist, or pluralist advocacy of her adult poetry in Duffy's children's poems, we are on the wrong trail. She rarely uses the dramatic monologue, unless the speaker is a rhyme, a glove, or a park, but she does take the reader on a romp with words and thus staves off the repressive conditioning she recounts in 'Litany' (*MT* 9). In 'The Play's the Thing: Word-Play and Poetry', Robert DiNapoli similarly argues for the crucial power of poems to open up imaginative and linguistic possibilities, and thereby ward off the reductive codes of conventional discourse: 'The language we learn as young children encodes and embeds those values in our dawning consciousness. We need a kind of linguistic clowning to open up the closed circle of over-determined meaning we've backed into unawares. Hence our need for the poet, who is our juggler, our linguistic prestidigitator who "plays" with words in just about every sense of the word "play"' (2014: 37).

CHILDHOOD: 'MY COUNTRY. // I WANT IT BACK'

'All childhood is an emigration', muses the adult voice in 'Originally' (*TOC* 7). Biographically, it refers to the Duffys' move from Scotland to England that the poet expands to the continual sense of loss that accompanies growing up. The title to her volume, *The Other Country*, is taken from the opening to L.P. Hartley's *The Go-Between* (1953): 'The past is a foreign country: they do things differently there'. In her constructions of childhood, Duffy records how children experience 'differently' each developmental phase and how these continue to be revisited and revised as an adult. 'The Light Gatherer' (*FG* 59–60) lyrically recreates the epiphany that a newborn creature brings: 'You fell from a star / into my lap'. The mother's uplift is uncontainable in words and presented through symbols of dazzling light and precious jewels; yet, she foresees tears as well as bright smiles ahead, prescient that the 'tunnel of years' will tarnish the baby's purity. In 'Originally', the train ride from Glasgow to Stafford is sketched by symbols that depict a five-year-old's feelings of being both small and growing: a 'loose tooth', falling through the countryside that sped past the window, the 'red room' of the individual railway carriage, and the reassuring presence of her parents and younger brothers. Growing up was subsequently accelerated when life in the new place involved moving beyond the hermetically sealed safety of the family. Trying to fit in, communicate, and escape bullying, the children had to lose their Scottish accent and dialect: 'I remember my tongue / shedding its skin like a snake, my voice / in the classroom sounding just like the rest.' The 'skelf of shame' uses the Scottish for splinter, a word the Midlands schoolteacher could not understand, to describe the hidden pain of renouncing her roots. This cultural displacement—the lost 'sense of first space / and the right place'—leaves a lifelong legacy so that '*where do you come from?*' is forever a vexed question. Duffy is again self-reflexive at the end of 'Hometown' (*TOC* 10) where the ghosts of the older and younger selves pass each other in 'an empty marketplace': 'I imagine myself // to be older and away, or remember myself / younger, not loving this tuneless, flat bell / marking the time. Or moved to tears by its same sound.'

Angelica Michelis discusses the recalls of childhood in 'Originally' and 'Hometown' according to Freud's theory of 'afterwardness' (2003: 91–2). Freud was referring to childhood trauma, and sexual trauma in particular, but it is a useful term for how we repeatedly rearrange and rewrite the past. In recording the significant phases of school, Duffy skilfully orchestrates the voices of her younger and older selves. 'In Mrs Tilscher's Class' (*TOC* 8) chronicles how a small person magnifies her immediate environment—the high windows, the school day punctuated by the hand bell that a lucky child could ring, the milk at playtime, the uniqueness of each curriculum subject, feeling loved by the teacher, and the boosting reward of a gold star. The mature self looks back at how the school year went round inexorably and how the ten-year-olds grew swiftly in pre-pubescent awareness—a 'rough boy' relayed the facts of life behind the bike sheds—and a new sense that adults could do bad things, signalled by tales of Ian Brady and Myra Hindley who had been arrested after their spate of murders in Greater Manchester, October 1965. 'Stafford Afternoons' (*MT* 11) vividly depicts the oddness, size, and sounds, of the world from a child's viewpoint: 'In a cul-de-sac, a strange boy threw a stone. / I crawled through a hedge into long grass / at the edge of a small wood, lonely and thrilled. / The green silence gulped once and swallowed me whole.' It also addresses the impact of experience on innocence as the ten-year-old encounters a flasher when she wanders across a bridge over the newly built M6. She did not mention the incident to anyone, perhaps out of shame or fear of a scolding. The gap between adult and child also comes across in 'Sit at Peace' (*TOC* 9), presumably a familiar command that clashed with the child's emergent subjectivity that she only realizes in retrospect. Linking it to 'Litany' (*MT* 9), Jane Thomas reads the poem through gendered spectacles as an account of being 'trained in femininity' against which the girl chafes and thus climbs the tree in tomboyish freedom (2003: 135–6). Either way, through memory, the woman reviews sitting on a back doorstep shelling peas, being thwacked by a girl bully, and being told to do jigsaws, collect stamps, and not to ask questions. Yet, this sense of distance from 'them' was muddled as 'they' rescued her after falling from a 'Parachute Tree'. It is only in looking back that the woman recognizes her competing impulses for dependence and independence.

'Sit at Peace' is subtle in exploring how a child works out their relationship to adults, specifically the connection between love and discipline that makes more sense in 'afterwardness'. Looking back in 'The Good Teachers' (*MT* 16), Duffy characterizes a beloved English teacher by 'Her kind intelligent green eye. Her cruel blue one.' The poem consists of an amusing list of the secondary school spinsters captured in a photograph viewed through a glass frame. These women disapproved of any teenage interests that would distract the girls from study. Consequently, their rebellion felt a natural rite of passage at the time but in retrospect it seems more like a performance of being grown-up. 'You roll the waistband / of your skirt over and over, all leg, all / dumb insolence, smoke-rings.' The present tense here accentuates memory's conflation of past and present time. 'Head of English' (*SFN* 12) is the dramatic monologue of a traditionalist teacher whose narrow view of literature—she approves Keats and Kipling—is symptomatic of her conservative outlook. The voice remembering the woman highlights how inculcating dogma that the students would parrot back deprived the girls of proper development. On the other hand, 'Remembering a Teacher' (aka 'Death of a Teacher', *NSP* 134), 'the poem that so infuriated Oxford's Professor of Poetry' (Gayle 2012), elegiacally recasts the enduring value that a different kind of English teacher added to the thirteen-year-old's experience:

Teaching

is endless love; the poems by heart, prayers; the lists
lovely on the learning tongue; the lessons, just as you said,

for life. Under the gambling trees, the gold light thins and burns,
the edge of a page of a book, precious, waiting to be turned

The long lines mirror the trees swaying outside at which the pupil would stare, the eternal nature of the teacher's efforts, the child and teacher reaching out to one another, and memory's mental shifting between past and present selves.

In interview, Duffy asserts what we see in these poems: "'the kind of otherness and callousness of childhood, I'd like to explore. I'd quite like to have the eyes and ears again'" (Armstrong 1993). Agonizingly, the speaker in 'How' (*Pamphlet* 20–1) finds the source of her wasted life, the 'haemorrhage of years', in licking the shoes of a schoolgirl bully, 'to earn the approval of Helen Maguire, / pretty, spiteful Helen Maguire'. 'Twins' (*PNP* 10) relates with graphic detail the taste of fear in being outnumbered by a pair of bullies—'*There's two of us*'—and the pain of humiliation: 'When I slipped, the gravel bit at my knees'. The closing line, 'and what they did to me then they did to me twice' means both the unnerving likeness and solidarity of the twins and also how the trauma replays in the victim's 'afterwardness'. Here, the 'otherness and callousness of childhood' lie in children's cruelty to each other, while elsewhere, they stem from maltreatment by adults. 'Welltread' (*MT* 14), in suitably stiff quatrains, seems set a century earlier but the vivid emotions transport it to any time or place. The voice deconstructs the emotional lesions caused by an authoritarian headmaster who terrorized pupils and their parents by dishing out Victorian corporal punishments. She recalls how the autocrat falsely accused her of a crime and caned her hand: 'The memory brings me to my feet / as a foul wound.' As discussed in Chap. 2, 'Confession' (*MT* 15), printed on the next page to 'Welltread', also dramatizes the indelible imprints of childhood trauma: 'on your knees let's hear that wee voice / recite transgression in the manner approved ... *Forgive me* ...'. The lack of punctuation enacts the chaos in the child's mind and the enduring scars of the priest's tyranny. Childhood's most disconcerting 'otherness and callousness' occur in abuse from close relatives. 'Lizzie, Six' and 'We Remember Your Childhood Well', discussed in Chap. 3, stage how the adults' voices overwhelm a vulnerable child's ability to defend themself or authenticate their version of events. As Whitley states: 'The power of the poems resides primarily in their revealing a dark and troubled underside to childhood, their implicit challenge to the complacent nostrums of a society that does not want to acknowledge how difficult and traumatic the relation between child and adult experience can be' (2007: 105).

'Model Village' (*SM* 21–2) offsets the evolution of a child into pretty language with the perverse and murderous impulses that adults hide. It opens: 'See the cows placed just so on the green hill. / Cows say *Moo*. The sheep look like little clouds, / don't they? Sheep say *Baa*. Grass is green'. The diction and tone sound like a child internalizing the voice of an adult reading the story aloud. Discussing the poem, Stan Smith comments on how learning the words and sounds of animals 'rehearses the catechisms by which the child is interpolated to such a specific linguistic identity ... creating a "model" reality in the head which then shapes all the self's negotiations with the "real"' (2003: 159–60). The 'real' with which the child has to negotiate is presented in the chilling scenarios that alternate with each passage from the storybook: '*I poisoned her, but no one knows. Mother, I said, / drink your tea. Arsenic. Four sugars.*'

Crucially, however, the normal journey from a sleeping babe to speech, to sexual awakening, and then to the psychological complexities of adulthood, is reinforced not blurred. Unhealthy grown-ups might resist this passage but the portrayal of their stunted development is not altogether unsympathetic. In 'Boy' (*TOC* 29), a man is still looking to be mothered, and 'The Captain of the 1964 *Top of the Form* Team' (*MT* 7) is spoken by someone 'who has never recovered from not being fourteen any more' (Duffy, Brown and Patterson 2003: 61). We can read a political edginess to the signifiers of privilege, 'The blazer. / The badge. The tie', and to the year, 1964, when Harold Wilson's Labour government was elected. However, Fiona Sampson approves how the poem 'refuses to be tempted by risky or expansive explanation' but 'moves as if on rails to its destination, disappointed middle-age' (2012: 122). The speaker contrasts the excitement of the televised school competition 'Top of the Form', when he felt 'brainy', famous, excited, and stimulated by the era's pop songs, to his dull existence with a 'stale wife' and 'thick kids'. More central is the poem's affective power in recapturing how a child's vitality—'the clever smell of my satchel', 'I lived in a kind of fizzing hope'—mixes with the sadness of its passing: 'My country. // I want it back.'

'Children, I remember …'

As in her adult poems, Duffy's poems for children locate childhood as a 'country' in which to do things differently. Duffy attests that children have 'innocence as birthrights' that is both protected and damaged as they grow: 'The language of innocence attracts to itself (as love, in its different way, does) the language of poetry—rhyme, rhythms, nonsense, beauty, lyricism, magic, fun—and this language spools out from the nursery rhyme to the fairy tale' (Duffy, *Daily Telegraph* 2005). Like the lilting lullaby 'Song' (102), the joyously lyrical 'A Child's Sleep' (269) presents the doting gaze of a parent towards their daughter's vulnerability: 'And she was the spirit that lives / in the heart of such woods; / without time, without history, / wordlessly good.' Innocence is to be protected in 'Don't be Scared' (79), a comforting series of reassuring images that start with 'the dark is only a blanket'. As children progress, however, language and perception jostle for synchronicity: '"The way things branded the senses; which now they don't do to the same extent. The way language itself seemed new and odd, artificial or censoring"' (Duffy, Stabler 1991: 124). This infectious perceptual vividness is captured in 'The Oldest Girl in the World' (*NCPC* 9–11): 'Truly, believe me, I could all the time see / every insect that crawled in a bush, every bird that hid in a tree, individually. //… Can't see a sniff of it now.' The 'Oldest Girl' speaks to young ears—'Children, I remember'—and impresses their peculiar powers of apprehension. Some poems accordingly reflect the child's different sense of time and their absorption in the moment. For example, spellbound by rain, an only child imagines its source as the sky's tears ('The Invention of Rain' 233), or a child on a beach revels in 'magic castles made by my hands' ('Sand' 36). 'Time Transfixed' animates René Magritte's surrealist painting of the fireplace from which a steam train emerges. The child longs to be old enough to board the train and 'chuff away to to- / morrow, yesterday, today' (214). In '-/-/99' (139), she charmingly begs, 'postman, postman, be as slow as you like', as if he might delay the century's end. A child in 'Brave Enough' (159) wishes to sit with her friend in a tree forever and 'not grow older, richer, wiser, sadder, by one day', the sequence of adverbs signifying the connection between age, money, experience, and sadness.

Duffy both colludes and toys with the practice of teaching children to name things as their rightful passage into social language. In 'A Week as my Hometown' (255–7), learning the days of the week is secondary to the imaginative pleasure of pretending to be a building or place. Monday's entry is 'Rain. I'm the Library, round-shouldered, my stone brow / frowning at pigeons, my windows steamed up'. The lengthy sequences, 'The Birds, the Fish and the Insects' (55–64) and 'The Fruit, the Vegetables, the Flowers and the Trees' (117–30), introduce the variety of each species in the manner of a *Ladybird* book, but the question and answer method turns the lists into a game: 'Which is the most friendly of the fruits? / Is it an apple?' The interactive play with names over-rides the facts: Carp is 'the most dissatisfied' fish, Flounder is 'the most bewildered', Pollock, 'the most vulgar', and the Wren is the 'most architectural of the birds'. As here, the joke often requires knowledge and vocabulary beyond the years of a young child, proving how Duffy never talks down but offers different levels of engagement for different biological and intellectual ages. 'The Alphabest 2019' (113–14) might be educational but the references are as much to the dreams of adults—'a brand new car' or 'the winning slip'—as to a child's orbit—'the fairy on the storybook page'. DiNapoli argues for the benefits of playful language, to which children are peculiarly receptive: '[it] shows us a contrarian wonder lurking within the mundane, not the tears but the jolly japes in things. ... Through sharing poetry with their children, adults can revive an uncommon delight and vision. Words bunch and tangle to form shapes of meaning both unexpected and pleasing. They play for us, asking only that we join in' (2014: 38).

Muller-Zettlemann outlines the intellectual play in Duffy's defamiliarizing antics, such as placing ordinary creatures in odd contexts and subverting narrative expectations. 'The Thief, the Priest and the Golden Coin', for example, is a 'literary hoax' in that it sets up the ingredients of a magical story that the lack of action fails to deliver but, 'it may initiate certain meta-textual reflections and, what is more important, delight its readers with its intriguing sound' (Muller-Zettlemann 2003: 190). 'The Written Queen' (259) enacts how the poem's speaker can create the character, 'line by line, once / upon a time', and 'Translation' (168) spoils the Cinderella plot by stressing its origins in other versions and by showing what happens if two words, 'vair' (sable) and 'verre' (glass), are mistranslated: 'And so Cinderella, / her slipper a furry tail, / was trapped in a fairy tale / (no translator being dafter) / happily / ever / after.' Thus, 'Apart from exposing common narrative patterns to examination, the poem's radical devaluation of its story-level automatically directs the reader's attention to the non-semantic, material aspects of the text' (Muller-Zettlemann 2003: 190). Similarly, the girl in 'A Bad Princess' (45) resembles a teenager who stomps around 'looking for trouble / diamond tiara, satin dress, hair an absolute mess' and 'The Giantess' (43), featuring a grotesque creature that looks for little girls as pets, is more amusing than gruesome by feminizing a stock storybook character. A talking glove begins life on a queen but due to a marring stain is passed on to a maid then a pickpocket who is caught by the police, and 'You-Know-who was exhibit One', confides the glove to the reader. Exaggerating the fictional device of restoring order, the glove gets reunited with its other hand ('The Glove' 159–60). 'Queens' (38–40), depicting a fat and thin queen trying to make friends, demystifies any fairy-tale idealism for the queens are full of human foibles. The magic number of the title to 'Three' (42) sets up the enchanting dimension to a tale in which a child meets a king, a giantess, and an invisible boy. However, the prosaic conclusion, in which he or she addresses themself or an audience—'These are three of the people that I met yesterday'—foregrounds the storytelling frame. These devices thus underline a young reader's knowledge of the gap between the world they inhabit and their fantasies. In similar vein, 'Tales of the Expected' (87–8) parody popular archetypes of gothic horror stories then dismiss them as supernatural nonsense. In the first poem of the sequence, the eerie ghost story is undercut by the commentary, 'so legend had it. But no-one believed it', and 'Ghoul School' similarly establishes a mature stance towards make-believe: 'The teachers aren't ghouls'. At the same time, arousing negative capability, the narrator affords some imaginative thrills through striking imagery and rhyme: 'The school isn't a ghost ship / floating away from the town ... / nobody left on board ... / a bell ringing for the drowned.'

The suspension of conventional norms experienced through language, especially through rhyme, equates to a child's free play in their discrete space and time capsule. Rieder insists how clever artistry 'establishes an interlude where the children ... find themselves metaphorically suspended from the conventional world but still secure in the reassurance of the non-sense world's finitude, its balance of imaginative possibility and formal limits, and the certainty that the game always comes to an end' (1998: 59). Based on the large four-poster bed housed in London's Victoria and Albert museum, 'The Great Bed of Ware' (100–1) is sheer imaginative play but is rounded off by a return to normality: 'How do I know this? / I was there / I was the spy / in the great bed of Ware!' 'Be Very Afraid' (81) encourages a child to invent their own strange creatures—'the Spotted Pyjama Spider' or 'the Hanging Lightcord Snake'—around familiar objects in their bedroom, and thus to control the distinction between actual and make-believe dimensions. 'The Moon' (149) is an endearing account by a child who takes the moon as their best friend but finally the moon returns to the sky. In 'Night Writing' (270), the small hours are a metaphor for poems but 'dawn is a rubber' and 'The Babysitters' 90-2 has Elvis Presley as the sitter but he departs, slyly leaving a pair of blue suede shoes as a souvenir. The speaker in 'Meeting Midnight' (3) travels to the mysterious time that is iconic to fairy stories but returns home where, 'The next day I bumped into half past four / He was a bore'.

Thus, the flights of fantasy operate within the vapid but reassuring solidity of the real world. 'Numbers' (134–8) and 'Counting to a Billion' (141–5) are lists that tempt a reader to puzzle over the logic, but, as Rieder argues of the limerick, a formula 'provides the child with a strictly rule-bound, reliable, and therefore reassuring set of boundaries within which to experience the fantastically extravagant and sometimes threatening contents of the poems' (1998: 48).[1] The plot of the prose poem, 'Brave Dave' (29), is not a bundle of laughs for 'well bred Fred is dead' but the fun is all in the rhyme. 'Peggy Guggenheim', 'co-written by Ella Duffy', has a simple structure but the subject is a complex woman who might not be an ideal role model for a girl. However, any outside reference to Guggenheim's high living is masked by the joy of rhyming her name: 'favourite poem has to rhyme / with Peggy, Peggy Guggenheim' (237).

The king of nonsense verse, Edward Lear, averred, '"The critics are very silly to see politics in such bosh: not but that bosh requires a good deal of care, for it is a *sine qua non* in writing for children to keep what they have to read perfectly clear & bright, & incapable of any meaning but one of sheer nonsense"' (Lear 1988: 228). Duffy's nonsense verse, as in 'The Architect of Cheese' (253), 'Dimples' (169), 'Opposites' (172), or 'Irish Rats Rhymed to Death' (170), certainly frees language from its contexts and makes of it a playground. However, some poems do address life's realities but without compressing the natural development of chronological age. The funeral for a stick insect called Courgette values and parodies the practice of burying children's pets with due solemnity (54). 'Maiden Names' (236) relates the child's discovery that her parents and grandparents had another name, symptomatic of another life, before their marriages. 'Your Grandmother' (13), loosely based on Duffy's mother,

[1] Rieder cites references to Liza Ede (1987) 'An Introduction to the Nonsense Literature of Edward Lear and Lewis Carroll', *Explorations in the Field of Nonsense*, ed. Wim Tigges (Amsterdam: Rodopi), pp. 7–60 and X.J. Kennedy (1990) 'Disorder and Security in Nonsense Verse for Children,' *The Lion and the Unicorn* 13: 28–33.

depicts her as the young, free, and single belle of the ball and parallels her adult poem, 'Before You Were Mine' (*MT* 13). 'Rooty Tooty' (12) celebrates parents as youths who played the guitar, danced, and fell in love, while in 'The Who' (13) the child mocks their anachronistic cultural references.

Enabling children to make free with language safeguards the otherness of their worlds yet builds a confidence that prepares them for the uncertainties and challenges of what is to come: 'the play, if you like—of pattern and meaning we call poetry' is vital if children are 'to come to terms with all the pleasures, pains, hopes and horrors which life on this planet affords' (DiNapoli 2014: 36). 'Tight' (65) consists of a three-lined verse pattern and coheres through repetition, alliteration, and assonance but the statements mix the safe with the subversive, the light-hearted with the serious: 'Valentine's Day is tight if you're all alone. / History is tight on Anon. / Le feu de joie was tight on Saint Joan.' Issues of social conscience, such as 'Pollution is tight on briny ocean waves' and 'Heavy snow is tight on pavement art', weave with concerns that are closer to a young reader, 'A windless day is tight on flying kites' or 'Swear-boxes are tight on saying f****'. As here, sometimes social transgression is rehearsed innocuously through language—'Polite society is *well* tight on the fart' (65). The repetition of the key word in 'Please' (217), toying with the phrase 'pretty please', like Gertrude Stein's famous 'a rose is a rose is a rose', rescues the term from overuse, and, in the case of 'please' of its attendant imperatives for polite speech, an imperative scrutinized for its stranglehold on the developing girl in Duffy's 'Litany' (*MT* 9). In the seven-page 'No Stone Unturned' (262–8), the repetitive formula of 'pebble, stone, brick, rock, and boulder' is an enchanting incantation that illustrates how 'from the most appalling pun to the most magnificent poetic diction, all our living language use is woven from a dense, humming swarm of interconnected words, their literal and figurative meanings, and their radiating, ramifying networks of associations' (DiNapoli 2014: 35).

Whereas Philip warns against silly verse that is fun but vacuous and often based on the pun (1996: xxviii), DiNapoli examines how 'the humble lamentable pun rides on the back of a cognitive glitch, a mental and linguistic hiccup we experience as we perceive an unexpected phonological resemblance between two otherwise unrelated words' (34). He argues for the 'guilty pleasure' in how a semantic tension is created and resolved at the same time. Duffy's puns in 'The Manchester Cows' (95–9) are wonderfully absurd, often debunking high culture; in Part 8 we have 'Haikow' and Part 9 introduces the 'Great Cow Artists', 'Picowsso' and 'Moonet'. Similarly, in 'Johann Sebastian Baa' (104) we experience how 'two terms of a well- (or ill-) wrought pun can set in motion a long chain of associations and resonances, which in turn can gel into new meanings' (DiNapoli 2014: 34). 'Friends' (154) consists in groan-inducing couplings such as, 'Miss Fog, Miss Road, met on a walk / Long time no see'. The groan is, however, only fake pain for, 'We laugh at the very unlikeliness of it all' and finding or recovering meanings is always pleasurable (DiNapoli 2014: 34).

The fun is also in opening up vistas, 'like a child tearing gleefully through a field, net in hand, after a swarm of elusive butterflies, the chase after the poem's dancing meanings will afford you more pleasure (and exercise) than any one capture' (DiNapoli 2014: 34). The sober point, however, is that 'Language that isn't playful in these ways, that seeks to communicate one and only one meaning, is the equivalent of an acoustically dead space, like an audiologist's testing booth. This is the language of the legal contract, the instruction manual and the directory' (2014: 35). 'Mrs Hamilton's Register' (109) fortifies young readers against such acoustically dead space by making a poem from the daily roll call, creating a beautiful meaning for each girl's name—'Grace and beauty? / Annie here'—and 'Boys' (25) plays with common associations of men's names, such as the Stanley Knife or Big Ben. Rieder argues: 'Nonsense verse separates itself from the "real" world, letting loose a number of possibilities, including dangerous and violent ones, and at the same time disconnecting those possibilities from the real world, that is, from what goes on after the game is over' (1998: 49). The macabre series on skeletons, where they become the colour of their food ('The Red Skeleton' 201) or get tangled up trying to embrace ('Cuddling Skeletons' 202) is simply quirky, 'disconnecting those possibilities from the real world'. Similarly, 'Fine Weather' (75) imagines the life of dead people in their graves and 'Numbers' (138) ends with someone lying in a coffin, but the reader knows these are just games on the page. 'Five Girls' (27–8) relates each of their troubles but, in the quasi-limerick form, the rhyme dominates any sense. In 'Halo' (132), nasty kids snatch the girl's halo and lob it into a tree but the basic narrative premise is self-reflexively far-fetched. In 'The Childminders' (89), the image of a dead boy has the chilling quality of Roald Dahl's short story, 'The Landlady', but the familiarity of the cliché, 'bored to death', any scary air of mystery.

So, any political poignancy is in empowering the child reader to own and manipulate language in ways that shift between or combine certainty and ambiguity, formulae and deviation. Whereas Lear, writing in the nineteenth century, addressed 'the most basic social conventions with which children struggle[d], such as those governing eating, dressing, grooming, and talking' (Rieder 1998: 51), in Duffy's day, children's struggles are more around image and confidence. Accordingly, 'So Shy' (192) consists in a series of compassionate scenarios that might encourage a reader to face their fears. 'Boo! To a goose!' (80) is a literal take on a silly phrase but the girl dares all sorts of things. 'Know All' (8) satirizes and deflates pretentiousness and the double negative of the last line, 'I DON'T KNOW NOWT', repeats the speaker's hollow boasts, which his poor grammar only echoes. 'Ask Oscar' (164) emulates a problem page for boys who have questions about exams, love, spots, and ghosts. In 'Walk' (231), the light metre and repeated assonance balance the narrative logic in which a speaker looks on at people enjoying their lives but feels apart: 'The wedding guests / are somewhere else, / like happiness'. With similarly mature psychology, 'A Worry' (84–5) verbalizes the condition of anxiety without a platitudinous solution. 'A Cigarette' (161) offers a voyage of the imagination as the cigarette grows in size to a wand, a tree, a beanstalk, and finally the 'size of death', but concludes, 'No friend of mine gave me a cigarette'. As here, there are occasional morals in terms of social codes, such as not smoking, not staying up late, and not stealing. In 'The Theft' (228) a laddish youth speaks the homily, 'Don't steal, kids, it ain't worth it', and 'Crikey Dick' (174) amusingly advises how to let off steam without swearing or throwing a brick through a window. As in her adult poems, Duffy dramatizes how materialism and greed deaden the imagination. 'Cucumbers' (131) makes money seem dull by substituting the vegetable for shared currency while 'Zero' (146) imagines a fruitless spending spree with an imaginary coin then discovering that the sun, moon, and stars are available for free. However, the 'Seven Deadly Adjectives' (68–74) replace the archetypal sins of covetousness, pride, and so on with Sly, Argumentative, Selfish, Moody, Two-faced, Boastful, and Lazy. These can be taken morally, as destructive human attributes, but also creatively, as words to avoid in writing a story.

As Stuart Kelly comments, '[Duffy's] works for children, such as *The Lost Happy Endings*, explore how to be different, how to be unshackled from the past, and how to turn old stereotypes inside out' (2009). The speaker of 'Lies' (5) is not appealing but he invites some sympathy for seeking an alternative to a stifling normality 'where mothers come and go / with plates of cakes / and TV sets shuffle their bright cartoons' (6).

There is, however, something unsettling when the liar speaks seductively to a girl who has a 'split strawberry mouth, moist and mute' but we can argue that the dodgy speaker lets the reader know he is just pretending: 'I turn up the collar of my coat / and narrow my eyes'.

Many poems do prepare readers for the untidiness of life where happy endings cannot be guaranteed. 'Jamjar' (226) is a story of a girl who falls through the jar's bottom, like Alice into Wonderland, but she ends up scooped out by a witch. The images in 'The Ocean's Blanket' (35) are conventional symbols for sea life but finish sadly: 'The ocean's blanket is made of sunken ships / and we are drowned, are drowned. / Beneath the ocean's blanket we will not be found.' In 'Quicksand' (83), the terror of disappearing into quicksand is mitigated by knowing the narrator's account is only a fantasy of what 'might-have-been'. 'Late' (4) is the story of an eight-year-old that disobeys the warnings, stays out, falls into a grave, and freezes. Disturbingly, she prays but no help comes and the moon and stars remain coolly indifferent to her plight, as if the universe is uncaring. Typically, however, the disconcerting lack of any ending, let alone a happy one, is anaesthetized by the rhymes: 'She froze. She had a blue nose'. 'A Child's Song' (106) is also troubling in its allusions to how the elements engulf the child and how the advent of darkness prefigures death. Again, however, the rhymes rescue the vision from too much realism: 'Wind, wind, under my coat, / you will snuff me out. / I know your game, wind, / your hand's at my throat.' 'Lost' (225) leaves a child in a hostile wood to be swallowed by the dark, but the voice is detached and quizzical, as if outside its own story: 'Who knows if a witch isn't a heap of leaves and old twigs, / hunched and sleeping under a bush?' Due to its scary narrative, critics discuss 'Whirlpool' (86) for the way it confronts a pile of childhood horrors. Muller-Zettlemann reads it as an allegorical 'dissolution of the self' (197) while Whitley poses that while the imagery is compelling, Duffy refuses to enmesh bad experience in a social situation, but rather foregrounds its source in ballad, myth, or folklore. Additionally, the climax is expressed 'through a fairy tale image of transformation, words metamorphosed, with a mixture of dumb horror and beauty, into "silver fish"' (Whitley 2007: 109). Whitley further argues that the danger in Duffy's children's poetry 'at a profound and troubling level' is part of a broader understanding that the delineation of terror is 'a crucial element in developing the power of the imagination' (2007: 104, 107).

Reviewing Duffy's collected poems for children, Michael Rosen comments, 'To tell the truth, she gives the impression of not being afraid of talking about anything, whether that's monsters, ghosts, quicksand or the taboo subjects which in the past have been told to stand outside the door of children's literature. CAD welcomes in forbidden words, love and sex' (Rosen 2009). The 'love and sex' are what we might expect, given the erotic quality of her lyrics for adults, but, in a culture concerned about age compression, Duffy pretty much leaves romance and sex for teenagers and adults (Whitley 2007: 114). Spared the prejudices and barriers of labels, children in her poems are emotionally uninhibited and their love is innocent: a girl hugs a tree ('Girl and Tree', 156) and adversaries are reconciled in 'A Crow and a Scarecrow Fell in Love' (157). Love between a mother and child is celebrated in tender lyrics; there is love for and from a teacher and for school (108); there are kisses from grandma, 'Granddad loved groovy gran', and a boy who kisses a girl has 'sharp freckles' (44). 'The Loch Ness Monster's Husband' (49)' wittily appropriates lines from 'I'm a Believer' by the pop group, The Monkeys, 'Ah thought love / was only true in fairy tales', to prove that love *can* be true. However, there is no more happily-ever-after marriage in these poems than in Duffy's adult volumes. 'A Bad Princess' (45) is rewarded with a 'dull young prince' and the Duchess of Ice who loves the Duke of Fire melts when she kisses him (41). 'Vows' (47) is a list poem that mocks a bride and groom trying to choose the right spouse. 'Henrietta, the Eighth' (50) reverses the notorious English king's prerogative to dispose of his wives and the woman kills off her husbands for being boring, lazy, crazy, defiant, lying, old, or snooping. The symbols for wedding anniversaries are moved to friendship in 'The Good Friend of Melanie Moon' (151–2) in which Duffy sows the seeds of same-sex love as a valid option, but she also blows them away, for after sixty years, 'my friendship with Melanie Moon / was over and done'. In 'Brave Enough' (159), a girl wishes to be tied to her girlfriend for life. Only the fantasy of 'Meeting Midnight' (3) has a sexual undertone, for Midnight is a woman dressed in 'a full length dark blue raincoat with a hood' who smokes a manly cheroot, has a strong scent, and kisses the girl, One O'clock, 'full on the lips'.

One critic's objection to finding 'adult poems misplaced in a children's collection' is not due to any smut but due to Duffy's radical play with language: '"Prior Knowledge" should be expelled from it at once; its deviousness turns poetry into puzzlement' (Hollindale 2009: 371). Conversely, while she is never linguistically or culturally conservative,

Rosen suggests that Duffy is the 'teacher's friend' because of her poems' rosy hue on school (2009). Certainly, they frequently encourage a curious child to pursue knowledge but never for showing off nor to restrict learning to the curriculum. 'Your School' (115–16) celebrates how knowledge is made available and 'The Laugh of Your Class' (110–11) knits learning with fun. 'Elvis! Shakespeare! Picasso! Virginia Woolf!' (242) both mimics and undermines the importance of having the right answers in class. A child can learn about art from 'Picasso's Blue Paintings' (248–2) but 'The Good Child's Guide to Rock 'n' Roll' (14–22) inducts readers into equally important popular culture. Central and vital, of course, is poetry. 'The Hat' (243–7) is a lively tour through the heritage of poets that includes women, Americans, and Scots. Each one is portrayed through niche characteristics, starting with, 'I was on Chaucer's head when he said He was a verray / parfit gentil knyght, and tossed me into the air', and ending with Ted Hughes, 'man in black who growled / with a sudden sharp hot stink of fox'. Elsewhere, poetry sneaks in to poems in various guises: 'there's a dog reading poetry under a lamp' (189) or 'with this ruby ring / I me wed / to passion, poems, magic spells' ('The Rings' 258), and 'inside a book, at home, / was a poem // Inside the poem, curled / was a world' (180).

'LAUREATE FOR ALL THE FAMILY'

Duffy circumscribes childhood by a sequence of experiences through which each individual passes and by dramatizing how we rearrange and rewrite these phases in the lingering 'afterwardness' that memory affords. Some of her adult poems chime with a children's version, such as 'Rings' (*NCPC* 258) with 'The Rings' (*Bees* 24) or 'Cockermouth and Workington' (*Bees* 55), that plays with the letter 'f', with 'F for Fox' (*NCPC* 182). The question and answer format of the poems on species is taken up in 'Big Ask' (*Bees* 9–10). 'Nippy Maclachlan' (*NCPC* 183), about a witch-like woman on 'the Border' (presumably the edge of mental and social normality), corresponds to 'The Pendle Witches' (*RL* 14–15). Both poems expose the deadly powers of local myth and gossip: 'Do you think Nippy McLachlan is real?' Bees, that frequent the volume of that name, are also busy in many children's poems, notably 'The Queen's Bees' (*NCPC* 51) and the reference to 'colony collapse disorder' in 'Tight' (*NCPC* 65). Some poems, such as 'A Child's Sleep' (*NSP* 133; *NCPC* 269) and 'The Invention of Rain' (*Pamphlet* 44; *NCPC* 233) occur in both adult and children's volumes. 'The Cord' (*FG* 61–2) dedicated to Ella, which describes a girl seeking her umbilical cord, could equally be in the children's collection and Hollindale concedes that 'Star and Moon' (*NCPC* 212) allows adult and child to share the poignant transience of early parenthood' (2009). *The Mirror* labelled Duffy 'the first poet laureate for the whole family' when it printed some of her children's poems (4 May 2009). As already mentioned, many include language games that all the family can enjoy whereas others just bypass age differences. 'Chocs' (*NCPC* 194), for example, describes the surreptitious foray into a box of *Moonlight* in a child's voice but the temptation is universal. 'Moth' (*NCPC* 53) reassures a person of any size that the insect is just a harmless 'butterfly's dark twin' for 'she can only hurt herself / flying too close to the light, / burning her wings'. However, an older reader can also invoke the myth of Icarus who over-stretched his limits—and who is mocked by his wife in 'Mrs Icarus' (*WW* 54). The series of dog poems presents a family debate around the pros and cons of a canine pet (*NCPC* 186–91).

Poems on Christmas especially appeal to all the family. 'Christmas Eve' (*RL* 44) is the internal monologue of a parent watching her daughter feel the magic of anticipation that rekindles her own childhood wonder. Since 2009, Duffy has edited the Christmas pamphlets by Candlestick Press (*The Twelve Poems of Christmas*), stating that they are 'the most original way of delivering poetry since Poems on the Underground' and 'the best, most poetic solution there could possibly be to card-and-present buying at Christmas' (2009: Introduction). The Christmas poems revive stories in ways that are marketed for and appeal to young and old, as witnessed by the reviews on Amazon's webpages. Commissioned to modernize 'The Night before Christmas' by Clement C. Moore, Duffy asserts that her version, 'Another Night before Christmas' (2010), 'concerns itself with innocence and belief' (*Daily Telegraph* 10 December 2005). Winterson concurs, 'I love the way the poem manages to include cashpoints and mobile phones, homeless people, stray dogs and satellites. It is contemporary, it happens in an ordinary town, but the ordinary town is where miracles happen too' (2005). *The Independent*'s reviewer of *Bethlehem: A Christmas Poem* (2012) explores the balance of scepticism and hope in poets writing about Christmas down the ages: 'Bowing to a literary tradition of her own, Duffy lets us see that interpretations differ, but that the birth-cry is true: "one wept at a miracle; another was hoping it might be so". Believers, doubters—and hopers—will all enjoy this gift' (Tonkin 2013). In 'Wenceslas: A Christmas Poem' (2012), Duffy embellishes the carol's account of a king who sends his servant to bring in a freezing pauper but retains the carol's core message: 'Then Wenceslas sat the poor man down, / poured Winter's Wine, / and carved him a sumptuous slice / of the Christmas Pie ... / as prayers hope You would, and I.' The magnanimous gesture is humanity's response to the poor man's prayer, '*Something Understood*', Duffy's intertextual reference to George Herbert's sonnet 'Prayer' that resonates with literary and spiritually minded readers. As the blurb on the book edition of 'Wenceslas' also captures, the poem demonstrates Duffy's 'music of being human': 'In reimagining the much-loved carol of King Wenceslas, Carol Ann Duffy's wonderful new poem offers merriment and festive cheer, but also celebrates what is truly important at this special time of year: the simple acts of kindness that each of us can show another.'

Compassion and kindness are also the values in Duffy's other narrative poems for Christmas, initially printed with illustrations in *The Guardian*. The protagonist of 'Mrs Scrooge' (2009) is a champion of environmental concern, living simply and refuting consumerism. She embraces the love between family and friends who congregate on Christmas Day in a scene where Charles Dickens's *A Christmas Carol* meets the popular film, *It's a Wonderful Life*. For the adult reader, there is plenty to think about, such as the cruelty of turkey farming, the tension between progress and conservation in projects such as Heathrow's Runway Three, and whether individual actions matter: '"The Polar Ice Cap melting," said the Ghost, / "Can mankind save it?" / "Yes, we can!" cried Mrs Scrooge. "We must!" / "I bring encouragement from Scrooge's dust," replied the Ghost. / "Never give up. Don't think one ordinary human life / can make no difference—for it can!" It is Tiny Tim who voices the real moral as he toasts his grandmother who '"taught us all / to value everything! / To give ourselves! / To live as if each day was Christmas Day!"' The emphasis on community is also there in 'A Christmas Truce' which combines a compelling plot with the moving dramatization of historical accounts—'a short history lesson to make children understand and grown men weep' (Guest 2011). For Duffy, the 'music' is always part and parcel of illuminating 'the human'. In collaboration with Sasha Johnson Manning, she wrote the vocal score of The Manchester Carols, first performed by children from several Manchester schools at The Royal Northern College of Music in 2007, again in 2008, and published in 2009. They are used by choirs of all ages and bring out the relevance of the Christmas story in ways that retain the mystery for believers and the very humane elements for those who are not. As Kate Wilkinson sums up: 'From the short lyric, to the character narrative, to the subverted carol, Duffy draws upon the traditions of both religious and secular verse to create something new, a public poetry that avoids the clichés of Christmas' (2014).

Philip perceives childhood's 'inextricable tangle of happy and sad feelings' (1996: xxviii). Arguably, these mixed emotions continue and intensify through adulthood but they can be untangled by precise yet playful poetic expression. What DiNapoli says of poetry for children is the most fitting finale to the study of Duffy's work that above all insists on the place of poetry in our times. He argues that although human communities have always possessed a variety of 'customs, social structures, religions and technologies', they have all produced poetry in some form. Like Walter Ong, he argues that poetry came long before letters, literacy, or literature, and it is only newer cultures that think they can do without it:

> Most of us scarcely realize our loss, and, given the speed with which the relaying of information has so come to dominate our work and leisure, awareness of that loss may soon pass out of mind altogether. On top of this deep tectonic displacement, the culture of information is at root a prose culture, discursive and expository. Its growing domination of the production and reception of text may one day finish the job of reducing poetry to merely a queer assortment of verbal artefacts humans once produced and valued. (DiNapoli 2014: 36)

This extract neatly fits how Duffy talks from and to 'our times'. She wishes children and adults to know that poetry can '"speak of all their suffering or all their joy. ... it's how we explain ourselves, how we bear witness, how we tell the truth. It's the form in language where that can be done. It can offer a lot of consolation. It's a form of secular prayer and it's the point in language where one is most truthful. We use poetry when we want to speak our souls or our hearts, both as writers and readers, don't we?"' (Duffy, Dougary 2011).

REFERENCES

1996 *Grimm tales* (London: Faber and Faber).
1997 *More Grimm tales* (London: Faber and Faber).
1999 *Meeting midnight*, Illustrated by Eileen Cooper (London: Faber and Faber).
2004 *Beasts and beauties: Eight tales from Europe* (London: Faber).
2009 *Mrs Scrooge: A Christmas tale*, Illustrated by Posy Simmonds (London: Picador); Illustrated by Beth Adams (New York: Simon & Schuster).
2009 *New & collected poetry for children* (London: Faber and Faber).

2010 *Another night before Christmas* (London: Picador).

2012 *Rats' tales*, adapted for stage by Melly Still (London: Faber and Faber).

2012 *Wenceslas: A Christmas poem*, Illustrated by Stuart Kolakovic (London: Picador).

2009 *The twelve poems of Christmas* [and for each subsequent year until 2019] (Nottingham: Candlestick Press).

2005 'The Most Natural Gift', *Daily Telegraph*, 10 December.

Armstrong, Amanda. 1993. Potent poetry. Interview with Carol Ann Duffy. *Writers' Monthly*, October.

Brown, Clare, and Don Patterson (eds.). 2003. *Don't ask me what I mean: Poets in their own words*. London: Picador.

DiNapoli, Robert. 2014. The play's the thing: Word-play and poetry. *P.N. Review* 40(4): 34–38.

Dougary, Ginny. 2011. Poetry is the music of being human. It's how we bear witness. *Times*, October 1.

Forbes, Peter. 2002. Winning lines. *Guardian*, August 31,pp. 20–23.

Gayle, Damien. 2012. Poet Laureate compared to Mills & Boon romance writers in stinging attack by rival. *Daily Mail*, January 31.

Guest, Katy. 2011. Christmas books of the year. *Independent on Sunday*, December 18.

Hollindale, Peter. 2009. The Signal Award 2000, Chambers, 371–372.

Kelly, Stuart. 2009. A toast to the poisoned chalice. *Scotland on Sunday*, May 3.

Lear, Edward. 1988. In *Selected letters*, ed. Vivien Noakes. Oxford: Clarendon Press.

Liddell, Gordon, and Anne Gifford. 2001. *New Scottish poetry*. London: Heinemann.

Michelis, Angelica. 2003. "Me not know what these people mean": Gender and national identity in Carol Ann Duffy's Poetry, 77–98. Michelis and Rowland.

Müller-Zettlemann, Eva. 2003. "Skeleton, Moon, Poet": Carol Ann Duffy's Poetry for children, 186–201. Michelis and Rowland.

Orbach, Susie. 2010. *Bodies*. London: Profile Books.

Paterson, Christina. 2009. Carol Ann Duffy: "I was told to get a proper job": The Big Interview. *Independent,* July 10.

Philip, Neil (ed.). 1996. *The new oxford book of children's verse*. Oxford: Oxford University Press.

Rice, John (ed.). 2001. *Scottish poems*. London: Macmillan Children's Books.

Rieder, John. 1998. Edward Lear's limericks: The function of children's nonsense poetry. *Children's Literature* 26: 47–61.

Rosen, Michael. 2009. Cool, too, for school. *Guardian*, October 31.

Sampson, Fiona. 2012. *Beyond the lyric: A map of contemporary British poetry*. London: Chatto & Windus.

Smith, Stan. 2003. "What like is it?": Duffy's *différance*, 143–168. Michelis and Rowland.

Stabler, Jane. 1991. Interview with Carol Ann Duffy. *Verse* 8(2): 124–128.

Styles, Morag. 1998. *From the garden to the street: Three hundred years of poetry for children*. London: Continuum.

Thomas, Jane. 2003. "The chant of magic words repeatedly": Gender as linguistic act in the poetry of Carol Ann Duffy, 121–142. Michelis and Rowland.

Thomas, Joseph. 2011. Poetry and childhood. *The Lion and the Unicorn* 35(1): 93–102.

Tonkin, Boyd. 2013. Review of *Bethlehem: A Christmas poem. Independent*, December 6.

Whitley, David. 2007. Childhood and modernity: Dark themes in Carol Ann Duffy's poetry for children. *Children's Literature in Education* 38(2): 103–114.

Wilkinson, Kate. 2014. Carol Ann Duffy: A great public poet who deserves her public honour. *Guardian*, December 31.

Winterson, Jeanette. 2005. Prepare for Santa. *Guardian*, December 17, *Review*.

Winterson, Jeanette. 2009. Can you move diagonally? Interview with the Poet Laureate, Carol Ann Duffy. *Times*, August 29.

Wroe, Nicholas. 2007. The great performer. *Guardian*, May 26. *Review* 11.

Bibliography

Works by Carol Ann Duffy

1974 *Fleshweathercock and other poems* (Walton on Thames: Outposts).

1977 *Beauty and the beast*, with Adrian Henri (Liverpool: Glasshouse Press).

1982 *Fifth last song* (Liverpool: Headland).

1985 *Standing female nude* (London: Anvil).

1986. *Thrown voices* (London: Turret Books).

1987 *Selling Manhattan* (London: Anvil).

1990 *The other country* (London: Anvil).

1992 *William and the ex-prime minister* (London: Anvil).

1993 *Mean time* (London: Anvil).

1994 *Selected poems* (Harmondsworth: Penguin).

1995 *Penguin modern poets 2: Carol Ann Duffy, Vicki Feaver, Eavan Boland* (Harmondsworth: Penguin).

1996 *Grimm tales* (London: Faber and Faber).

1996 *The Salmon Carol Ann Duffy: Selected poems* (County Clare: Salmon Poetry).

1997 *More Grimm tales* (London: Faber and Faber).

1998 *The Pamphlet* (London: Anvil).

1999 *Meeting midnight*, Illustrated by Eileen Cooper (London: Faber and Faber).

1999 *The world's wife* (London: Anvil).

2000 *The oldest girl in the world* (London: Faber and Faber).

2002 *Feminine gospels* (London: Picador).

2002 *Queen Munch and Queen Nibble*, Illustrated by Lydia Monks (London: Macmillan Children's Books).

2002 *Underwater Farmyard*, Illustrated by Joel Stewart (London: Macmillan Children's Books).

© The Editor(s) (if applicable) and The Author(s) 2016
J. Dowson, *Carol Ann Duffy*,
DOI 10.1057/978-1-137-41563-9

2003 *The good child's guide to rock 'n' roll* (London: Faber and Faber).
2003 *The skipping-rope snake*, Illustrated by Lydia Monks (London: Macmillan Children's Books).
2003 *The stolen childhood and other dark fairy tales* (Harmondsworth: Puffin).
2003 *Collected Grimm tales* (London: Faber and Faber).
2004 *Doris the giant*, Illustrated by Annabel Hudson (Harmondsworth: Puffin).
2004 *Beasts and beauties: Eight tales from Europe* (London: Faber).
2004 *New selected poems 1984–2004* (London: Picador).
2005 *Another night before Christmas* (London: John Murray).
2005 *Moon zoo*, Illustrated by Joel Stewart (London: Macmillan Children's Books).
2005 *Rapture* (London: Picador).
2006 *The lost happy endings*, Illustrated by Jane Ray (Harmondsworth: Penguin).
2007 *The hat* (London: Faber and Faber).
2007 *The tear thief* (Oxford: Barefoot Books).
2009 *Mrs Scrooge: A Christmas tale*, Illustrated by Posy Simmonds (London: Picador); Illustrated by Beth Adams (New York: Simon & Schuster).
2009 *New & collected poetry for children* (London: Faber and Faber).
2009 *The Princess's blankets*, Illustrated by Catherine Hyde (Dorking: Templar).
2010 *Love poems* (London: Picador).
2010 *The gift*, Illustrated by Rob Ryan (Oxford: Barefoot Books).
2010 *Another night before Christmas* (London: Picador).
2011 *The bees* (London: Picador).
2011 *The Christmas truce*, Illustrated by David Roberts (London: Picador).
2012 *Near* (London: Faber and Faber).
2012 *Rats' tales*, adapted for stage by Melly Still (London: Faber and Faber).
2012 *Wenceslas: A Christmas poem*, Illustrated by Stuart Kolakovic (London: Picador).
2013 *Bethlehem* (London: Picador).
2014 *Ritual lighting: Laureate poems*, artwork by Stephen Raw (London: Picador).
2014 *Faery tales*, Illustrated by Tomislav Tomic (London: Faber and Faber).
2014 *Dorothy Wordsworth's Christmas birthday* (London: Picador).
2015 *Everyman* (London: Faber and Faber).
2015 *Collected poems* (London: Picador).

WORKS EDITED BY CAROL ANN DUFFY

1992 *I wouldn't thank you for a valentine* (London: Viking).
1995 *Anvil new poets 2 no. 2* (London: Anvil).
1996 *Stopping for death* (London: Viking).
1999 *Time's tidings: Greeting the 21st century* (London: Anvil).
2001 *Hand in hand: An anthology of love poetry* (London: Picador).
2004 *Out of fashion: An anthology of poems* (London: Faber and Faber).

2004 *Overheard on a saltmarsh: Poets' favourite poems* (London: Macmillan Children's Books).
2007 *Answering back: Living poets reply to the poetry of the past* (London: Picador).
2009 *The twelve poems of Christmas* [and for each subsequent year until 2019] (Nottingham: Candlestick Press).
2009 *To the moon: An anthology of lunar poetry* (London: Picador).
2012 *Jubilee lines: 60 poets for 60 years* (London: Faber and Faber).
2013 *1914: Poetry remembers* (London: Faber and Faber).

UNCOLLECTED POEMS BY CAROL ANN DUFFY

'McGonagall's Burd' (2002) *Sunday Herald*, 29 December.
'December' (2009) *Christmas Pamphlet* (Nottingham: Candlestick Press).
'Inside the Yurt (for Catherine Lockerbie)' (2009) *Times*, 18 August.
'Politics' (2009) *Guardian*, 13 June.
'The Twelve Days of Christmas' (2009) *Radio Times*, 8 December.
'Vigil' (2010) https://www.youtube.com/watch?v=JkDV_mqnJT4
'Democracy' (2010) *Guardian*, 7 May.
'A Cut Back' (2011) *Guardian*, 9 April.
'Remembering a Teacher' (2012) *Daily Mail*, 31 January 2012. [Aka 'Death of a Teacher', *NSP* 134].
'The Thames, London, 2012' (2012) *Guardian*, 27 April.
'Translating The British' (2012) *Mirror*, 11 August.
'22 Reasons for the Bedroom Tax' (2013) *Guardian*, 11 October.
'September 2014: *Tha gaol agam ort*' (2014) *Guardian*, 23 September.
'Richard' (2015) *Guardian*, 26 March.

ARTICLES AND INTERVIEWS (WITH AN UNNAMED INTERVIEWER) BY CAROL ANN DUFFY

1989 Interview for BBC English File (http://www.bbc.co.uk/poetryseason/poets/carol_ann_duffy.shtml).
1990 'Carol Ann Duffy', Interview, *Options*, June: 61.
1993 Interview, *Writer's Monthly*, October: 4–5.
1993 Poet's Comment on *Mean Time*, *Poetry Book Society Bulletin*, Summer: 8.
1994 'A Place of Escape', Interview, *Second Shift* 4: 20–2.
2001 'Introduction: Alter Egos: New Writing', *Mslexia* 8, Winter/Spring: 23–4.
2002 Poet's Comment on *Feminine Gospels*, *Poetry Book Society Bulletin*, Autumn: 10.
2005 Poet's Comment on *Rapture*, *Poetry Book Society Bulletin*, Autumn: 5.
2005 'The Most Natural Gift', *Daily Telegraph*, 10 December.
2008 'Winning Poets', *Mslexia* 38, July/August/September: 31–3.
2009 'Sisters in Poetry', *Guardian*, 2 May.

2009 'Exclusive: Poet Laureate Carol Ann Duffy's Poems for Children', *Mirror*, 4 May.

2009 'Exit Wounds', *Guardian*, 25 July: *Review* 2–4.

2010 'Poetry Is the Music of Being Human', *Times*, 30 January: *Saturday Review* 2.

2010 'As Tempting as Chocolates', *Daily Telegraph*, 13 February: *Saturday Review*: 20

2010 'Older and Wiser', *Guardian*, 13 March.

2010 'The Week in Books', *Guardian*, 1 May: *Review* 5.

2010 'Play up! Play up!', *Guardian*, 10 July.

2010 'Carols for Christmas', *Guardian*, 18 December: *Review* 2–4.

2011 Interview, *The Stylist:* 100.

2011 'Poems for a Wedding', *Guardian*, 23 April.

2012 Interview, *Times*, 29 September.

2012 'Choosing Sylvia's Poems', *Guardian*, 2 November.

CRITICAL WORKS (INCLUDING INTERVIEWS
WITH A NAMED INTERVIEWER)

Acheson, James, and Romana Huk (eds.). 1996. *Contemporary British poetry: Essays in theory and criticism.* New York: State University of New York Press.

Addley, Esther. 2008. Poet's rhyming riposte leaves Mrs Schofield "gobsmacked". *Guardian*, September 6.

Aitchison, James. 1990. Nightmare of our times. Review of *The Other Country*, *Glasgow Herald*, September 15.

Allnutt, Gillian, Fred D'Aguiar, Ken Edwards, and Eric Motram (eds.). 1988. *The new British poetry 1968–88.* Colorado: Paladin.

Ambrose, Alice (ed.). 1979. *Wittgenstein's lectures 1932–35.* Oxford: Blackwell.

Anderson, Hephzibah. 2005. Christmas Carol. *Observer*, December 4.

Armstrong, Amanda. 1993. Potent poetry. Interview with Carol Ann Duffy. *Writers' Monthly*, October.

Armstrong, Isobel, and Virginia Blain (eds.). 1999. *Women's poetry: Late Romantic to late Victorian: Gender and genre, 1830–1900.* Basingstoke: Macmillan.

Bakhtin, M.M. 1965. *Rabelais and His World*, Trans. H. Iswolksy, in Morris (1994), 195–206.

Bakhtin, M.M. 1981. In *The dialogic imagination: Four essays*, ed. Michael Holquist. Austin: University of Texas Press.

Barry, Peter. 2000. *Contemporary British poetry and the city.* Manchester: Manchester University Press.

Barry, Peter. 2002. Contemporary poetry and ekphrasis. *The Cambridge Quarterly* 31(2): 155–165.

Barry, Peter. 2006. *Poetry Wars: British poetry of the 1970s and the Battle over Earls Court.* Cambridge: Salt Publishing.

Bate, Jonathan. 2000. *The song of the earth*. London: Picador.

Baudrillard, Jean. 1988. In *Selected writings*, ed. M. Poster. Cambridge: Polity Press.

Bell, Jo. 2011. Landlines. *National Trust Magazine*, Spring: 48–52.

Bell, Jo. 2014. 'Jo Bell's always there awards #5', blog. *The Bell Jar*, May 19. http://belljarblog.wordpress.com/2014/05/19/jo-bells-always-there-awards-5/

Belsey, Catherine, and Jane Moore (eds.). 1997. *The feminist reader*. Malden: Blackwell.

Berger, John. 2008. *Ways of seeing*. London: Penguin Books.

Bertram, Vicki. 2004. *Gendering poetry: Contemporary women and men poets*. London: Rivers Oram/Pandora Press.

Boland, Eavan. 1993. Between me and the mass. Review of *Mean Time*, *Independent on Sunday*, July 25.

Boland, Eavan. 1994. Making the difference: Eroticism and ageing in the work of the woman poet. *P.N. Review* 20(4): 13–21.

Bradbury, Lorna. 2009. Can poetry change the world? *Daily Telegraph*, October. *Review* 3.

Bragg, Melvyn. 2009. Interview with Carol Ann Duffy. *South Bank Show, ITV Television*, December 6.

Bray, Elisa. 2005. The five minute interview with Carol Ann Duffy. *Independent*, August 13.

Breton, André. 1972. *Manifestoes of surrealism*. Michigan: Ann Arbor Press.

Brown, Mark. 2009. Carol Ann Duffy leaps into expenses row with first official poem as laureate. *Guardian*, June 13.

Brown, Jeffrey. 2014. Reporting poetry. *Poetry* 203(6): 567–573.

Brown, Clare, and Don Patterson (eds.). 2003. *Don't ask me what I mean: Poets in their own words*. London: Picador.

Brownjohn, Alan. 2012. Waggledance and whisky. Review of *The Bees*, *Times Literary Supplement*, February 10.

Bruce, Keith. 2003. It would make you sing the blues. *The Herald*, November 15.

Bryant, Marsha. 2011. *Women's poetry and popular culture*. New York: Palgrave.

Buckley, Marian. 1989. Interview with Carol Ann Duffy. *City Life Magazine*, June 15.

Burt, Stephen. 2002. Repetitive strains. *Times Literary Supplement*, September 27.

Butlin, Robert. 2004. Review of *New Selected Poems* and *Out of Fashion*, *Scottish Review of Books* 1.1.

Campbell, Siobhan. 2006. In search of rapture. *Poetry Ireland Review* 85: 87–89.

Caraher, Brian. 2011. *Carol Ann Duffy, Medbh McGuckian and ruptures in the lines of communication*, 179–195. Dowson.

Cardwell, Colin. 1999. Duffy's wife less ordinary. *Scotland on Sunday*, December 19.

Chambers, Nancy (ed.). 2009. *Poetry for children: The Signal Award 1979–2001.* Stroud: Thimble Press.

Chapman, Danielle. 2011. Review of *The Bees, Financial Times*, October 14.

Christianson, Aileen, and Alison Lumsden (eds.). 2000. *Contemporary Scottish women writers.* Edinburgh: Edinburgh University Press.

Cixous, Hélène. 1997. *Sorties: Out and out: Attacks/ways out/forays,* 91–103. Belsey and Moore.

Colton, Julian. 2012. Review of *The Bees, The Eildon Tree* 21, 46.

Constantine, David. 2004. Aspects of the Contemporary (i): What good does it do? *Magma* 29, Summer.

Cooke, Rachel. 2009. I still haven't written the best I can. Interview with Carol Ann Duffy. *Observer*, May 3.

Cowing, Emma. 2005a. Love in the dock. Review *of Rapture, The Scotsman,* September 17.

Cowing, Emma. 2005b. The 20 Scottish books everyone should read. *The Scotsman,* December 28.

Crawford, Robert, and Mick Imlah (eds.). 2000. *The new Penguin book of Scottish verse.* London: Allen Lane.

Culler, Jonathan. 1975. Poetics of the lyric. In *Structuralist poetics: Structuralism, linguistics and the study of literature,* 161–188. London: Routledge.

Darlington, Miriam. 2015. The virtuoso thrush plays his melodies of spring. *Times,* May 2.

De Castella, Tom. 2014. Whatever happened to the term New Man? *BBC News Magazine*, January 30. http://www.bbc.co.uk/news/magazine-25943326

De la Vega, Carla. 2012. Cultural Olympiad: Poetry in motion. *Vision,* June.

Debray, Régis. 2008. God and the political planet. *New Perspectives Quarterly* 25(4): 33–35.

DiNapoli, Robert. 2014. The play's the thing: Word-play and poetry. *P.N. Review* 40(4): 34–38.

Donaghy, Michael. 1991. Carol Ann Duffy. In *Contemporary poetry,* 244. London: St James Press.

Donne, John. 1977. In *Selected poems,* ed. John Hayward. Harmondsworth: Penguin.

Donnelly, Laura. 2013. Liverpool Care Pathway being "rebranded" not axed'. *Daily Telegraph,* December 1.

Dooley, Maura (ed.). 1997. *Making for Planet alice: New women poets.* Newcastle-upon-Tyne: Bloodaxe.

Dougary, Ginny. 2011. Poetry is the music of being human. It's how we bear witness. *Times,* October 1.

Dowson, Jane (ed.). 2011. *The Cambridge companion to twentieth-century British and Irish women's poetry.* Cambridge: Cambridge University Press.

Dowson, Jane, and Alice Entwistle. 2005. *A history of twentieth-century British women's poetry*. Cambridge: Cambridge University Press.

Draycott, Jane. 2004. Review of *Feminine Gospels, Poetry London* 47, Spring: 28.

Dudhnath, Keith. n.d. Review of *New and Collected Poems for Children*, *The Book Bag*. http://www.thebookbag.co.uk/reviews/index.php?title=New_and_Collected_Poems_for_Children_by_Carol_Ann_Duffy

Duncan, Lesley. 1999. A Lady to take charge of toad odes. *The Herald*, April 26.

Dunmore, Helen. 1999. Waiting for the world's wife. *Poetry Review* 89(2): 80–81.

Dunn, Douglas (ed.). 1992. *The Faber book of twentieth-century Scottish poetry*. London: Faber and Faber.

Edemariam, Aida. 2009. Carol Ann Duffy: "I don't have ambassadorial talents". *Guardian*, May 26.

Eldridge, Richard. 2010. Truth in poetry: Particulars and universals. In *A companion to the philosophy of literature*, ed. G.L. Hagberg and W. Jost, 385–398. Oxford: Wiley-Blackwell.

Ezard, John. 2003. Poet's poll crowns Larkin king of verse. *Guardian*, October 15.

Fanthorpe, U.A. 2010. *New and collected poems*, Preface by Carol Ann Duffy. London: Enitharmon.

Feinstein, Elaine. 2002. A casual kind of confidence. *Guardian*, September 14.

Ferguson, Brian. 2013. Scots-born poet laureate Duffy to be star of the show at palace exhibition. *Scotsman*, October 25.

Flood, Alison. 2009. Carol Ann Duffy becomes first female poet laureate. *Guardian*, May 1.

Flood, Alison. 2012a. Carol Ann Duffy is "wrong" about poetry says Sir Geoffrey Hill. *Guardian*, January 31.

Flood, Alison. 2012b. Poetry Parnassus to gather poets from every Olympic nation. *Guardian*, April 17.

Forbes, Peter. 1994. Talking about the new generation, Carol Ann Duffy. *Poetry Review* 84(1): 4–6, 111.

Forbes, Peter. 1995. Why the new popular poetry makes more sense. *Poetry Review* 85(3): 46–47.

Forbes, Peter. 1996/1997. Beyond the Bell Jar. *Poetry Review* 86(4): 3.

Forbes, Peter. 2001. Seven years on, Carol Ann Duffy. *Poetry Review: A New Generation Retrospective* 91(1): 3, 22.

Forbes, Peter. 2002 Winning lines. *Guardian*, August 31.

Forster, Julia. 2006. Critical openness: A study of poetry in public places. *Agenda*, July 5. http://www.agendapoetry.co.uk/documents/JuliaForster-Essaypdf.pdf

France, Linda (ed.). 1993. *Sixty women poets*. Newcastle-upon-Tyne: Bloodaxe.

Friedan, Betty. 1963. *The feminine mystique*. New York: Dell Publishing.

Fryatt, Kit. 2002/2003. Seeking and finding a difficulty. Review of *Feminine Gospels*, *Metre* 13: 83–84.

Gardner, Helen (ed.). 1975. *Gerard Manley Hopkins: Poems and prose.* Harmondsworth: Penguin.

Gayle, Damien. 2012. Poet Laureate compared to Mills & Boon romance writers in stinging attack by rival. *Daily Mail*, January 31.

Geyer, Margaret. 2014. Awesome response to Scottish referendum. *Guardian*, September 21.

Gifford, Terry. 1999. *Pastoral.* London: Routledge.

Gifford, Douglas. 2009. *Addressing the bard: Twelve contemporary poets respond to Robert Burns.* Edinburgh: Scottish Poetry Library.

Gifford, Douglas, and Dorothy McMillan. 1997. *A history of Scottish women's writing.* Edinburgh: Edinburgh University Press.

Goodyear, Ronnie, and Annie Morgan (eds.). 2011. *Soul feathers: An anthology to aid the work of Macmillan Cancer Support.* Stony Stanton: Indigo Dreams.

Goring, Rosemary. 2004. Review of *New Selected Poems. The Herald*, October 23.

Greenlaw, Lavinia. 2009. The public poet. *Granta*, May 5.

Greer, Germaine (ed.). 2001. *101 poems by 101 women.* London: Faber and Faber.

Greer, Germaine. 2009. I'd be happy if the new laureate blew all her money on the horses or invested in fetish gear. *Guardian*, May 11.

Greer, Germaine. 2010. Farewell to poetry's pal from Carol Ann Duffy, the nation's students, and me. *Guardian*, November 28.

Gregson, Ian. 1996. *Contemporary poetry and postmodernism: Dialogue and estrangement.* Basingstoke: Macmillan.

Gregson, Ian. 1999. *The male image: Representations of masculinity in postwar poetry.* Basingstoke: Macmillan.

Griffin, Jo. 2010. *The lonely society.* London: Mental Health Foundation.

Griffiths, Jane. 2005. Words for love. *Times Literary Supplement*, November 18.

Guest, Katy. 2009. The people's poet. *Independent on Sunday*, May 3.

Guest, Katy. 2011. Christmas books of the year. *Independent on Sunday*, December 18.

Habermas, Jürgen. 1994. *The Structural Transformation of the Public Sphere: An Inquiry into a Category of Bourgeois Society.* Trans. Thomas Burger with Fredrick Lawrence. Cambridge: Polity Press.

Hale, Dominic. 2012. Review of *The Bees, Cadaverine Magazine*, July 23.

Hardy, Thomas. 1993. *Selected poems.* Harmondsworth: Penguin.

Harris, T.J.G. 1993. WOW!. Review of *Mean Time, PN Review* 20, November/December 2, 58.

Harrison, Tony. 2000. *Laureate's block.* Harmondsworth: Penguin.

Heaney, Seamus. 2001. *North* [1975]. London: Faber and Faber.

Higgins, Charlotte. 2009. Carol Ann Duffy becomes first woman laureate. *Guardian*, May 1.

Hilpern, Kate. 2002. The Top Brass: The ten leading poets in Britain as chosen by their peers. *Independent,* October 7.

Hollindale, Peter. 2009. The Signal Award 2000, Chambers, 371–372.

Horner, Avril. 2003. "Small female skull": Patriarchy and philosophy in the poetry of Carol Ann Duffy, 99–120. Michelis and Rowland.

Hoyle, Ben. 2010. David Beckham injury immortalized by Poet Laureate. *Times*, March 17.

Hughes-Edwards, Mari. 2006. "The house … has cancer": The representation of domestic space in the poetry of Carol Ann Duffy. In *Our house: The representation of domestic space in modern culture*, ed. Gerry Smyth and Jo. Croft, 121–140. Amsterdam/New York: Rodopi.

Jameson, Fredric. 1991. *Postmodernism, or, the cultural logic of late capitalism*. London: Verso.

Jones, Ernest. 1955. *Sigmund Freud: Life and work*, vol. 2. London: Hogarth Press.

Jury, Louise. 2006. Judges in rapture as poet Duffy wins T. S. Eliot Prize. *Independent*, January 17.

Kellaway, Kate. 1993. When the moon is an onion and the tree sings minims. *Observer*, June 20.

Kellaway, Kate. 2005. I am in heaven, I am in hell. Review of *Rapture*, *Observer*, October 9.

Kellaway, Kate. 2011. Review of *The Bees*, *Observer*, November 6.

Kellner, Douglas. 2000. Habermas, the public sphere, and democracy: A critical intervention. In *Perspectives on Habermas*, ed. Lewis Hahn, 259–288. Chicago: Open Court Press.

Kelly, Stuart. 2009. A toast to the poisoned chalice. *Scotland on Sunday*, May 3.

Kennedy, David. 2012. *The ekphrastic encounter in contemporary British poetry and elsewhere*. Farnham/Burlington: Ashgate.

Kennedy, Maev. 2013. Bedroom tax brings out the beast in poet laureate. *Guardian*, October 11.

Khan, Urmee. 2010. Inspiration behind laureate's passion for romantic poetry. *Daily Telegraph*, February 13.

Kindersley, Tania, and Sarah Vine. 2009. *Backwards in high heels: The difficult art of being female*. London: Harper Collins.

Kinnahan, Linda. 1996. "Look for the doing words": Carol Ann Duffy and questions of convention, 245–268. Acheson and Huk.

Kinnahan, Linda A. 2000. Now I am Alien: Immigration and the discourse of nation in the poetry of Carol Ann Duffy, 208–225. Mark and Rees-Jones.

Kisiel, Ryan. 2010. Dunce's Corner Banned. *Daily Mail*, January 5.

Kristeva, Julia. 1997. Women's time, 201–216. Belsey and Moore.

Laird, Nick. 2005. The secret is to walk evading nothing. *Daily Telegraph*, November 13.

Larkin, Philip. 1990. In *Collected poems*, ed. Anthony Thwaite. London: Faber and Faber.

Lawless, James. 2009. *Clearing the tangled wood: Poetry as a way of seeing the world*. Palo Alto: Academic Press.

Lawson, Mark. 2011. Poet laureate Carol Ann Duffy. Interview, *Front Row*, BBC Radio 4, September 30. http://www.bbc.co.uk/programmes/b0151xt6

Lear, Edward. 1988. In *Selected letters*, ed. Vivien Noakes. Oxford: Clarendon Press.

Lesley, Jeffries, and Peter Sansom (eds.). 2001. *Contemporary poems: Some critical approaches*. Sheffield: Smith/Doorstop.

Leviston, Frances. 2005. Review of *Rapture, Tower Poetry*. http://www.towerpetry.org.uk/poetry-matters/poetry/poetry-archive/169-frances-leviston-reviews-rapture-by-carol-ann-duffy

Liddell, Gordon, and Anne Gifford. 2001. *New Scottish poetry*. London: Heinemann.

Linklater, Magnus. 2009. Carol Ann Duffy's tribute to departing head of Edinburgh book festival. *Times*, August 18.

Lochhead, Liz. 1991. *Bagpipe Muzak*. Harmondsworth: Penguin.

Lochhead, Liz. 2011a. *A choosing: The selected poems of Liz Lochhead*, Foreword by Carol Ann Duffy. Edinburgh: Polygon Books.

Lochhead, Liz. 2011b. Review of *The Bees, Guardian*, November 4.

Longley, Edna (ed.). 2003. *The Bloodaxe book of twentieth-century poetry*. Tarset: Bloodaxe.

Love, Tim. 2010. Popularising poetry in the UK. http://www2.eng.cam.ac.uk/~tpl/texts/popularisingpoetry.html

Low, Valentine. 2015. Royal birth leaves left-wing poet laureate with writer's block. *Times*, May 6.

Mackinnon, Lachlan. 1988. Review of *Selling Manhattan, Times Literary Supplement*, March 18–24.

MacNeice, Louis. 1964. *Selected poems*. London: Faber and Faber.

Maguire, Sarah. 2000. Poetry makes nothing happen. In *Strong words: Modern poets on modern poetry*, ed. W.N. Herbert and Matthew Hollis, 248–251. Tarset: Bloodaxe.

Mark, Alison, and Deryn Rees-Jones (eds.). 2000. *Contemporary women's poetry: Reading/writing/practice*. London: Macmillan.

Marre, Oliver. 2009. Carol Ann Duffy turns into a pub bore. *Daily Telegraph Blogs*, December 6.

May, William. 2011. Verbal and visual art in twentieth-century British women's poetry, 42–61. Dowson.

McAllister, Andrew. 1988. Carol Ann Duffy. *Bête Noir* 6, 69–77.

McClure, John A. 2007. *Partial faiths: Postsecular fiction in the age of Pynchon and Morrison*. Athens: University of Georgia Press.

McCrum, Robert. 2008. The royal family doesn't need a poet. *Guardian*, December 1.

McCulloch, Andrew. 2014. Nostalgia. *Times Literary Supplement*, December 2.

McGuinness, Patrick. 2000. Get rid of time and everything's dancing. Review of *The World's Wife*, *London Review of Books*, October 5, 15–16.

Meiklem, Peter John. 2009. Duffy: Poet in motion. *The Big Issue*, July 30–August 5, 7.

Mendelson, Charlotte. 2002. The gospel truth. Review of *Feminine Gospels*, *Observer*, October 12.

Michelis, Angelica. 2003. "Me not know what these people mean": Gender and national identity in Carol Ann Duffy's Poetry, 77–98. Michelis and Rowland.

Michelis, Angelica, and Antony Rowland (eds.). 2003. *The poetry of Carol Ann Duffy: 'Choosing tough words'*. Manchester: Manchester University Press.

Middleton, Peter. 2004. Poetry after 1970. In *The Cambridge history of twentieth-century literature*, ed. Laura Marcus and Peter Nicholls, 768–786. Cambridge: Cambridge University Press.

Miller, Phil. 2009. Scot is made first female Laureate. *The Herald*, May 2.

Miller, Kei. 2013. Not everyone was invited to the party. Blog, November 20. http://underthesaltireflag.com/2013/11/20/not-everyone-was-invited-to-the-party/

Miller-Mack, Ellen. 2013. Review of *Rapture*, *The Rumpus*, August 23. http://therumpus.net/2013/08/rapture-by-carol-ann-duffy/

Milne, W.S. 1995. Review of *Selected Poems*, *Outposts* 180/181, Spring/Summer: 157–158.

Mitchell, Adrian. 1964. *Poems*. London: Jonathan Cape.

Moi, Toril. 1997. Feminist, female, feminine, 104–116. Belsey and Moore.

Moi, Toril. 2004. From femininity to finitude: Freud, Lacan, and feminism. *Signs: Journal of Women in Culture and Society* 29(3): 841–878.

Moore, Matthew. 2009. Carol Ann Duffy is first woman poet. *Daily Telegraph*, May 1.

Moorhead, Joanne. 2011. Carol Ann Duffy: "Poems are a form of texting". *Guardian*, September 5.

Morley, David. 2006. Language's mercury. Review of *Rapture*, *Poetry Review* 96(1): 87–89.

Morris, Pam (ed.). 1994. *The Bakhtin reader: Selected writings of Bakhtin, Medvedev, Vološinov*. London: Edward Arnold.

Moss, Stephen. 2010. What is the future of Poetry? *Guardian*, June 18.

Mousley, Andy. 2013. *Literature and the human*. Abingdon: Routledge.

Mullan, John. 2013. Love poems by Carol Ann Duffy. *Guardian*, January 18.

Müller-Zettlemann, Eva. 2003. "Skeleton, Moon, Poet": Carol Ann Duffy's Poetry for children, 186–201. Michelis and Rowland.

Mulvey, Laura. 1975. Visual pleasure and narrative cinema. *Screen* 16(3): 6–18.

Nye, Robert. 1986. Bright new panes broken. Review of *Standing Female Nude*, *Times*, February 13.

Nye, Robert. 2002. The true love poet. *Scotsman*, August 31.

O'Brien, Sean. 1993. Illuminating manuscripts. *Sunday Times*, July 18.

O'Brien, Sean. 1998. *The deregulated muse: Essays on contemporary British and Irish poetry*. Newcastle on Tyne: Bloodaxe.

O'Connell, Alex. 2012. The poet who refuses to rest on her laureate. *Times*, November 3.

O'Driscoll. 1990. The day and ever. *Poetry Review* 80(3): 65–66.

O'Hagan, Sean. 2010. Shaped by War: Photographs by Don McCullin. *Observer*, February 7.

O'Riordan, Adam. 2009. The uses of erotic poetry. *Guardian*, September 16.

O'Rourke, Daniel (ed.). 2002. *Dream state: The new Scottish poets* [1994]. Edinburgh: Polygon.

Ong, Walter. 2002. *Orality and literacy: The technologizing of the word*. London: Routledge.

Orbach, Susie. 2005. *Hunger strike: The anorexic's struggle as a metaphor for our age* [1986]. London: Karnac Books.

Orbach, Susie. 2006. *Fat is a feminist issue*. London: Arrow Books.

Orbach, Susie. 2010. *Bodies*. London: Profile Books.

Owen, Wilfred. 1975. In *War poems and others*, ed. Dominic Hibberd. London: Chatto and Windus.

Oxley, William. 2005. Love's virtuoso. *Acumen* 53: 105–106.

Padel, Ruth. 1990. In otherness together. Review of *The Other Country*, *Times Literary Supplement*, May 11–17.

Padel, Ruth. 2002. *52 ways of looking at a poem*. London: Chatto and Windus.

Padel, Ruth. 2005. Review of *Rapture, Independent*, September 16.

Page, Benedict. 2011. Withdrawal of Poetry Book Society funding sparks outcry. *Guardian*, April 4.

Parry, Tom. 2012a. *Daily Mirror* launches "We Love Reading" campaign. *Mirror*, January 16.

Parry, Tom. 2012b. Translating the British: Poet laureate Carol Ann Duffy celebrates the Olympics. *Mirror*, August 11.

Paterson, Christina. 2009. Carol Ann Duffy: "I was told to get a proper job": The Big Interview. *Independent*, July 10.

Paton, Graeme. 2008. Poem banned from schools over knife crime fears. *Daily Telegraph*, September 3.

Philip, Neil (ed.). 1996. *The new oxford book of children's verse*. Oxford: Oxford University Press.

Plath, Sylvia. 2014. *Poems*, chosen by Carol Ann Duffy. London: Faber and Faber

Pollard, Clare. 2001. Getting poetry to confess. *Magma* 21: 41–44.

Preston, John. 2010. Carol Ann Duffy interview. *Daily Telegraph*, May 11.

Price, Leah. 2000. Elegant extracts. *London Review of Books* 3: 26–28.

Pugh, Sheenagh. 1999. Why? Review of *The Pamphlet, Thumbscrew* 13: 26–29.

Puss in Boots. 2012. Politics, politics. Review of *The Bees, Gutter* 6.

Quinn, Justin. 2000. The Larkin-Duffy line. *Poetry Review* 90(3): 4–8.

Rae, Simon (ed.). 1999. *News that stays news: The twentieth century in poems.* London: Faber and Faber.

Ramaswamy, Chitra. 2009. Crowning glory of jaffa cake sunsets. *Scotland on Sunday*, July 26, 10–11.

Redmond, John. 2007. Lyric adaptations: James Fenton, Craig Raine, Christopher Reid, Simon Armitage, Carol Ann Duffy. In *The Cambridge companion to twentieth-century English poetry*, ed. Neil Corcoran, 245–258. Cambridge: Cambridge University Press.

Rees Jones, Deryn. 1999. *Carol Ann Duffy.* Plymouth: Northcote House.

Rees-Jones, Deryn. 2005. *Consorting with angels: Essays on modern women poets.* Tarset: Bloodaxe.

Rees-Jones, Deryn (ed.). 2010. *Modern women poets.* Tarset: Bloodaxe.

Reid, Mark. 1992/3. Near misses are best. *Orbis* 1992/1993: 34–38.

Relich, Mario. 2011. Review of *The Bees, Scottish Review of Books* 8(1): 27–28.

Reynolds, Margaret. 2006. The end of the affair. *Guardian*, January 7.

Reynolds, Peggy (host). 2014. *Four women poets today*, produced by Beauty Rubens, BBC Radio 4, September 20.

Rice, John (ed.). 2001. *Scottish poems.* London: Macmillan Children's Books.

Rieder, John. 1998. Edward Lear's limericks: The function of children's nonsense poetry. *Children's Literature* 26: 47–61.

Roberts, Neil. 1999. Carol Ann Duffy: Outsidedness and Nostalgia. In *Narrative and voice in postwar poetry*, 184–194. Essex: Longman.

Roberts, Neil. 2003. Duffy, Eliot and impersonality, 33–46. Michelis and Rowland.

Roberts, Michael Symonns. 2008. Poetry in a post-secular age. *Poetry Review* 98(4): 69–75.

Robinson, Alan. 1988. *Instabilities in contemporary British poetry.* Basingstoke: Palgrave.

Rose, Jacqueline. 1982. Introduction to Lacan, "God and the *Jouissance* of The Woman". In *Feminine sexuality: Jacques Lacan and the ecole freudienne*, ed. Juliet Mitchell and Jacqueline Rose, 137–138. London: Macmillan.

Rosen, Michael. 2009. Cool, too, for school. *Guardian*, October 31.

Ross, Peter. 2012. Interview with Carol Ann Duffy. *The Scotsman*, December 2.

Rowland, Anthony. 2003. Love and masculinity in the poetry of Carol Ann Duffy, 56–76. Michelis and Rowland.

Rumens, Carole (ed.). 1990. *New women poets.* Newcastle-upon-Tyne: Bloodaxe.

Rumens, Carole (ed.). 1995. *Two women dancing: New and selected poems by Elizabeth Bartlett.* Tarset: Bloodaxe.

Rumens, Carole. 1999/2000. Trouble and strife. Review of *The World's Wife*, *Poetry Review* 89(4): 33–34.

Rumens, Carol. 2012. Review of *The Bees, The Yellow Nib* 7, 75.

Sampson, Fiona. 2012. *Beyond the lyric: A map of contemporary British poetry.* London: Chatto & Windus.

Sansom, Ian. 1995. Wayne's world. Review of *Selected Poems, London Review of Books,* July 6, 20.

Scannell, Vernon. 1987/1988. Review of *Selling Manhattan, Poetry Review* 77(4): 36–37.

Schmidt, Michael. 1998. *The lives of the poets.* London: Weidenfeld and Nicolson.

Sexton, David. 2011. Review of *The Bees, London Evening Standard,* September 22.

Shaw, Adrian. 2009. "The 12 days of Christmas": Poet laureate Carol Ann Duffy's grim version for our times. *Mirror,* December 7.

Simic, Charles. 1985. Notes on poetry and history [1984]. *The uncertain certainty,* 124–128. Ann Arbor: University of Michigan Press.

Simic, Charles. 1997. *The Orphan factory: Essays and memoirs.* Ann Arbor: University of Michigan Press.

Simmonds, Kathryn. 2014. The God allusion. In *Poetry News,* 5. London: The Poetry Society.

Simon, Paul. 1983. Train in the distance. *Hearts and bones.* Warner Bros, Burbank, California.

Sinfield, Alan. 1977. *Dramatic monologue.* London: Methuen.

Sissay, Lemn. 2012. Carol Ann Duffy and Geoffrey Hill: Truly poetic heavyweights. *Guardian,* January 31.

Smith, Stevie. 1981. In *Me again: The uncollected writings of Stevie Smith,* ed. Jack Barbera and William McBrien. London: Virago.

Smith, Laurie. 2000. With one bound she was free. Review of *The World's Wife, Magma* 16: 16–21.

Smith, Stan. 2003. "What like is it?": Duffy's *différance,* 143–168. Michelis and Rowland.

Smith, Stan. 2008. *Poetry and displacement.* Liverpool: Liverpool University Press.

Smith, Mark. 2009. Duffy's 12 Days of biting satire. *The Herald,* December 7.

Spice Girls. 1996. The 'Wannabe', co-written with Matt Rowe and Richard Stannard. *Spice.* Virgin Records, London.

Stabler, Jane. 1991. Interview with Carol Ann Duffy. *Verse* 8(2): 124–128.

Styles, Morag. 1998. *From the garden to the street: Three hundred years of poetry for children.* London: Continuum.

Thomas, Jane. 2003. "The chant of magic words repeatedly": Gender as linguistic act in the poetry of Carol Ann Duffy, 121–142. Michelis and Rowland.

Thomas, Joseph. 2011. Poetry and childhood. *The Lion and the Unicorn* 35(1): 93–102.

Thorpe, Adam. 1993. Light-bulbs and dangling sun. Review of *Mean Time, Observer,* November 21.

Thorpe, Vanessa. 2009. Laureate puts political spin on 12 days of Christmas. *Guardian,* December 6.

Thwaite, Anthony. 2004. Anglo-Irish accords. Review of *New Selected Poems*, *Sunday Telegraph*, October 17.

Tonkin, Boyd. 2010. A valentine strictly for grown ups. Review of *Love Poems*, *Independent*, February 8.

Tonkin, Boyd. 2013. Review of *Bethlehem: A Christmas poem*. *Independent*, December 6.

Viner, Katharine. 1999. Metre Maid. Interview with Carol Ann Duffy, *Guardian*, September 25.

Vološinov, V.N. 1994. *Marxism and the Philosophy of Language* [1929]. Trans. L. Matejka and I.R. Titunik, [1973], Morris, 50–61.

Wagner, Eric. 2009. Skill, talent and a great heart are more important than her gender. *Times*, May 2.

Wainwright, Jeffrey. 2003. Female metamorphoses: Carol Ann Duffy's Ovid, 47–55. Michelis and Rowland.

Wainwright, Martin. 2012. Poet laureate Carol Ann Duffy on the Pendle witches. *Guardian*, August 15.

Walmsley-Collins, Fiona. 2013. Readers' books of the year 2013: Part 3. *Guardian*, December 28.

Waugh, Patricia. 1989. *Feminine fictions: Revisiting the postmodern*. London: Routledge.

Wheeler, Stephen M. 1999. *A discourse of wonders: Audience and performance in Ovid's metamorphoses*. Philadelphia: University of Pennsylvania Press.

Whitley, David. 2007. Childhood and modernity: Dark themes in Carol Ann Duffy's poetry for children. *Children's Literature in Education* 38(2): 103–114.

Whyte, Christopher. 2004. *Modern Scottish poetry*. Edinburgh: Edinburgh University Press.

Wilkinson, Kate. 2014. Carol Ann Duffy: A great public poet who deserves her public honour. *Guardian*, December 31.

Williams, Nerys. 2011. *Contemporary poetry*. Edinburgh: Edinburgh University Press.

Winterson, Jeanette. 2005a. Interview with Carol Ann Duffy. *Times*, September 10. http://www.jeanettewinterson.com/journalism/carol-ann-duffy/

Winterson, Jeanette. 2005b. Prepare for Santa. *Guardian*, December 17, *Review*.

Winterson, Jeanette. 2009. Can you move diagonally? Interview with the Poet Laureate, Carol Ann Duffy. *Times*, August 29.

Winterson, Jeanette. 2015. On the poetry of Carol Ann Duffy—Of course it's political. *Guardian*, January 17.

Wolf, Naomi. 1991. *The beauty myth: How images of beauty are used against women*. London: Vintage.

Wood, Barry. 2005. Carol Ann Duffy: *The World's Wife*. Conversation with Carol Ann Duffy. http://www.sheerpoetry.co.uk/advanced/interviews/carol-ann-duffy-the-world-s-wife

Woods, Michael. 2003. "What it is like in words": Translation, reflection and refraction in the poetry of Carol Ann Duffy, 169–185. Anglelis and Rowland.

Woolf, Virginia. 1977. *A room of one's own*. London: Grafton.

Woolf, Virginia. 2002. *Moments of being: Autobiographical writings*. London: Pimlico.

Wroe, Nicholas. 2007. The great performer. *Guardian,* May 26. *Review* 11.

Wroe, Nicholas. 2014. Carol Ann Duffy on five years as poet laureate: "It has been a joy". *Guardian*, September 27.

Yeats, W.B. 2008. A general introduction for my work. In *The major works by W.B. Yeats*, ed. Edward Larissy. Oxford: Oxford University Press.

MEDIA

First female Poet Laureate named' (2009) *BBC News*, May 1. http://news.bbc.co.uk/1/hi/entertainment/8027767.stm

'Shipping forecast loses household name' (2002) *BBC News*, February 3. http://news.bbc.co.uk/1/hi/uk/1798629.stm

REFERENCES

Shakespeare, William. 1993. *The complete works,* ed. Jeremy Hylton. http://shakespeare.mit.edu

The Bible, New International Version. https://www.biblegateway.com

Index

INDEX TO WORKS BY CAROL ANN DUFFY.

BOOKS

J. Dowson, *Carol Ann Duffy*,
DOI 10.1057/978-1-137-41563-9